Local Content Oil and Gas Law in Africa

Examining local content law and policy in the oil and gas industry, this book uses Nigeria as a primary case study, comparing its approach to countries such as Brazil and Norway which have also adopted local content laws in relation to their oil and gas industries. In considering various aspects of local content law and policy as they apply to the oil and gas industry, the book examines the factors behind the formulation of local content policies by petroleum producing states, and the various strategies they have employed to implement them. It analyses arguments against local content requirements from the perspective of international trade and investment law, and from liberal market economic theorists, who argue against its overall usefulness. The book highlights salient aspects of the oil and gas industry such as regulation, national oil companies, treatment of minorities, and policy formulation and implementation.

Pereowei Subai is Senior Lecturer in Law at Niger Delta University, Bayelsa State, Nigeria.

Routledge Research in Energy Law and Regulation

Regulation in the European Electricity Sector
Maciej M. Sokolowski

Law and Green Energy Policies
Roy Partain

Nuclear Energy Regulation, Risk and The Environment
Abdullah Al Faruque

Local Content Oil and Gas Law in Africa
Lessons from Nigeria and Beyond
Pereowei Subai

Host Government Agreements and the Law in the Energy Sector
The case of Azerbaijan and Turkey
Hakan Sahin

Local Content Oil and Gas Law in Africa

Lessons from Nigeria and Beyond

Pereowei Subai

Routledge
Taylor & Francis Group
LONDON AND NEW YORK

First published 2019
by Routledge
2 Park Square, Milton Park, Abingdon, Oxon OX14 4RN

and by Routledge
605 Third Avenue, New York, NY 10017

First issued in paperback 2021

Routledge is an imprint of the Taylor & Francis Group, an informa business

Publisher's Note
The publisher has gone to great lengths to ensure the quality of this reprint but points out that some imperfections in the original copies may be apparent.

British Library Cataloguing-in-Publication Data
A catalogue record for this book is available from the British Library

Library of Congress Cataloging-in-Publication Data
Names: Subai, Pereowei, author.
Title: Local content oil and gas law in Africa : lessons from Nigeria and beyond / Pereowei Subai.
Description: New York, NY : Routledge, 2019. | Series: Routledge research in energy law and regulation | Includes bibliographical references and index.
Identifiers: LCCN 2018044921 | ISBN 9781138478619 (hbk)
Subjects: LCSH: Natural gas—Law and legislation—Africa. | Petroleum law and legislation—Africa. | Natural gas—Law and legislation—Nigeria. | Petroleum law and legislation—Nigeria.
Classification: LCC KQC817 .S83 2019 | DDC 343.609/26—dc23
LC record available at https://lccn.loc.gov/2018044921

Typeset in Galliard
by Taylor & Francis Books

ISBN 13: 978-1-03-224157-9 (pbk)
ISBN 13: 978-1-138-47861-9 (hbk)

DOI: 10.4324/9781351068086

This book is dedicated to my God and Father, who saved me and lifted me from the miry clay. To my wife Tamunodiepiriye, for her tireless support and love. To my children, Dotimi, Oyinmiebi, and Oyinkariebi, and to my niece Oyinteinade, for their love and encouragement. It is also dedicated to my dear mother, Mrs Mary Perekebena Fombo (nee Empere), through whom the Light came into my life.

Contents

Tables

Table of cases

Table of statutes and instruments

Nigeria

Foreign Enactments

Angola

Brazil

Ghana

Tanzania

Norway

International Instruments

Instruments under the WTO system

Table of abbreviations

AGRA	Associated Gas Reinjection Act 1979
ANP	National Agency for Petroleum, Natural Gas, and Biofuels (Agência Nacional do Petróleo)
ARRA	American Recovery and Reinvestment Act of 2009
ASCM	Agreement on Subsidies and Countervailing Measures
BIT	Bilateral Investment Treaty
BNDE	National Bank for Economic and Social Development
BPI	Brazilian Petroleum Industry
DPR	Department of Petroleum Resources
DSB	Dispute Settlement Body
E&P	Exploration and Production
E&T	Employment and Training
EEA	European Economic Area
EU	European Union
FGN	Federal Government of Nigeria
FPSO	Floating, Production, Storage, and Offloading Facility
GATS	General Agreement in Trade in Services
GATT	General Agreement on Tariffs and Trade
GDP	Gross Domestic Product
GMOU	Global Memorandum of Understanding
GPA	Agreement on Government Procurement
HHI	Hyundai Heavy Industries
IOC	International Oil Company
ISSF	Indigenous Supply and Service Firm
ITT	Invitation to Tender
JOA	Joint Operating Agreement
JOC	Joint Operating Committee
JQS	Joint Qualification System
JV	Joint Venture
LCR	Local Content Requirement
MIT	Multilateral Investment Treaty
NAFTA	North American Free Trade Agreement

NAOC	Nigerian Agip Oil Company
NAPIMS	National Petroleum Investment Management Services
NCD	Nigerian Content Division
NCCC	Nigerian Content Compliance Certificate
NCDMB	Nigerian Content Development and Monitoring Board
NCCF	Nigerian Content Consultative Forum
NCPR	Nigerian Content Performance Report
NCS	Norwegian Continental Shelf
NDDC	Niger Delta Development Commission
NDDB	Niger Delta Development Board
NDR	Niger Delta Region
NIMASA	Nigerian Maritime Administration and Safety Agency
NIPEX	Nigerian Petroleum Exchange
NLNG	Nigerian Liquefied Natural Gas Company Ltd
NNOC	Nigerian National Oil Corporation
NNPC	Nigerian National Petroleum Corporation
NOC	National Oil Company
NOGICDA	Nigerian Oil and Gas Industry Content Development Act 2010
NoPI	Norwegian Petroleum Industry
NOSDRA	National Oil Spill Detection and Regulatory Agency
NPD	Norwegian Petroleum Directorate
NPI	Nigerian Petroleum Industry
OECD	Organisation for Economic Co-operation and Development
OML	Oil Mining Lease
OMPADEC	Oil Minerals Producing Areas Development Commission
OPEC	Organisation of Petroleum Exporting Countries
OPL	Oil Prospecting License
OPTS	Oil Producers Trade Section
OSO	Offshore Supplies Office
OTC	Offshore Technology Conference
PEDEFOR	Incentive Programme for Supply Chain Competitiveness and the Development and Improvement of Suppliers to the Oil and Gas Sector
POC	Private Oil Company
PPC	Petroleum Producing Country
PPTA	Petroleum Profits Tax Act 1958
PROMINP	Mobilization Program of the National Petroleum Industry
PSC	Production Sharing Contract
PTDF	Petroleum Trust Development Fund
R&D	Research and Development
RRC	Resource Rich Country
RRR	Resource Rich Region
RSC	Risk Service Contract
SDFI	State's Direct Financial Interest
TRIMs	Trade Related Investment Measures

UK	United Kingdom
USA	United States of America
UTP	Universiti Teknologi Petronas
WTO	World Trade Organization

Acknowledgements

A work of this nature would be incomplete without my acknowledging some persons who have impacted my academic career significantly.

The following Vice Chancellors of the Niger Delta University (past and present), have been most helpful to me. Professor John C Buseri, who started me on my academic career, refused to accept my 'wine', but made me promise to give my best. Professor Chris Ikporukpo, for supporting my PhD aspirations in no small measure. Professor Samuel G Edoumiekumo, who approved my research leave in order to enable me to complete this book.

Special mention must be made of the following colleagues at the Law Faculty, Niger Delta University. Professor Johnson F Fekumo, father, teacher, mentor, and former faculty dean. Professor Solomon T Ebobrah, current dean: a constant inspiration and a trailblazer. Dr Sylvanus Abila, my head of department, my erstwhile dean of law Dr Damfebo K Derri for supporting me through my fledgling years. Dr Simon Amaduobogha, for believing in me, so quietly. Mrs Oruwari Grace Popoola, for her kind words and constant encouragement. Mr Mark Amakoromo, my 'partner', for your kind encouragement in writing this book. Mrs Gina Elivis-Imo, an inspiration. Mrs Tarikiye Angaye, former faculty officer, for her encouragement to me. Mrs Ikuromo Oruan, my quiet sister, who has always been there.

I also acknowledge all my students through the years, at the Faculty of Law, Niger Delta University, Department of History, Federal University Otuoke, and the school of Law, St Augustine University. Special mention must be made of Miss Eniye Igbanibo, who first read through this manuscript and made useful suggestions.

Special mention must be made of my friend Dr Uzuazo Etemire for his inspiration and support, and of Dr Fiona Batts of the St Augustine University of Tanzania, School of Law for her support in my progress. Professor Festus O Emiri, who started me on the path to publishing. The Shell Club, Port Harcourt, for providing me a quiet and enabling working environment. In this regards, mention must be made to Miss Stella Ijeoma Onumaegbu the Club librarian, for her support and assistance. I acknowledge the quite support of my father in law and mother in law, Pastor and Mrs Lazarus Johnson, for their love and support. Special mention must be made of the editorial team at Routledge. Particularly,

Brianna Ascher, Nicola Sharpe, Siobhan Poole, Hannah Lovelock, Julia Hanney and Heather Jones, who were most cordial, patient and supportive of my work from the beginning. Lastly, I wish to mention the support of my wife, helper, and 'proof reader' Tamunodiepiriye Subai, who read through this manuscript, fished out my mistakes, made useful suggestions, and believed in me when I doubted myself.

May God bless you all.

Introduction

Countries all over the world are endowed with non-renewable natural resources in vast quantities. Some of these resources, which are trapped under the sea, in rocks, and in the ground, are worth billions of dollars.[1] This accounts for why the discovery of huge deposits of natural resources naturally evokes optimism that economic transformation and development, as well as poverty reduction, will result from their exploitation.[2] The experience of quite a number of these resource rich countries (RRCs), especially among the developing nations of Africa, and in some parts of South America, has however demonstrated that ownership of vast natural resources is one thing, translating them into sustainable prosperity and a higher standard of living for their citizens, is another thing entirely. For while natural resource extraction almost certainly increases the revenue base of RRCs, the challenge has been how to manage these inflows efficiently. Creating that vital link between natural resources and economic prosperity, has proved to be an uphill task for quite a number of these countries due to factors such as weak leadership, the absence of sustainable frameworks for the promotion of accountability and transparency in the management of resource revenues, etc.

Weak management of natural resources and the benefits which accrue from them, can have adverse consequences on RRCs. First, it may result in over dependence on resource revenues, the fallout of which may be a staple trap, and the neglect of other equally important economic sectors. Furthermore, the inability to create direct linkages from resource revenues to the rest of a country's economy and its citizenry, may result in economic stagnation, and the so-called 'Dutch Disease'.[3] In the worst case scenario, the poor management of natural resource and resource revenues may result into the so-called 'resource curse', with its varied manifestations in corruption, war, conflicts, poverty, and political instability.[4]

It is not gloomy for all RRCs, however. Some of them have been able to create sustainable links between their natural resources and their citizens. By prudent

1 Except otherwise indicated, references in this book to dollars refer to US dollars, and references to pounds refer to British pounds.
2 See Kakonge, 2011.
3 See Polterovich and Popov, 2005.
4 See Idemudia, 2012; see also Kurtz, 2011.

management and focused leadership, countries such as Norway, Qatar, Kuwait, and Saudi Arabia, have attained the highest standards of living for their citizens. Furthermore, several RRCs have established sovereign wealth funds with the aim of saving and investing resource based revenues to act as an economic buffer in times of volatile price fluctuations in the market, enable economic diversification from resource dependence, and to cater for the interests of future generations. Still, others have strengthened regulation in order to guarantee sustainable extraction of those resources. Of late, some countries, which are particularly rich in petroleum, have turned to local content requirements as a further means of optimising their natural resources.[5]

The local content strategy is prominent among a number of Africa's petroleum producing countries (PPCs) such as Nigeria, Ghana, Angola, Kenya, Uganda, Tanzania, and Equatorial Guinea, as well as in some of their non-African counterparts like Brazil, Saudi Arabia, Indonesia, Oman, and Jordan. Some of these countries have resorted to legislation as a means of requiring petroleum firms operating in their terrains to utilise locally produced goods and services, while others rely largely on contracts, or a combination of both, to drive local content. This book examines local content oil and gas law in Africa, using the upstream aspects of the Nigerian petroleum industry (NPI), as its primary case study. In order to achieve its objective, it analyses Nigeria's local content policies and laws, but in so doing, extracts lessons, where necessary from other African countries such as Angola, Ghana, etc., as well as non-African countries such as Norway, Brazil, Malaysia, Saudi Arabia, etc., in a view to enabling a deeper appreciation of the workings of local content laws in the petroleum industry.

Nigeria is used as the primary case study in this book for a number of reasons. First, because of the country's prominent place in the petroleum industry in Africa. Situated on the West African Coast, Nigeria is a regional power as far as ownership and production of crude oil are concerned. With an estimated 37 billion barrels of crude oil it remains Africa's largest crude oil producer, besides having the second largest deposits in the continent, after Libya. In terms of natural gas deposits, however, Nigeria can be considered a global power. Home to an estimated 192,065 trillion cubic feet deposits of natural gas, it is ranked ninth in the world in terms of gas ownership.[6] The second reason Nigeria is chosen as a case study is because of its extensive experience as a PPC. Nigeria became a petroleum exporting country in 1958 and has thus had years of experience in the petroleum industry, from which valuable lessons can be extracted for other new entrants into the petroleum industry such as Ghana, Tanzania, and Uganda. The third reason is because of Nigeria's dominant place in Africa, as the continent's largest economy, coupled with its vast and unrivalled population.[7] Lastly, because of the unique nature of Nigeria's local content strategy which has seen it blaze a trail in the

5 For further reading on the management of petroleum resources, see Al-Kassim, 2006.

6 British Petroleum, 2017.

7 Nigeria has the biggest economy in Africa by nominal gross domestic product, and is by far the most populous country in the continent.

codification of local content legislation and the establishment of an institutional local content regulator separate and entirely different from its petroleum industry regulator.

The book is divided into ten chapters. Chapter 1 lays a theoretical framework for the understanding of various local content policies and strategies that have been adopted among PPCs, while reviewing arguments for and against local content requirements. Chapter 2 focuses on institutional and legal frameworks for local content development, while Chapter 3 is an overview of the historical development of local content in Nigeria. Chapters 4, 5, 6, and 7 examine the Nigerian Oil and Gas Industry Content Development Act 2010. It examines its provisions, prospects, drawbacks, implementation, enforcement, and legality in the light of international trade law. Chapter 8 analyses the role of national oil companies in local content development, while Chapter 9 analyses the role of a specialised local content in the development of resource rich regions of RRCs, using the Niger Delta region of Nigeria as a case study. The book is concluded in chapter 10.

Bibliography

Al-Kassim F, *Managing Petroleum Resources: The 'Norwegian Model' in a Broad Perspective* (Oxford Institute of Energy Studies, Oxford, 2006).

British Petroleum, 'BP Statistical Review of World Energy' (2017) https://www.bp.com/content/dam/bp/en/corporate/pdf/energy-economics/statistical-review-2017/bp-statistical-review-of-world-energy-2017-full-report.pdf, accessed 11 March 2018.

Idemudia U, 'The Resource Curse and the Decentralization of Oil Revenue: the Case of Nigeria' (2012) 35 *Journal of Cleaner Production*, 183.

Kakonge JO, 'Challenges of Managing Expectations of Newly Emerging Oil and Gas Producers of the South' (2011) 4(2) *Journal of World Energy Law & Business*, 124.

Kurtz MJ, 'Conditioning the "Resource Curse": Globalization, Human Capital, and Growth in Oil-Rich, Nations' (2011) 44(6) *Comparative Political Studies*, 747.

Polterovich V and Popov V, 'Resource Abundance, Globalization, and Economic Development' (2005) *New Economic School, Research Project 2005–2006* https://pages.nes.ru/english/research/projects/proposal/2005–2006/PolterovichPopov.doc, accessed 9 January 2016.

1 Local content in petroleum producing countries: strategies and approaches

1.1 Background to the rise of local content requirements in petroleum producing countries

Petroleum resources are usually trapped in underground or sea basins.[1] For purposes of administration and extraction, these basins are usually divided into geographic parcels or blocks. Rights or licenses to explore for and develop these blocks are customarily awarded by petroleum producing countries (PPCs) to exploration and production (E&P) firms or national oil companies (NOCs), either discretionarily or after a competitive bidding process.[2] The firms to which these E&P rights are awarded may be referred to as 'concessionaires' or, in some cases, as operators or contractors.[3] These concessionaires do not work alone, though. From the time they commence exploration activities to the point of extraction, production, transportation, and eventual abandonment of the concession, concessionaires would require the assistance of a number of service and supply firms which would operate as subcontractors, under their co-ordination.[4]

In other words, while established concessionaires such as Shell or Mobil will focus on their core mandate of oil and gas production, they will decidedly require 'external support' in areas such as fabrication, construction, and engineering, from supply and service firms. This will require them to make major investment and operational decisions in the award of contracts to these supply and service firms. For example, in order to explore an oil block, a concessionaire may require external support in gathering seismic data, as well as in drilling, and field appraisals. Offshore firms may also require floating, production, storage and offloading facilities (FPSOs) as well as external support in the laying of underground cables and pipelines.[5] Field operation and production services, such as well services, facilities hire, and operations and maintenance, may also be

1 References to petroleum in this book also includes mineral oils, related hydrocarbons, and natural gas. See also s.15 of Nigeria's Petroleum Act of 1969.
2 See Dam, 1965, at p 58.
3 Within the context of this book, a concessionaire is a person or company to whom the right to explore for, and produce, petroleum has been granted by a sovereign state.
4 Heum, 2003, at p 5.
5 See Easo and Wallace, 2014.

required from third parties.[6] Other ancillary services required by concessionaires in their operations, include: banking, law, insurance, catering, and transportation. These contracts usually run into billions of dollars in payment for services rendered as well as for equipment that would have to be manufactured or acquired.[7] It is therefore understandable that a PPC which desires to optimize the benefits associated with its petroleum industry would seek to ensure that a large chunk of these contracts are executed locally by indigenous firms.

The irony is that international oil companies (IOCs), particularly firms such as Shell, Total, Mobil, Chevron, etc., which are domiciled mainly in America and Europe, have dominated the petroleum industries of a number of PPCs. In Africa, for example, they dominate extensively in countries such as Angola, Nigeria, Equatorial Guinea, and Gabon. In addition to this, the most critical supplies and services required in upstream projects are outsourced to European- and American-based service and supply firms such as Schlumberger, Wilbros, Transocean, Baker Huges, Weatherford International, and Halliburton.[8] The fall out of the dominance of foreign-based firms in a number of developing PPCs is a low indigenous participation by the citizens of those countries. For many of these PPCs, colonial, financial, and technological factors, as will be shown to be present, are largely responsible for weak local content in their petroleum industries.

Perhaps the first is the colonial factor, which shaped the interactions between most PPCs and IOCs prior to their being independent after the Second World War. Virtually every PPC in Africa, for example, was at one time or the other colonised by a European power. Nigeria and Sudan were colonised by Britain; Angola and Equatorial Guinea by Portugal; Algeria and Gabon by France, etc. And while PPCs in the Middle East were not colonised like African countries, a number of them were actually governed under a mandate system supervised by the League of Nations following the defeat of the Ottomans in the First World War.[9] Colonial dominance in Africa saw the petroleum resources of colonial territories subjected to extensive and

6 See Hewitt, 2008, at p 179.

7 For instance in 2016 alone, the Nigerian National Petroleum Corporation's (NNPC) joint venture obligation for capital and operating expenditures stood at $8.55 billion alone. This figure does not include expenditures by its production sharing contract (PSC) partners, nor those of sole risk operators in the NPI. See NNPC, 'Monthly Financial and Operations Report' (January, 2017) http://nnpcgroup.com/Portals/0/Monthly%20Financial%20and%20Operations%20Data/Full%20Reports/NNPC%20Monthly%20Financial%20&%20Operations%20Report%20for%20the%20month%20of%20January%202017.pdf, accessed 24 April 2017.

8 Of late, Chinese, Korean, and Indian firms have also entered into Africa. Some of these firms such as Samsung and Hyundai are also playing critical roles in petroleum industries across Africa, and are challenging the almost exclusive dominance once held by American and European firms.

9 Syria for instance was placed under the authority of France, and Iraq under Britain. See generally Haas, 1952. See also Stansfield, 2013.

exploitative control by the colonial powers, primarily Britain, Portugal, and France. These countries gave to IOCs which were owned or managed by their nationals or subjects, extensive dominance over the natural resources of their colonies with scant regard for the interests of these territories. Because these firms were largely regarded as extensions of their home states, they became heir, naturally perhaps, to concessions whose terms bordered on near ownership of any petroleum they discovered in these colonial territories. For example, a concession granted to Shell-BP by the British government in 1937 covered the whole Nigerian land mass. Besides, the concession was for an unduly long period of time.[10] These privileges gave Shell-BP a stronghold over the NPI and ensured that Nigeria, which became politically independent in 1960, remained 'tied' to the yoke of arrangements designed to secure British dominance over its petroleum industry, post-independence.[11] In a similar vein, Algeria, which fought a bitter liberation war with its French masters, obtained its independence only after it made significant concessions designed to safeguard the interests of French petroleum firms,[12] which were already operating in Algeria at the time.[13]

The second factor is that PPCs lacked, and still lack, the financial wherewithal to fund major petroleum-related projects as well as the technological capacity to explore, extract, and process their petroleum deposits.[14] This explained why for a time, many were contented with corporate taxes and minor social initiatives of foreign firms. The issue was that IOCs, and their supply and service counterparts operating in Africa and elsewhere, understandably repatriated most of their profits away from the countries in which they operate, to their home countries. This meant that the outsourcing of critical jobs in the petroleum industry resulted in the loss of revenues to host PPCs. For instance, it has been estimated that of the $18 billion spent annually for petroleum contracts in Nigeria, less than 20 percent is retained internally.[15] Moreover, it has been reported that the country lost

10 Concessions awarded before the Second World War in the Middle East were very extensive and gave virtual control to IOCs. For instance, the average concession signed between IOCs and Iran, Iraq, Kuwait, and Saudi Arabia had an average lifespan of 82 years. The areas covered were also extensive. For instance, in all four countries, IOCs had total control over an average of 88 percent of the national area. This included all of Iraq and Kuwait. This was coupled with the absence of relinquishment clauses. These firms could sit on their acreages without doing nothing. Lastly, there, the fiscal terms meant that the IOCs were only required to pay paltry sums to host governments, see Stevens, 2008, p 11. See also, Hossein, 1979, p 5.

11 See Joffe, 2009.

12 Except otherwise stated in this book, references to 'petroleum firms' means all firms involved in the petroleum industries, whether they are offshore, producing, exploration, downstream, or service firms.

13 Concessions made to the French were later reneged upon, however, when Houari Boumediane took over office as president in a military coup. See Sueur, 2013.

14 A company is in oil and gas production if it is awarded contracts for E&P, as against service companies which are involved in various stages of the production process such as seismic operations, pipelines fabrication, construction of storage facilities, and tank farms, etc. See generally, Raymond and Lefler, 2006.

15 See Balouga, 2012.

$380 billion to capital flight due to its weak local content in the petroleum industry from 1956 to 2006, besides losing the opportunity to create two million jobs.[16] Besides loss of revenues, it deprived local African industries of opportunities to develop capacity and expertise through hands-on experience, as well as loss of opportunities for technology transfer.

But the dominance of IOCs was not to go unchallenged forever. The end of the Second World War saw a rise in the clamour for greater control of natural resources by developing countries. Newly independent African and Middle Eastern countries teamed up with some South American countries to clamour for permanent sovereignty over their natural resources. They were given impetus by the passage of some United Nations resolutions, notably 1803 of 1962 and 2158 of 1966.[17] Led by Venezuela, Iran, Iraq, Kuwait, and Saudi Arabia, which together controlled (and still control) most of the world's petroleum deposits, they arranged themselves under the banner of the Organisation of Petroleum Exporting Countries (OPEC) which was formed in 1960.

OPEC's primary aim was the protection of its members' interests and for control of the petroleum industry.[18] It canvassed for better terms of engagement with IOCs and pushed for the stabilisation of petroleum prices.[19] The rise of OPEC resulted in the decline of the control of IOCs over the global petroleum industry. Emboldened by its formation, some PPCs expropriated the assets of IOCs operating in their countries,[20] while others renegotiated downwards the terms under which they operated or increased the royalties and taxes payable by IOCs.[21] In pursuance to OPEC's directives, a number of these countries began to directly participate in their petroleum industries via NOCs.[22]

16 Wabote, 2018; Okafor, 2011; see also 'Nigerian Content Act: Stakeholders Share their Experience 3 Years On' (2012) NCDMB http://www.ncdmb.gov.ng/index.php/public-relations/news-updates/134-nigerian-content-act-stakeholders-share-experience-3years-on, accessed 21 November 2012.

17 While resolution 1803 recognised the permanent sovereignty of states over their natural resources, resolution 2158 advised host countries to secure maximum exploitation of natural resources by the accelerated acquisition of full control over production operations, management and marketing. See also UN General Assembly, *Permanent sovereignty over natural resources*, 17 December 1973, A/RES/3171, http://www.refworld.org/docid/3b00f1c64.html, accessed 16 May 2018.

18 See Johnston, 2008, at p 34.

19 See Adelman, 1972.

20 For instance, in 1938, Mexico established Pemex by expropriating the interests of European and American firms, while Iran nationalised the assets of BP in the 1950s. See Samples and Vittor, 2011. See also Joffe et al, 2009, p 5.

21 For example, California-Arabian Standard Oil (CASOC) (later Saudi Aramco), under threat of nationalization, agreed to share profits with the Saudi Arabia government on a 50:50 basis. See Citino, 2002. Many PPCs began to demand better fiscal terms, royalties, and the right to share in the profits of IOCs. Furthermore, new contractual terms such as joint ventures, PSCs, and service contracts were executed between PPCs and IOCs. See Seymour, 1980.

22 OPEC's 'General Agreement on Participation' required its members to acquire a 'sensible' level of partition in oil operations, beginning at 25 percent, and increasing gradually to 51 percent. See Parra, 2005; see also Columbia Centre, 'Local content:

The growth of NOCs effectually challenged the dominance of IOCs significantly and gave PPCs greater say in their petroleum industries all over the world. Today, NOCs control over 75 percent of the world's petroleum resources, although most continue to partner with IOCs.[23] In spite of these developments, the outsourcing of crucial jobs has continued in developing PPCs all over the world. In essence, foreign service and supply firms continue to play dominant roles in the petroleum industries of quite a number of PPCs all over the world, with attendant loss of revenues and opportunities for development of technical capacity as well as jobs.

Keen to arrest the outsourcing of critically important jobs in their petroleum industries, some PPCs have resorted to local content development through the formulation of local content policies. Initially, these local content policies were confined to the creation of backward linkages through the supply to local economies via technology transfer, job creation, and the increase of local ownership. Recently, several PPCs have increasingly sought to create forward linkages such as processing petroleum products prior to export as well.[24] To that end, a number of them have established refineries and petrochemical industries, and ventured into the production of fertilizers. Still, some other local content policies are now formulated with the aim of diversifying the petroleum industry beyond the oil and gas sector value chain.[25]

Lately, some African PPCs such as Nigeria, Angola, and Equatorial Guinea have resorted to imposing more deliberate local content requirements (LCRs) on petroleum firms operating in their terrains in order to encourage local participation. To that end they have formulated policies, devised initiatives, or required firms to comply with minimum local content either via contract or legislation. New entrants to the petroleum industry such as Ghana, Tanzania, Uganda, and Kenya have also welcomed the local content movement. These countries have either formulated LCRs, or are in the process of doing so.[26] But what is local content, and what form does it assume?

Simply put, it is conditioning the grant of benefits on the use of local goods and/or services in producing goods and/or services in a particular country or locality.[27] It ranges from deliberate government patronage of local industries in the award of procurement contracts, to requiring firms operating in a particular country or locality to utilise specified percentages of local goods and services in their operations. Furthermore, local content development may entail the design of government processes in order to discourage the influx of foreign firms, in a bid to

Angola' 2014 http://www.eisourcebook.org/cms/December%202015/Angola%20Petroleum%20Local%20Content%20Analysis.pdf, accessed 12 May 2017.

23 See Pinto, 2013.

24 See White, 2017.

25 See Tordo, Racy and Arfaa, 2011, at p 8; see also Auty, 2001.

26 Interestingly, the rise of local content measures in the petroleum industry is not unique to Africa alone. Countries in the Middle East have also sought to increase local content lately, as well as Brazil and Russia. See Olawuyi, 2017.

27 See Hestermeyer and Nielsen, 2014, at p 565.

promote domestic industries. In relation to the petroleum industry, the term is all-encompassing, gathering to itself the extent to which human and material resources, as well as services provided in a PPC, are employed and utilised in a country's petroleum industry.[28] As such, a PPC may require concessionaires or service firms operating in its domain, to attain minimum local content targets, which may be measured as a percentage of investment, hours worked, equipment supplied, or jobs created in the industry. A PPC may, in addition, require foreign-based firms operating on its turf to establish subsidiaries locally, or to engage in local production of the goods they require for their operations in that country.

Local content policies as designed by PPCs may be implemented through government-related initiatives, or local requirements contained in legislations or contracts. Some LCRs are comprehensive, embracing material aspects of the petroleum industry with a view to optimising the derivables from the value chain.[29] They usually cover broad categories such as employment, the development of local firms, as well as the promotion and utilisation of local supply and service industries.

LCRs on employment, for instance, may require concessionaries or service firms to recruit an appreciable number of their employees from their host countries in order to promote the integration of the citizens of those countries into their petroleum industries. They may also require these firms to have internal policies on personnel development, training, and job succession, etc.[30] In addition to securing employment of their citizens, PPCs may push for the direct participation of indigenous firms in the more capital- and technology-intensive aspects of their petroleum industries. This aspect of local content may thus require the formulation of policies deliberately aimed at promoting indigenous supply and service firms (ISSFs), as well as indigenous E&P firms.

Thus a PPC may choose to award petroleum concessions to indigenous E&P firms, or on more favourable and preferential terms in order to encourage their participation in the industry. For example, in 1991 Nigeria commenced the award of petroleum concessions to local E&P firms on a discretionary basis. This policy

28 In a similar vein, s.106 of the Nigerian Oil and Gas Industry Content Development Act 2010 (NOGICDA) defines it as the as the 'quantum of value added to or created in the Nigerian economy by a systematic development of capacity and capabilities through the deliberate utilization of Nigerian human, material resources and services in the Nigerian Oil and Gas Industry. See also reg.49 of Ghana's Petroleum (Local Content and Local Participation) Regulation, 2013. See Accenture, 'Developing local content Programs' (2009) http://www.criticaleye.com/insights-servfile.cfm?id=833 accessed 28 October 2017.

29 Ovadia, 2015.

30 See s.28 of NOGICDA 2010, for example, which requires PPCs to prepare and submit local content plans bordering on training, employment, and investment in-country. Similarly, Art.86 of Angola's Petroleum Activities Law of 2004 (Law 10/04), under which foreigners may only be employed where there Angolan citizens do not have the requisite qualifications and experiences. While Art.4 of the Decree on the Rules to Observe in Recruitment, Integration, Training and Development of Workers from the Oil Sector of 2009, (Decree 17/09) of Angola also provides that the hiring of foreign workers can only be done with the prior authorization of the Ministry of Petroleum.

was implemented notwithstanding the fact that most of the initial awardees, at the time, lacked the requisite experience to prequalify for the grant of petroleum concessions. Although Nigeria's discretionary award of petroleum concessions to local firms was later subjected to some abuses, it heralded the entrance of indigenous E&P firms in the core aspects of the NPI, which for decades before had then been the exclusive preserve of IOCs. Furthermore, Nigeria awards marginal oil fields to indigenous E&P firms on relatively liberal terms in order to enable their participation in the operation of oil fields which are regarded as not being too capital or financially intensive, or commercially attractive to IOCs.[31]

A PPC may also require or encourage foreign supply or service firms to partner with ISSFs in fabrication contracts in order to encourage their participation in critically important projects in their petroleum industries. For example, in 2013, LADOL, an indigenous logistics firm, was jointly awarded a contract for the construction and installation of an FPSO for Total in its Egina oilfield, valued at about $3.5 billion. A PPC may, in addition, reserve certain jobs in the petroleum industry for ISSFs in order to encourage their participation. As such, concessionaires may be required to utilize only local firms in certain aspects of their operation. For example, amendments to Algeria's 2005 Hydrocarbons Law reserved transportation of petroleum for Sonatrach, the country's NOC, or to any firm in which it has a 51 percent stake.[32]

The third aspect of local content development may entail requiring petroleum firms to source a certain percentage of the materials and services they require in-country, with a view to promoting local industries. To that end, PPCs may grant incentives to firms which comply with their directives in the form of tax reliefs. Compliance may be used as a basis for the award of further concessions or jobs in the future, as well.[33] On the other hand, they may impose sanctions on defaulters which may entail banning concessionaires and service firms from bidding for jobs or licenses in the future, or imposing stiff fines for non-compliance.[34]

31 To date, the FGN has awarded about 30 marginal oil fields to indigenous firms. See Department of Petroleum Resources, 'Oil and Gas Annual Report (2016) https://dpr.gov.ng/index/wp-content/uploads/2016/01/2016-Oil-Gas-Industry-Annual-Report.pdf, accessed 6 March 2016; see also Ezeani and Nwuke, 2017. See also 'FG Kicks off Second Marginal Fields Bid Round ...Assures of Transparency and Accountability in Bid Process' http://www.nnpcgroup.com/PublicRelations/NNPCinthenews/tabid/92/articleType/ArticleView/articleId/479/FG-Kicks-off-Second-Marginal-Fields-Bid-Round-Assures-of-Transparency-and-Accountability-in-Bid-Process.aspx, accessed 28 October 2017.

32 See Krotoff and Bonnefoy, 2006.

33 See s.48 of NOGICDA. See also s.13(i) of the Petroleum Profits Tax Act 1958 (PPTA). The PPTA in effect disallows concessionaries from claiming capital allowances for the importation of certain goods which could have been purchased in Nigeria. Under Arts 12, 14 and 20 of Angola's Decree-Law 17/09, certain financial contributions are deductible for tax purposes if they are geared towards local content compliance.

34 See s.68 of NOGICDA for instance, under which failure to comply with Nigeria's LCRs may result in the termination of a contract awarded to a firm in the NPI.

It was demonstrated above that LCRs have risen not only in African PPCs, but also in other countries of the world which are rich in natural resources. They have risen because a number of RRCs believe that certain benefits may accrue to them if they optimise local participation in their petroleum industries. Some of these perceived benefits are now explored in detail.

1.2 Perceived benefits of local content

Local content measures are often imposed in the hope that if properly implemented and complied with, they would translate into numerous benefits for PPCs. The employment of an appreciable number of a country's citizens in its petroleum industry for example, is expected to have a multiplier effect on a larger number of the population, through funds retention in-country, personal income taxes, and manpower development, etc. Countries that adopt local content measures expect that the involvement of local firms in their petroleum industries will translate into the retention of billions of dollars of profits in-country in addition to the taxes that these firms would pay to their state governments. Again, local firms may expectedly create jobs for a large number of the citizens of PPCs which would have been outsourced abroad. For example, the 650,000 barrels of crude oil per day refinery currently being built by the Dangote group is expected to create an estimated 4,000 jobs for Nigerians.[35] These jobs, where so created, would not only generate personal income taxes for states and local governments by employing a significant percentage of employees, but also these employees, many of whom are residents of Nigeria, would spend their earnings in the country, which would boost other sectors of the economy as well.

There are also expectations that a strong local content would impact other segments of the economy through linkages with related sectors. Because the petroleum industry is capital- and technology-intensive, an appreciable local content will, over time, result in the development of technological capacity through sustained investment in research, technology transfer, etc. This will invariably impact other related industrial and financial sectors of PPC such as manufacturing, shipping, transportation, construction, and fabrication.[36] The capacity generated by these firms may be exported to foreign terrains, and by so doing may be able to generate taxes for their home states, and repatriate their profits back home.[37]

35 Yusuf, 2018.
36 Neff, 2005.
37 For example, Sahara Energy, an indigenous Nigerian firm, has a presence in Africa, the Caribbean, Asia, and Europe. Sahara Energy, 'About Us' http://www.sahara-group.com/about_us.html, accessed 29 January 2018; while Televeras also has operations in Equatorial Guinea and Ivory Coast, M Nsehe, 'Nigerian Energy Group Televeras and ExxonMobil Win Oil Blocks in Equatorial Guinea' *Forbes* (7 June 2017) https://www.forbes.com/sites/mfonobongnsehe/2017/06/07/nigerian-energy-group-taleveras-and-exxonmobil-win-oil-blocks-in-equatorial-guinea/, accessed 29 January 2018; similarly, Atlas-Oranto Petroleum has operations in Equatorial Guinea, Ghana, South Sudan, Benin, Senegal, Sao Tome, and Uganda. See Oranto Petroleum, 'Portfolio' http://atlas-oranto.com/portfolio/, accessed 29 January 2018.

In addition to the above perceived benefits, the development of human capacity by virtue of a strong local content in the petroleum industry will invariably create a human resources pool, from which academics, and policy makers with hands-on experience, can be sourced.[38] A vibrant human resources pool will inexorably address regulatory gaps, by ensuring that critically important regulatory offices are manned by adequately equipped personnel.[39]

PPCs which seek to improve their local content in order to reap the perceived benefits outlined above, would however have to design their strategies properly if they are to attain success in that regard. As a matter of first importance, they would have to formulate well thought out policies, and combine them with workable legal frameworks. Local content policies, which are firm statements of intent, would guide their practices and procedures in the implementation of their local content goals. Such policies would state matters of principle and action, and outline what is to be done, and by whom.[40] Without a properly articulated policy, attaining arriving at a definite criteria to measure their successes or failures will be difficult, if not impossible. In other words, the extent to which PPCs have achieved their policy objectives may be a starting point in assessing how successful they have been in the implementation of their local content agenda.

Such policies will have to be clear, comprehensive, and achievable, in the light of several factors, such as: the location of petroleum deposits (onshore, swam, offshore, or deep offshore). Other factors a PPC may consider in formulating its local content policy in the petroleum industry would include the financial and technical capacities of its local industries, the extent to which it depends on petroleum for the funding of its budgets, the size of its petroleum reserves, etc.

Local content policies and the measures used in implementing them invariably vary from country to country. While some are protectionist, strict and top-down in nature, others are mild, collaborative, bottom-up, and flexible, still some other PPCs endeavour to adopt a hybrid of both protectionism and liberalised approaches. A proper appreciation of the features and distinctions of the protectionist and liberalised approaches is important since a policy approach that may be suitable for Nigeria, may be unsuitable for Egypt or Russia, as the case may be. These two approaches, their suitability, and the factors which inform their adoption by PPC, are the focus of the following analysis.

1.3 Approaches to local content development

1.3.1 The protectionist approach

As the name implies, protectionism refers to government measures that are aimed at protecting local petroleum firms and sectors from foreign competition. These

38 A ready example is that of Kesiye Simbi Wabote, who, prior to his appointment as the current executive secretary of the Nigerian Content Development Monitoring Board, was a top executive of Shell Petroleum Development Company of Nigeria.

39 See also Amanze-Nwachukwu, 2012.

40 University of Sydney, 'What is a Policy' http://sydney.edu.au/legal/policy/what/index.shtml, accessed 16 June 2013.

measures may take several forms. First, a government may limit the extent of the participation of foreign firms in its petroleum industry, or it may set very ambitious and extensive local content targets which concessionaires, contractors and other operators would be required to comply with. These measures may be implemented through rigid, top-down regulations, and defaulters may be visited with stiff sanctions.[41] Other protectionist measures may take the form of tariffs and duties imposed on imported goods, as well as extremely harsh labour laws which prohibit or severely limit foreigners from operating or working in a PPC.

Critics of protectionist measures argue that they cause delays in petroleum operations, besides making countries which adopt them unattractive to foreign investors.[42] Furthermore, in order to get around rigid and sometimes 'impossible' protectionist measures, some firms (local and foreign) may resort to creative compliance, or bribery of regulators. Commenting on which the Organisation for Economic Co-operation and Development (OECD), observes that '... as the technicality and complexity of regulation increases, so does the possibility for less scrupulous players to find loopholes in specific rules and engage in "creative compliance"'.[43] And besides predisposing regulators to corruption, protectionism, by reserving certain rights for NOCs, ISSFs, and indigenous E&P firms, may result in their being uncompetitive and inefficient. This is more likely to be the case if such firms 'enjoy' state-conferred benefits as a matter of right. Some PPCs which have adopted protectionist local content measures include Nigeria, Brazil, and Indonesia. Certain elements of Brazil's protectionism are considered presently, while the Nigerian experience is examined in subsequent chapters.[44]

Brazil, like most South American countries has always had a strong nationalistic fervour. This has played out in its protectionist approach to its petroleum industry. The country first discovered petroleum in commercial quantities in 1939. In 1953 it enacted Law 2004, which excluded private participation (foreign and local) from most of the Brazilian petroleum industry (BPI) and conferred exclusive monopoly upstream rights on its NOC, Petróleo Brasileiro SA ('Petrobras'). This monopoly was later extended to most aspects of the downstream sub-sector of the BPI as well. Thus Petrobras was made to operate without upstream competition for over 40 years. Between 1995 and 1997, however, Brazil liberalised its petroleum industry in order to address liquidity constraints which it faced at the time.[45] It

41 See Takechi and Kiyono, 2005. See also Gu and Yabuuchi, 2003.

42 See Nwaokoro, 2012. See also Atsegbua, 2012.

43 OECD, 'Reducing the Risk of Policy Failure: Challenges for Regulatory Compliance' (2000) http://www.oecd.org/gov/regulatorypolicy/1910833.pdf, accessed 4 January 2017.

44 Nigeria's local content policy is embodied in NOGICDA, the contents of which are examined in more detail in Chapter 5.

45 In 1995, Constitutional Amendment No. 9 amended some aspects of Brazil's 1988 constitution, which like Law 2004/1953, had made illegal certain service contracts which Brazil had entered into with foreign firms in the 1970s and in the 1980s as being in contravention of Brazil's ban on foreign participation. The amendment paved way for the liberalisation of the BPI, which was brought into force in 1997, following the enactment of Law 9478. See also Ribeiro, 2009.

stripped Petrobras of its monopoly rights in the upstream by repealing Law 2004/1953, and partially privatised it in 2000. Furthermore, Brazil opened up the BPI to private firms (foreign and local). These firms were for the first time allowed to bid for petroleum concessions in an open and competitive bidding process. Furthermore, Brazil established the National Agency for Petroleum, Natural Gas, and Biofuels (ANP) as a separate and independent body to oversee and regulate the industry.

These reforms did not remove the country's protectionist attitude to its petroleum resources however. First, LCRs which were published by the ANP were heavily tilted to favour local firms operating in the BPI.[46] Furthermore, Petrobras remained the de facto monopoly over the BPI, despite the influx of new actors such as Shell and Chevron. The so-called liberalisation attempt was put to the test in 2007, when Brazil discovered giant offshore fields trapped in a pre-salt layer.[47] In response to the euphoria that greeted these findings, Brazil returned to its monopoly days. In 2010, it transited to a special and unique production sharing regime for most of its pre-salt fields. To that end it enacted Law 12.351/2010 which stipulated that the pre-salt fields would be operated under production sharing arrangements as against the concessionary framework which had regulated Brazil's interactions with concessionaires, pre-2010.

Article 10 of Law 12.351 law authorised the Brazilian Ministry of Mines and Energy to enter into production sharing contracts (PSCs) with petroleum firms under an auction system administered by the ANP. The average age of these PSCs was 35 years. Petrobras was given a minimum stake of 35 percent in all PSCs that would be entered into between the Brazilian state, and E&P firms. The firm was made exclusive operator of all pre-alt PSCs as well.[48] In the same year, Brazil enacted Law 12.276 of 2010 (the 'onerous assignment law'), which arbitrarily

46 CMS Law-Now, 'Reforms to Brazilian Local Content Policy' (2016), http://www.cms-lawnow.com/ealerts/2016/02/reforms-to-brazilian-local-content-policy, accessed 28 October 2017.

47 The pre-salt region refers to giant offshore oil fields estimated to be between 50 and 100 billion barrels of crude oil. At conservative estimates, however, they are still estimated to triple Brazil's current petroleum reserves which are in excess of 10 billion barrels of crude oil. See Cortes, 2011. See also Millard, 2011.

48 Brazil enacted Law 12.351 in 2010, which sets out the framework for PSC in the pre-salt. Interestingly, prior to the PSC Law, firms in Brazil operated through either the concession system or through a regime for the transfer of rights to Petrobras. With the PSC Law, the country now has three separate systems under which petroleum firms operate in the country. See PPSA, 'PPSA's Roles in the New Regulatory Regime for the Brazilian Pre-Salt' (2014) https://www.braziltexas.org/assets/files/oswaldo%20Bratecc%20Workshop_PPSA_Oswaldo%20Pedrosa_May%207%202014_v1.pdf, accessed 6 January 2017. Article 10 of Law 12.351 authorises the Brazilian Ministry of Mines and Energy to enter into PSCs with petroleum firms under an auction system administered by the ANP. With this law, Brazil departed from its traditional RSCs and concessionary contracts. Its PSCs are for a 35-year duration. Millard and Lima, 2013. This law was, however, deemed a clog on the wheel of the progress of the firm which became overwhelmed by its responsibilities in the vast pre-salt region. The government enacted Law 13.365/2016 to address some of those challenges. The new law makes

assigned oil blocks to Petrobras which were estimated to contain over five billion barrels of crude oil in the pre-salt fields. The onerous assignment was not free, though, as the firm was required to pay over $43 billion to the Brazilian state – most of which were in securities.

This about-turn in policy saw Brazil abandon all pretensions to the liberalisation of the BPI in the wake of its pre-salt finds. Petrobras' exclusive operatorship as well as its huge onerous concessions were, however, deemed to be a clog on the wheel of the progress of the firm. They over-stretched the capabilities of the firm to a point of near breakdown. Overwhelmed by its burdens, and immense operational responsibilities in the vast pre-salt region and elsewhere, the firm came to the point of near bankruptcy. In order to address the limitations which Petrobras faced in the pre-salt, the Brazilian government enacted Law 13.365 in 2016. The new law made the firm the preferred operator in pre-salt PSCs, but removed the mandatory operatorship component. By so doing it, paved the way for other experienced E&P firms to operate in the pre-salt fields as well.[49]

Apart from the challenges which Petrobras faced in the pre-salt, Brazil's stringent local content laws also made the BPI unattractive for foreign investors. In an age where PPCs have sprawled all over the globe and are competing for limited capital, Brazil found its pre-salt projections falling apart. Keen to reverse this trend, it capitulated to pressures and to reason: from 2017 Brazil began to reverse some of its strict and protectionist local content policies. Thus it removed local content as a bidding criteria for its 14th bidding round which was held in 2017, in order to attract foreign investors, while retrospectively relaxing some LCRs in blocks awarded as far back as 2005.[50]

The protectionist approach to local content is popular among several developing PPCs. From Nigeria, Ghana, Indonesia, Brazil, Angola, to Tanzania, these countries have shown a strong preference for introducing protectionist measures as a direct strategy of furthering domestic participation in their petroleum industries. And others such as Uganda and Kenya are about to adopt similar frameworks.[51] Several factors should, however, be considered before a PPC should decide whether to adopt protectionism. These factors include: the country's financial and technical capacity, the extent of its reserves and their location, as well as the international trade implications of protectionism. Because of their importance locally and internationally, they require in-depth assessment by policy makers in countries which seek to adopt this approach in developing their local content. Some of these factors are now considered.

First is the issue of technical and financial capacity. The petroleum industry is technology- and capital-intensive. It requires advanced drilling technologies and

Petrobras the preferred operator with the choice to choose which block it wishes to operate in the pre-salt, but it is no longer a mandatory operator.

49 See generally, Subai, 2018.

50 CMS Law, 'Brazil Proposes Relaxation of Local Content Requirements' (2017) http://www.cms-lawnow.com/ealerts/2017/02/brazil-proposes-relaxation-of-local-content-requirements, accessed 5 September 2017.

51 See Ovadia, 2016.

the combination of various forms of scientific and engineering capacities. In addition, the industry requires billions of dollars from strong financial institutions as well as vibrant service, supply, fabrication, construction, and manufacturing sectors. This makes reliance on foreign technology and capital inevitable most of the time not only for developing PPCs incidentally, but also for developed PPCs such as Norway, the United Kingdom (UK), and Australia. This means that developing countries which have relatively weak financial and technological capacities may invariably have to rely on foreign firms and funds at least to some extent, in order to develop their petroleum resources. It may therefore not be very suitable for them to adopt strict protectionist approaches in their petroleum industries, perhaps not until they are able to develop strong manufacturing sectors, vibrant local supply and service firms, as well as efficient indigenous E&P firms.

While some PPCs with relative capacity such as Russia, China, Brazil, or more developed ones such as America, the UK, and Australia, may be better suited for protectionism, in practice they still rely on foreign capital and technology to extract and develop their petroleum resources. What is being established here, is that excluding foreign participation or adopting a very strict local content approach may have unintended consequences as the Brazilian example demonstrates. Similar to Brazil, Algeria at one time, decided to 'go it alone' in its petroleum industry. Thus it excluded foreign firms from operating on its turf and placed all its hopes on its NOC, Sonatrach. Despite the firm's relative competence, in no time it became obvious that because of the country's weak financial and technical capacity, excluding foreign participation was not going to work.[52] These realities eventually 'forced' Algeria to open up its petroleum sector in 2005.[53]

Another important factor to be considered before adopting a protectionist approach to local content is the extent of petroleum reserves owned by the PPC in question. Essentially, countries with fewer petroleum deposits may easily afford protectionism, in contrast to countries with abundant deposits, which would inevitably have to rely on foreign input and capital if they are to profitably exploit their resources. Pretentions to exclusive or very strict protectionism may only stifle the growth of a PPC such as Saudi Arabia or Venezuela, each of which has crude oil deposits in excess of 200 billion barrels. These countries may be contrasted with Ivory Coast, whose reserves are less than 200 million barrels of crude oil, or Tunisia, which has an estimated 0.4 billion barrels of crude oil.[54]

52 See Alvarez, 2010.

53 In 2006, though, Algeria's president, A Bouteflika, via a 2006 Order ('the 2006 Hydrocarbons Order'), amended portions of the 2005 Act in a bid to reallocate to the firm, a majority stake in all upstream and downstream activities. Furthermore, only Sonatrach and other local firms, in which it owned at least a 51 percent share, were allowed to undertake transportation or refining activities in the sector. For more on this, see Subai, 2018.

54 Source: British Petroleum, 'BP Statistical Review of World Energy', https://www.bp.com/content/dam/bp/en/corporate/pdf/energy-economics/statistical-review-2017/bp-statistical-review-of-world-energy-2017-full-report.pdf, accessed 11 March 2018.

These factors explain why Brazil could have afforded exclusive protectionism as at 1953, having discovered only about 15 million barrels of crude oil at the time, while Norway was 'forced' to open up its industry from inception to foreign participation, since its initial discoveries were in excess of one billion barrels of crude oil.[55]

Then there is the issue of the location or situation of petroleum deposits. A PPC considering protectionism has to ascertain whether the deposits are offshore or onshore. In essence, the harsher the terrain in which petroleum resources are trapped, the higher the technology and funds required to extract them. While it may be easy for a developing country, acting via its NOC or indigenous firms, to extract onshore petroleum, these firms may struggle to operate offshore or in ultra-deep terrains, which would require FPSOs, underground cables and pipelines, and advanced drilling technologies. In effect, offshore operations often entail the use of highly specialised equipment as well as higher costs. Strict protectionist rules may therefore delay and increase significantly the costs of these projects if the equipment or the goods required are not available locally.[56]

In most instances, the technology for offshore projects may only be possessed by experienced IOCs such as Shell, Chevron, Eni, etc., and their service counterparts such as Wilbros and Baker Hughes, or by very established and capable NOCs such as Petrobras and Statoil. Location of reserves should therefore be taken into consideration before determining whether or not to adopt strict protectionism or whether to open up a PPC to IOCs and foreign service firms. For instance, virtually all of Norway's petroleum resources are trapped offshore. This meant that any pretensions to protectionism in 1969 when the Norwegian petroleum industry was born, were impossible and impracticable, given that the country did not have an NOC or vibrant E&P firms, at the time.[57]

Lastly, the extent to which petroleum contributes to the gross domestic product (GDP) of a PPC should also be taken into consideration in determining whether or not to adopt protectionist local content measures. This is because there are certain economic repercussions in adopting protectionism. For example, it may slow production especially if its strict nature scares away foreign investors or slows the operations of petroleum firms. This will invariably affect government earnings. PPCs such as the United States of America (USA) and the UK, in which petroleum revenues contribute less than 3 percent to annual GDP may more readily afford protectionism, in contrast to petroleum-reliant economies such as Saudi Arabia and Kuwait, where petroleum revenues contribute as much as 50 percent of GDP.

55 Norway, 'Norwegian Oil Production through 35 Years' http://www.energybc.ca/cache/oil2/www.norway.org/ARCHIVE/business/businessnews/oilproduction/index.html, accessed 14 March 2017.

56 See Pereira, Gergio and Amorium, 2017, where the authors note cost and time implications of Brazil's local content laws in its pre-salt regions.

57 Norsk Hydro a Norwegian firm which had had extensive experience in the hydropower industry was, however, just entering into the petroleum business at the time.

Lastly, PPCs which seek to adopt protectionism should consider whether such measures have implications under international trade law. As shown in Chapter 7, most countries of the world are signatories to some form of multilateral or bilateral free trade agreements which discourage protectionist measures. Breach of these measures may result in a backlash in sanctions and retaliatory measures. These factors should therefore be considered before embarking on protectionist local content measures.

1.3.2 The liberalised approach to local content

In contrast to protectionism, the liberalised approach to local content development is more flexible, bottom-up, and less mandatory in nature. Countries that adopt this approach seek to develop local content gradually by promoting collaboration between indigenous firms and their foreign-based counterparts on a voluntary basis. Such countries typically endeavour to create a level playing field for local and foreign firms to function freely. As such, rather than rely on stringent LCRs for example, a PPC that seeks to develop its local content through collaboration, may encourage foreign petroleum firms to patronise local supply and service firms, or to enter into partnership arrangements with them. Furthermore, it would endeavour to create a favourable and attractive climate for such firms in order to encourage them to domicile their operations in-country or to establish subsidiaries in its terrain. A number of Western PPCs such as Canada, Norway, Australia, and the UK, which champion the free market ideology, are more collaborative in their approach to local content development. This explains the absence of mandatory LCRs. And, perhaps with the exception of Norway, states that adopt this approach oftentimes refrain from directly participating in their petroleum industries through NOCs.

And while such countries may seek to give some support to local firms, perhaps the most notable feature of the liberalised approach is that less reliance is placed on prohibitive measures, while the emphasis is placed on a pacifist approach. Hence these countries encourage local suppliers by building their capacities to compete, while simultaneously inviting foreign firms to invest in-country. It may be argued that PPCs such as Norway and the UK can afford to adopt this approach because they have been able to develop some level of in-country capacity, in the form of vibrant E&P firms, strong manufacturing sectors, as well as developed services and supply sectors. Thus assured of the ability of their local industries to compete favourably with foreign firms, they are under less pressure to 'protect' local industries from foreign competition. The UK approach to local content development is now reviewed.

The UK is a PPC. Most of its petroleum resources are situated on the UK side of the North Sea. Perhaps because of its status as a developed country, the UK did not adopt the protectionist route to local content development, but opened its petroleum industry to American and European firms to operate and compete freely on the North Sea. That notwithstanding, the UK government was somewhat involved in the industry through British Petroleum (BP), in which it had some shares, and later through the British National Oil Company which was established in 1975. The UK government's refusal to stipulate strict local content measures, however, saw UK supply and service firms being side-lined by American firms in the vital aspects of petroleum operations in the North Sea. A fact that was confirmed by a study conducted in the early 1970s. In response, the UK government established the Offshore Supplies Office (OSO) in 1973.[58] Its primary aim was to increase the local content in the UK's petroleum industry from about 30 percent to 70 percent, through a 'full and fair opportunity' policy that would ensure that UK-based firms were given fair opportunities to compete with foreign firms, on an equal footing.

Rather than rely on targets and sanctions, however, the OSO first set about evaluating the local content in the UK petroleum industry, following which it developed initiatives aimed at capacity building as a means of addressing perceived deficiencies. Then it set about monitoring and auditing purchasing procedures of petroleum firms in the North Sea, while requiring such firms to submit quarterly reports of contracts they intended to award, along with a list of the contractors they intended to use, as well as a list of firms which bided for jobs unsuccessfully.[59] The OSO was thus able to determine if UK firms were side-lined in the contracting process. Other measures were geared towards the stimulation of the development of new UK-based suppliers, and the promotion of collaborations between local and foreign based firms, export promotion, and the stimulation of research and development (R&D), were adopted as well. Due largely to the efforts of the OSO, over time, the local content in the UK petroleum industry grew from about 30 percent prior 1973, to about 60 percent in 1977, and about 87 percent by 1988.[60]

As the UK example demonstrates, capacity building initiatives are often the hallmark of countries that adopt the liberalised approach to local content. These countries invest heavily in infrastructure, research, as well as in the development of viable manufacturing, construction and technology-related sub-sectors to act as feeders to their petroleum industries. The same thread runs across the USA, Canada, Norway, and Australia.

The issue is whether this approach would be suitable for developing countries that lack the capacity of their developed counterparts. Ideally, it may be argued that PPCs such as Gabon and Sudan which struggle with adequate in-country capacity in the form of strong petroleum companies, a vibrant manufacturing and construction base, strong banks, etc., should adopt the liberalised approach to local content. This is because such countries may inevitably require foreign 'support' for the development of their petroleum resources, until such a time as their

58 International Management and Engineering Group of Britain Limited, 1972. See also, Smith, 2011.

59 See Klueh et al, 2009.

60 Oxford Analytica, 'The Impact of Pre-Salt: a Long Term Perspective' (2010), a report prepared for Petrobras http://www.oxan.com/.../cr/.../OxfordAnalyticaPetrobrasPreSalt.pdf , accessed 19 November 2017.

local industries are able to tackle more significant challenges. Hence the stipulation of stringent LCRs may discourage such investments. Rather, such countries should, within a given time frame, seek to develop in-country capacity through sustained investment in the development of human capacity, and its services and manufacturing sectors, but in the interim, should refrain from adopting protectionist measures.[61] The risk in adopting such an approach in developing countries such as Gabon or Sudan, however, is that unrestrained liberalisation may stifle the growth of local firms, which would almost certainly be unable to compete with more vibrant foreign firms.

1.4 Between protectionism and the liberalised approach

The pertinent question then for developing PPCs of Africa is: which approach is better suited for local content development? Should countries such as Nigeria, Ghana, and Angola open their petroleum sectors to local and foreign firms to compete freely or should they resort to protectionism? The answer is not so clear cut. The desire to protect local firms from strong foreign competition is not without its merits, which explains why a number of developing and emerging economies resort to some form of protectionism not only in their extractive industries, but also in areas such as shipping, car manufacturing and assembling, and construction, etc. Thus while protectionism has its drawbacks, it also has its benefits.

It enabled the development of Brazil's Petrobras develop into an oil giant, but almost crippled the same industry in later years. Again, it should be mentioned that some of the champions of free markets have benefitted immensely in the past from some level of protectionism. Statoil of Norway (recently renamed Equinor ASA), for example, benefited immensely from state patronage from 1972 until Norway joined the European Economic Area (EEA) in 1994 and was thus required to open up its petroleum sector to free competition among EEA members. Protectionism has had some positive benefits for Nigeria as well, as is shown subsequently,[62] and its potential for addressing perceived unfairness in trade among nations informed President Donald Trump's expressed desire to 'dump' the North American Free Trade Agreement (NAFTA).[63] Lastly, it is worth noting that the majority of the countries which have refrained from adopting protectionism did not do so out of sheer belief in the benefits of liberalism, but mainly because they were 'forced' to do so in the interest of free trade and its attendant benefits. That said, the liberalised approach has its merits as well. It 'compels' local firms to rely on their competitiveness rather than on state patronage and protection, which impels

61 See the Draft Local Content Policy for the Tanzanian Oil and Gas Industry (2014), https://mem.go.tz/wp- content/uploads/2014/05/07.05.2014local-content-policy-of-tanzania-for-oil-gas-industry.pdf, accessed 30 June 2017.

62 The impact of Nigeria's local content strategy is dealt with in greater detail in Chapters 4 and 5.

63 Wingrove and Olorunnipa, 2018.

them to greater efficiency. Furthermore, it enables countries to attract foreign investment, while ensuring that they do not breach their international free trade obligations.

Protectionism, however, has its drawbacks. Champions of free markets have argued against their perceived benefits and legality in the light of international free trade laws, while also pointing out that protectionism may actually have negative economic implications for countries which adopt them. Additionally, foreign-based firms are quick to point out that they are onerous, harsh, and unrealistic. In a similar vein, some legal scholars have argued that LCRs stand the risk of violating international trade and investment laws. Some of the arguments against protectionism are considered in detail presently, while the arguments on the legality of protectionist local content measures are examined in Chapter 7.

1.5 Some arguments against protectionist local content approaches

Despite their immense popularity, protectionist local content measures are not always welcomed among free trade advocates and some scholars who have argued that they impose economic costs and delays on operators, while their overall economic impact remain uncertain. Grossman for example states that '... content protection and content preference may fail to attain the noneconomic objectives of the policy maker'.[64] Others argue that LCRs place a huge burden on industries which seek to expand by compelling the utilisation of locally manufactured goods and services rather than allowing them select providers on the basis of quality and cost.[65] It has also been suggested that the support conferred by LCRs on local producers is variable and opaque, and that government officials may have little or no understanding of the rate of protection actually conferred.[66] And that by insulating local firms from foreign competition, local content measures may give rise to lags in the adoption of new technologies, which eventually undermines the goal of nourishing high-tech infant industries.[67]

Then there is the contention that LCRs may adversely impact on downstream producers in terms of quality and price,[68] and are susceptible to corruption and favouritism, especially where a local industry has relatively few vibrant firms. Another argument has been put forward as well – that, at best, the empirical evidence demonstrates that LCRs stand the risk of building inefficient national industries, at enormous welfare costs.[69] In effect, the much touted economic benefits of local content are called into question by scholars who argue that LCRs sacrifice quality in preference for incompetent indigenous firms or services.[70] And

64 See Grossman, 1981.
65 See Hestermeyer and Nielsen, 2014, at p 554.
66 Cimino, Hufbauer and Schott, 2018.
67 Cimino, Hufbauer and Schott, 2018.
68 Hestermeyer and Nielsen, 2014, at p 591.
69 See Pursell, 2001.
70 See Kolstad and Kinyodo, 2017.

that they may translate into soaring operational costs, delays in project implementation, and bureaucratic rigidity, which may render compliance difficult.[71]

Rather than resort to protectionism, advocates of liberalism argue that PPCs should strengthen local industries and make their environment attractive to foreign-based petroleum firms.[72] That market-driven local procurement should be carried out in economically viable forms, tailored to the local corporate environment, rather than being enforced through policy-based regulations. To that end, some scholars have singled out Norway as an ideal model and a success story which developed its local content via the enhancement of its domestic knowledge base and via arrangements which allowed for a dynamic industrial and technological development.[73] Thus rather than rely on local content targets and mandatory stipulations, PPCs should gradually expand domestic competencies and capabilities to competitive levels.[74] Some other scholars have argued that in the place of local content measures, countries should refocus their efforts to lever natural resources in the creation of broad-based economic opportunities.[75]

As plausible as the above arguments sound, they fly in the face of the experience of many PPCs. First, building capacity over time is often difficult in the face of unrestrained foreign competition, which makes it next to impossible for local firms to function and develop unassisted by some level of government protection. And as shown earlier in the previous section, the much touted Norwegian local content success did not develop without some form of government preferences and protection. Secondly, although Norway did not necessarily have petroleum industry experience as at 1969, it was already a relatively developed country at that time. It already had viable local firms operating either in its hydro industries or in shipping. Norsk Hydro for instance, which entered the petroleum industry in the late 1960s, already had extensive experience in the hydroelectric business, which it started as far back as 1905.[76] This background enabled thus enabled the country to build indigenous capacity and a strong NOC within a very short time by relying on a hybrid of protectionism and the liberalised approach. Thus although its service sector was largely liberalised, Norway still conferred on its NOC Statoil certain automatic rights in its upstream. For example, the firm was granted a 50 percent stake in all concessions awarded to foreign firms in the 1970s and 1980s.[77] Again, while conceding that deficiencies in the design and implementation of local content programs may result in increased costs, delays and invariably impact revenue, local content also has the potential of delivering measurable benefits, if correctly designed and implemented, taking into cognisance country-specific factors.

71 Valle, 2015; see also See Tordo, Racy and Arfaa, 2011, at p 9.

72 See Kolstad and Kinyodo, 2017, at p 5; see also Ramdoo, 2015.

73 Ramdoo, 2015, at p 3.

74 Heum, 2008, at p 4.

75 See Besada and Martin, 2015.

76 Norsk Hydro, 'Our History' http://www.hydro.com/en/about-hydro/Our-history/, accessed 30 June 2017.

77 See Cameron, 1984–1985.

Again, although the UK's petroleum industry was largely liberalised, initial efforts were yet taken to favour the country's peculiar interests. Like Norway, in the fifties and sixties for example, the country used its discretion in awarding petroleum licenses to favour indigenous firms and firms from countries which were directly or indirectly linked to the UK. In its allocation of petroleum licenses in the North Sea, for instance, firms with ties to the UK were deliberately favoured. For example, 30 percent of petroleum blocks awarded were reserved for firms with ties to the UK, and another 10 percent to firms with ties to Canada. Naturally, this meant that considerations of fairness and equal treatment which form the bedrock of the liberal market ideology were subjected to more objective considerations of 'national interest'. Thus petroleum licenses in the UK were not necessarily awarded to the most efficient and competitive firms without catering for domestic interests.[78] It may well be instructive to reiterate again that, unlike Norway and the UK, many developing PPCs such as Nigeria, Gabon, South Sudan, and Ghana, do not already have technological competence, hence some form of 'protection' of domestic industries is not without its merits. Such protection should, however, be 'matched' with a dogged commitment to the development of local capacity.

It is conceded that unduly restrictive local content policies may stifle competition or result in inefficient domestic monopolies. But again this may only occur in PPCs such as Gabon, Ghana, Tanzania, and Sudan, which may not have viable local firms to compete among themselves. In contrast, however, protectionist local content measures may not necessarily weaken competition in PPCs such as the USA, China, Brazil, India, or Indonesia which are large, and have local firms that are able to compete among themselves. The USA, for example, besides having a large population, is home to some of the most globally competitive IOCs and supply and service firms. Hence even if the US petroleum industry is 'protected' through local content measures, its local firms would still have to compete among themselves for petroleum licenses and contracts.

Again it is conceded that local content measures may result in competitiveness in countries where petroleum licenses and contracts are awarded arbitrarily and not through a competitive process. In practice, however, a country adopting a local content measure may stipulate that contracts or licenses should only be awarded to capable local firms through a fair, transparent and competitive process. Such requirements additionally give room for foreign participation, with the caveat, however, that local firms be preferred if they have competent personnel and demonstrate adequate capacity, and that indigenously produced goods and services comply with international standards. Again, local firms may only be patronised in contracting where their bids do not exceed what is offered by their foreign counterparts above a specified threshold.[79] These requirements essentially

78 Dam, 1965, at p 66.

79 S.16 of NOGICDA for instance, provides Nigerian firms must have capacity to execute jobs in the NPI before they may be claim entitlement to preferential treatments. Furthermore, the value they bid for must not exceed the lowest value bid by other firms, by 10 percent. See also art.26.1 of Angola's Petroleum Activities Law, which stipulates that Sonangol and its associates, and any other entities that co-operate with them in

mean that domestic petroleum firms which do not develop some level of capacity may 'lose' out to foreign firms or to local competitors.[80] As such, rather than 'demotivate' them, they are spurred to develop capacity in order to remain in business and take advantage of opportunities open to them by local content policies.

In addition, protectionist local content measures may be suitable for developing countries, whose local industries have long been stifled by the dominance of IOCs and their foreign service counterparts. The Nigerian experience, as shown later in the book, will demonstrate that foreign firms operating in the petroleum industry may not be naturally predisposed towards strengthening local firms or in furthering domestic capacity. This accounts for the reason why Nigerian content remained low for a long period of time until the Nigerian government formulated a local content policy and took steps to bring it into actualisation.[81]

1.6 Conclusion

This chapter has attempted to lay the foundation for rest of this book. It demonstrated that because of the intense financial and technological nature of the petroleum industry, several developing PPCs inevitably rely extensively on foreign E&P firms and their service and supply counterparts, which has resulted in a weak local content in most of them. And that in their desire to reverse the trend, several PPCs have resorted to LCRs designed to boost domestic participation and create linkages between their petroleum industries and their broader economies. The chapter also attempted to conceptualise local content in general terms, while highlighting its perceived benefits. Protectionist and liberalised approaches to local content development, their merits and demerits, and the circumstances under which they may be applied, were also examined. Lastly, some arguments against local content measures were also analysed. The experiences of Norway, the UK, and Brazil in developing local content were considered as well.

One crucial lesson that can be extracted from the experiences of the above countries with respect to the development of local content is that there is the need for PPCs to be deliberate, committed to, and focused on, the implementation of whatever strategy they adopt. This would first of all require the formulation of well thought out policies, followed by strategic legal and institutional frameworks to guide policy implementation. In settling for a legal framework, for example, PPCs would have to determine whether to rely on (statutory or contractual)

carrying out petroleum operations, are to acquire materials, equipment, machinery, and consumer goods of national production, of the same or approximately the same quality and that are available for sale and delivery in due time, at prices that are no more than 10 percent higher than the imported items including transportation and insurance costs and customs charges due. Similar provisions are contained in art.23.1 of Equatorial Guinea's model PSC.

80 See s.3(2) of NOGICDA, See also *Arco v NAOC and others*, FH/PH/CS/02/2015. Discussed more fully in Chapter 3.

81 See Chapter 4, which explores the historical aspects of local content in Nigeria.

frameworks. Then they would have to settle for a suitable institutional framework to drive their local content policies. Some PPCs opt for NOCs, while others rely almost exclusively on government regulators, still others combine both NOCs and regulatory institutions. Whatever approach is adopted by a PPC should be realistic, having factored in the peculiar circumstances faced by the country. These factors should include a proper appreciation of the historical and peculiar settings of a PPC which seeks to erect local content frameworks, their in-country capabilities, as well the overall objectives which under-girds its policies. It is thus pertinent to appreciate that an approach that may result in positive outcomes for country A, may be unsuitable and unsuccessful if transplanted to country B. Going forward and developing this theme further, Chapter 2 evaluates legal and institutional frameworks for local content development.

Bibliography

Adelman MA, *The World Petroleum Market* (Johns Hopkins University Press, Baltimore, 1972).

Al-Kassim F, *Managing Petroleum Resources: The 'Norwegian Model' in a Broad Perspective* (Oxford Institute of Energy Studies, Oxford, 2006).

Alvarez AM, 'Reintierism in the Algerian Economy Based on Oil and Natural Gas' (2010) 38(10) *Energy Policy*, 6338.

Amanze-Nwachukwu C, 'Why DPR Can't Efficiently Regulate Oil Sector' *Thisday* (13 December 2012) http://www.thisdaylive.com/articles/why-dpr-can-t-efficiently-regulate-oil-sector/104909/, accessed 9 September 2017.

Atsegbua LA, 'The Nigerian Oil and Gas Industry Content Development Act 2010: an examination of its Regulatory Framework' (2012) 36(4) *OPEC Energy Review*, 479.

Auty RM, *Resource Abundance and Economic Development* (Oxford University Press, Oxford, 2001).

Balouga J, 'Nigerian Local Content: Challenges and Prospects' (2012) (Third Quarter) *International Association of Energy Economics*, 23 http://www.iaee.org/en/publications/newsletterdl.aspx?id=176, accessed 11 November 2012.

Besada H and Martin P, 'Mining Codes in Africa: Emergence of a "Fourth Generation"?' (2015) 28(2) *Cambridge Review of International Affairs*, 263.

Cameron P, 'North Sea Oil Licensing: Comparisons and Contrasts' (1984–1985) 4 *Oil & Gas L. & Tax. Rev.*, 99.

Cimino C, Hufbauer GC and Schott JJ, 'A Proposed Code to Discipline Local Content Requirements' (2014) *Policy Brief No. PB14-6*, Petersen Institute for International Economics, https://piie.com/publications/pb/pb14-6.pdf, accessed 18 June 2018.

Citino NJ, *From Arab Nationalism to OPEC: Eisenhower, King Saúd, and the Making of U.S.-Saudi Relations* (Indiana University Press, Bloomington, 2002).

Cortes K, 'Brazil to Auction Pre-Salt Oil Fields after Royalties', *Bloomberg* (7 January 2011), http://www.bloomberg.comlnews/2011-01-07/brazil-to-auction-pre-salt-oil-fields-after-roalties-updatel-.html, accessed 17 January 2017.

Dam KW, 'Oil and Gas Licensing and the North Sea' (1965) 8 *Journal of Law and Economics*, 51.

Easo J and Wallace A, 'Understanding Local Content Policies in Africa's Petroleum Sector' (2014), http://www.worldlawgroup.com, accessed 28 October 2017.

Ezeani EC and Nwuke C, 'Local content and the Marginal Fields Programme: Challenges for Indigenous Participation in the Nigerian Oil Industry' (2017) 15(1) *OGEL*, 1.

Grossman GM, 'The Theory of Domestic Content Protection and Content Preference' (1981) 96(4) *Quarterly Journal of Economics*, 583.

Gu W and Yabuuchi S, 'Local Content Requirements and Urban Unemployment' (2003) 12 *Intl. Rev. Econ. & Fin.*, 481.

Haas E, 'The Reconciliation of Conflicting Colonial Policy Aims: Acceptance of the League of Nations mandate system [Analysis of the Franco-British Motivations Leading to the Acceptance of the Mandate System after the First World War]' (1952) 6 *International Organization*, 521.

Hestermeyer HP and Nielsen L, 'The Legality of Local Content Measures under WTO' (2014) *Journal of World Trade*, 553.

Heum P et al, 'Enhancement of Local Content in the Upstream Oil and Gas Industry in Nigeria: A comprehensive and Viable Policy Approach' (2003) *SNF Report No. 25/03*, SNF: Institute for Research in Economics and Business Administration http://extrayendotransparencia.grupofaro.org/wp-content/uploads/2014/12/Enhancement-of-LC-in-the-upstream-oil-and-gas-industry-in-Nigeria.pdf, accessed 12 November 2016.

Heum P, 'Local Content Development: Experiences from Oil and Gas Activities in Norway' (2008) *SNF Working Paper No. 02/08* https://brage.bibsys.no/xmlui/bitstream/handle/11250/166156/1/A02_08.pdf, accessed 22 November 2016.

Hewitt T, 'Who is to Blame: Allocating Liability in Upstream Project Contracts' (2008) 26 *J. Energy Nat. Resources L.*, 177.

Hossein K, *Law and Policy in Petroleum Development: Changing Relations between Transnationals and Governments* (Nichols, Dubuque, 1979).

Idemudia U, 'The Resource Curse and the Decentralization of Oil Revenue: the Case of Nigeria' (2012) 35 *Journal of Cleaner Production*, 183.

International Management and Engineering Group of Britain Limited, *Study of Potential Benefits to British Industry from Offshore Oil and Gas Developments* (HMSO, London, 1972).

Joffe G et al, 'Expropriation of Oil and Gas Investments: Historical, legal and economic perspectives in a New Age of Resource Nationalism' (2009) 2(1) *Journal of World Energy Law & Business*, 4.

Johnston D, 'Changing Fiscal Landscape' (2008) 1(1) *Journal of World Energy Law & Business*, 31.

Kakonge JO, 'Challenges of Managing Expectations of Newly Emerging Oil and Gas Producers of the South' (2011) 4(2) *Journal of World Energy Law & Business*, 124.

Klueh UH et al, 'Policies to Improve the Local Impact from Hydrocarbon Extraction: Observations on West Africa and Possible Lessons for Central Asia' (2009) 37 *Energy Policy*, 1128.

Kolstad I and Kinyodo A, 'Alternatives to Local Content Requirements in Resource-Rich Countries' (2017) 45(4) *Oxford Development Studies*, 409.

Krotoff K and Bonnefoy N, 'Hydrocarbons Legislation in Algeria: Back to Square One?' (2006) http://www.la.utexas.edu/users/chenry/oil/2006/syll-2006%20Hydrocarbons%20Law%20Algeria.pdf, accessed 8 August 2017.

Kurtz MJ, 'Conditioning the "Resource Curse": Globalization, Human Capital, and Growth in Oil-Rich, Nations' (2011) 44(6) *Comparative Political Studies*, 747.

Millard P, 'Brazil Oil Fields May Hold More Than Twice Estimates' *Bloomberg* (19 January 2011) http://www.bloomberg.com/news/2011-01-19/brazil-oil-fields-may-hold-more-than-tw ice-estimated-reserves, accessed 9 March 2017.

Millard P and Lima MS, 'Brazil's Debt Crunch Buoys Exxon's Prospects in Brazil' *Bloomberg* (12 April 2013) http://www.bloomberg.com/news/2013-04-11/petrobras-debt-crunch-buoys-exxon-s-prospects-in-brazil-energy.html, accessed 8 April 2018.

Neff S, 'Memorandum on International Best Practice in Development of Local Content in the Energy Sector' (2005) Presented to the Nigeria National Stakeholders Working Group http://www.neiti.org.ng/sites/default/files/page/uploads/local-content-5-9-051.pdf, accessed 6 February 2018.

Nwaokoro JE, 'Signed, Sealed but will it Deliver? Nigeria's local content Bill and Cross-Sectoral Growth' (2012) 4(1) *Journal of World Energy Law & Business*, 56.

Okafor C, 'Local Content: Nigeria Loses $380 Billion to Expatriates' *Thisday* (21 December 2011).

Olawuyi DS, 'Local Content Requirements in Oil and Gas Contracts: Regional Trends in the Middle East and North Africa' (2017) 36(1) *JERNL*, 30.

Ovadia JS, 'Local Content Policies and Petro-Development in Sub-Saharan Africa: A Comparative Analysis' (2016) 49 *Resources Policy*, 27.

Ovadia JS, 'The Role of Local Content Policies in Natural Resource-based Development' (2015) *Austrian Development Policy*, 37 http://www.oefse.at/fileadmin/content/Downloads/Publikationen/Oepol/Artikel2015/Teil1_03_Ovadia.pdf, accessed 4 June 2018.

Parra F, *Oil Politics – A Modern History of Petroleum* (Tauris & Co Ltd, New York, 2005).

Pereira EG, Gergio F and Amorium L, 'The Brazilian pre-salt case: Governmental Interference and Challenges for Potential Joint Ventures' (2017) 35(4) *Journal of Energy & Natural Resources Law*, 456.

Pinto GE, 'Upstream Oil and Gas Legal Frameworks: Brazil and the United States Compared' (2013) 115 *W. Va. L. Rev.*, 999.

Polterovich V and Popov V, 'Resource Abundance, Globalization, and Economic Development' (2005) *New Economic School, Research Project 2005–2006* https://pages.nes.ru/english/research/projects/proposal/2005–2006/PolterovichPopov.doc, accessed 9 January 2016.

Pursell G, 'The Australian Experience with Local Content Programs in the Auto Industry-Some Lessons for India and other Developing Countries' (2001) 35(2) *Journal of World Trade*, 379.

Ramdoo I, 'Unpacking Local Content Requirements in the Extractive Sector: What Implications for the Global Trade and Investment Frameworks?' (2015) *E15 Expert Group on Trade and Investment in Extractive Industries, Think Piece*, http://e15initiative.org/wp-content/uploads/2015/07/Extractive-Ramdoo-FINAL.pdf, accessed 9 January 2017.

Raymond MS and Leffler LF, *Oil & Gas Production in Nontechnical Language* (3rd edn, Penwell Books, London, 2006).

Ribeiro MR, 'Sovereignty over Natural Resources Investment Law and Expropriation: The case of Bolivia and Brazil' (2009) 2 *Journal of World Energy Law & Business*, 139.

Samples TR and Vittor JL, 'Energy Reform and the Future of Mexico's Oil Industry: The Pemex Bidding Rounds and Integrated Service Contracts' (2011) 7(2) *Texas Journal of Oil Gas & Energy*, 215.

Seymour I, *OPEC: Instrument of Change* (Macmillan, London, 1980).

Smith NJ, *The Sea of Lost Opportunity: North Sea Oil and Gas, and the Offshore Supplies Office* (Elsevier, 2011).

Stansfield G, 'The Unravelling of the Post-first World War State System? The Kurdistan Region of Iraq and the Transformation of the Middle East' (2013) 89(2) *International Affairs*, 259.

Stevens P, 'National Oil Companies and International Oil Companies in the Middle East: Under the Shadow of Government and the Resource Nationalism Cycle' (2008) 1(1) *Journal of World Energy Law & Business*, 5.

Subai P, 'Petroleum Sector Liberalisation and direct state participation: lessons from Brazil' (2018) 6(1) *African Nazarene University Law Journal*, 92.

Sueur JDL, *Algeria since 1989: Between Terror and Democracy* (Zed Books, London, 2013).

Takechi K and Kiyono K, 'Local Content Protection: Specific-Factor Model For Intermediate Goods Production and Market Segmentation (2005) 15 *Japan and the World Economy*, 69.

Tordo S, Tracy BS and Arfaa N, 'NOCs and Value Creation' (2011) *World Bank Working Paper No. 218* http://siteresources.worldbank.org/INTOGMC/Resources/9780821388310.pdf, accessed 2 January 2016.

Valle S, 'Brazil's Local Content Rules to be Eased to Spur Oil Projects' *World Oil* (2015) http://www.worldoil.com/news/2015/5/12/brazils-local-content-rules-to-be-eased-to-spur-oil-projects, accessed 8 March 2018.

Wabote S, 'Eight Years of Local Content Act' *The Nation* (23 April 2018) http://thenationonlineng.net/eight-years-of-local-content-act/, accessed 9 June 2018.

White S, 'Regulating for Local Content: Limitations of Legal and Regulatory Instruments in Promoting Small Scale Suppliers in Extractive Industries in Developing Economies' (2017) *The Extractive Industries and Society*, 262.

Wingrove J and Olorunnipa T, 'Trump Repeats He'd Quit NAFTA and May Seek Separate Talks' *Bloomberg* (8 June 2018) https://www.bloomberg.com/news/articles/2018-06-08/trump-says-he-ll-quit-nafta-if-countries-can-t-reach-new-deal, accessed 15 August 2018.

Wu G and Yabuuchi S, 'Local Content Requirements and Urban Unemployment' (2003) 12 *Intl. Rev. Econ. & Fin.*, 481.

Yusuf Y, 'Dangote Refinery to Create 4000 Jobs, Crash Prices' *Leadership* (14 December 2017) https://leadership.ng/2017/12/14/dangote-refinery-create-4000-jobs-crash-prices/, accessed 18 August 2018.

2 Legal and institutional frameworks for local content development

2.1 Legal frameworks and strategies

Protectionist local content requirements (LCRs) are typically contained in contracts or in statutes. As demonstrated in Chapter 1, petroleum producing countries (PPCs) which opt for the liberalised approach to local content development do not usually rely on mandatory directives and strict local content stipulations, but emphasise the creation of enabling environments for petroleum firms to operate in, while at the same time encouraging collaborations between local and foreign firms. In addition, these countries rely on government-led initiatives aimed at developing local capacity, as a means of motivating local firms to take on challenging roles in the petroleum industry. On the other hand, the vast majority of developing PPCs are more inclined to set local content targets which petroleum firms are mandated to comply with. These countries rely on strict, top-down LCRs which are aimed primarily at protecting local industries from foreign competition.

Irrespective of whether a country relies on protectionism or the liberal approach, it is likely to require strategic legal and institutional frameworks to serve as vehicles for the advancement of its local content agenda. If the legal framework is protectionist, it would most likely require petroleum firms (local and foreign), to employ local citizens, and purchase their equipment in-country. Furthermore, the country would impose sanctions or stiff fines on defaulting firms or confer tax reliefs on locally produced goods and services in order to strengthen them. PPCs which adopt the liberalised approach to local content do not ordinarily apply command and comply strategies, thus they place less reliance on laws in furthering their local content. Still, these countries may utilise laws to drive certain content initiatives such as manpower development, technology acquisition, and the provision of favourable loans for local suppliers. In addition, they may use the instrumentality of law to confer tax incentives on local firms in order to attract them to domicile their operations in-country.

This chapter concentrates, however, on protectionist local content measures, which are ordinarily contained in statutes (Nigeria, Ghana, Tanzania), contracts (Equatorial Guinea, Jordan, Qatar, Lebanon, Syria), or a combination of both, (Brazil, Angola).

The legal framework (contract or statute) is arguably the most important aspect of protectionism. This is because it would outline in binding written stipulations, the level of compliance required from firms operating in a PPC as well as the consequences for breaching them. This explains why foreign firms which desire to operate in a PPC would be concerned not only about the fiscal terms involved in investing abroad, but also about LCRs. The features, suitability, and nature of the contractual and statutory approaches will now be considered in detail.

The contractual legal framework for local content entails inserting LCRs in contracts rather than in statutes. Thus a country which partners with international oil companies (IOCs) or other exploration and production (E&P) firms through its national oil company (NOC) may insert LCRs in joint ventures (JVs), or production sharing contracts (PSCs) and thus require petroleum firms (which are often the operators) in such collaborations, and their sub-contractors, to utilize local goods and services provided they are readily available, do not exceed a certain price margin, and meet industry standards. For instance, article 14(4) of Angola's Draft PSC which is used by NOC, Sociedade Nacional de Combustíveis de Angola-Empresa Pública ('Sonangol'), in its engagement with IOCs, provides that operators and their subcontractors shall:

> Contract local contractors, as long as their services are similar in quality and availability to those available on the international market and the prices of their services, when subject to the same tax charges, are no more than ten percent (10%) higher compared to the prices charged by foreign contractors for identical services;
>
> Acquire materials, equipment, machinery and consumable goods of national production, insofar as their quantity, quality and delivery dates are similar to those of such materials, equipment, machinery and consumable goods available on the international market. However, such obligation does not apply in those cases in which the local prices for such goods are more than ten percent (10%) higher compared to the prices for imported goods, before charging Customs Duties but after the respective costs for transportation and insurance have been included.

Similarly, article 23.1 of Equatorial Guinea's model PSC requires contractors and their subcontractors to give preference to:

> Equatorial guinean services, materials, equipment, consumables and other goods whose quality and time of delivery are comparable to those available internationally, provided that the cost in Equatorial Guinea is no more than ten percent (10%) above the cost of similar services, materials, equipment, consumables and other goods available internationally.

Through contractual provisions, PPCs may also obligate petroleum firms to train and employ a significant number of local personnel. Article 23.2 of Equatorial Guinea's model PSC, for example, contains robust requirements in that regard.

Similarly, oil mining leases (OMLs) executed between Nigeria and IOCs pre-1969 had contained some requirements geared towards securing non-skilled employment for Nigerians.[1] Petroleum firms which are contracted directly to operate in PPCs through sole risk concessionary arrangements which do not entail collaborations with NOCs, may also be required to make local content commitments in their course of bidding for such jobs. In order to pre-qualify for such contracts, bidders may have to commit to the development of that country's local expertise and know-how. For example, up until 2017 when it conducted its 14th bidding round, Brazil had made local content a significant criteria in determining whether or not to award E&P licenses to bidding firms.[2]

In the legislative approach to local content, on the other hand, a PPC may insert LCRs in a primary statute or in a subsidiary legislation. In the past, a petroleum law may have contained some minor LCRs, but recently, there is a tendency of codifying LCRs in a separate law. This code would typically contain most of what petroleum firms operating in a terrain would be required to comply with. This approach is championed by Nigeria, whose LCRs are codified in the Nigerian Oil and Gas Industry Content Development Act 2010 (NOGICDA). It would appear that the legislative approach is attractive to some African PPCs, which have sought to emulate it since the passage of NOGICDA by Nigeria's central legislature.[3] Unlike the contractual approach, the statutory approach is not company specific, but applies to all operators, irrespective of ownership structure, or nationality. Furthermore, it is binding on a wider scope of participants. NOGICDA is, for example, binding on the Nigerian state, as well as on the country's NOC: the Nigerian National Petroleum Corporation (NNPC).[4] The statutory approach relegates contractual arrangements to the background, and in overriding them, sets specific local content targets for petroleum firms, which are, in some cases, backed with sanctions.[5] It is necessary at this stage to analyse the merits and demerits of each of these approaches

The main advantage of the contractual approach is its flexibility, variability, and the fact that it is company specific.[6] A government which opts for this approach is therefore at liberty to enter into customised contracts with contractors, taking into cognisance their unique capabilities, strengths, and weaknesses. In contrast to

1 See for instance, Clause 17(1) of OML 92, see also Oguine, 2011, at p 406.
2 CMS Law, 'Brazil Proposes Relaxation of Local Content Requirements' (2017) http://www.cms-lawnow.com/ealerts/2017/02/brazil-proposes-relaxation-of-local-content-requirements, accessed 5 September 2017.
3 See for instance, Ghana's Petroleum (Local Content and Local Participation) Regulation, 2013. The same approach is being mulled by Uganda, Kenya, Congo Brazzaville, and other African countries: NCDMB, 'Kenya, others to emulate Nigeria's Local Content policy' (2015) http://www.ncdmb.gov.ng/index.php/newsupdates/news-updates/6604-kenya-others-to-emulate-nigeria-s-local-content-policy, accessed 8 November 2017.
4 Ss 1 and 2 of NOGICDA.
5 See for instance s.68 of NOGICDA.
6 In practice, many PPCs have model contracts which apply across board to bidding companies, see Martin and Park, 2010.

statutes, LCRs which are contained in contracts may be easily waived by an NOC or by the government, where necessary to enable the PPC and its partners adapt to changing times and address challenges as they arise. The issue is that, in practice, this flexibility usually works against the PPC, especially where its NOC/regulator is weak and unable to stand its ground in its dealings with petroleum firms. For example, although Nigeria adopted this approach for most of its pre-2010 era, its NOC was unable to insist on the patronage of Nigerian goods and services. The contractual approach may, however, be better suited for PPCs which have vibrant institutions. For example, Sonangol of Angola, while weak as an operator, is strong as a regulator of the Angolan petroleum industry and has been able to further that country's local content by relying significantly on this approach.[7] In effect, legislative LCRs may be more suitable for countries which have weak NOCs and are thus more likely to capitulate easily to their IOCs partners in granting undeserved waivers.

Relying on contractual arrangements for the furtherance of local content also has the advantage or disadvantage of being confidential. This means that the terms of these requirements may not be readily accessible to the public, or to relevant stakeholders. While the confidentiality may be suitable for the PPCs and their partners, on the other hand, their not being accessible to the public means that it will not be easy for the public in general to challenge their infringements. Then there is the issue of enforcement. Local content terms which are contained in contracts are ordinarily unenforceable by third parties, even if they are its direct beneficiaries. This is because the privity of contract doctrine bars persons who do not furnish consideration in exchange for commitments made for their benefit, from enforcing those benefits in a court of law.[8] Again, this may be an advantage for the parties in that it prevents vexatious litigations from meddlesome interlopers. On the other hand, should the government, acting through an NOC or a regulatory agency be lax in enforcing the terms of the contract, relevant stakeholders may find that they are unable to enforce such LCRs in court. On the other hand, statutory LCRs may, in certain instances, be enforced by third parties through public interest litigation. This would be the case if the law directly empowers interested stakeholders to enforce obligations imposed on petroleum firms, or if the court considers it so.[9]

7 Although the firm relies extensively on the contractual approach in its interaction with IOCs, Angola also has some local content laws which are contained in: the General Petroleum Activities Law, No. 10/2004, a Customs and Taxation Law No. 11/04. There is also Decree No. 48/2006, which contains Rules and Procedures of Public Procurement Competitions in the Petroleum Sector. There is also the Training Law, No. 116/2008 which relates to capacity building for local content development, another Training Decree Law, No. 17/2009, and there is an Executive Decree, No. 14/2010, which relates to the Functioning and Management of the Petroleum Training Fund.

8 See *Thomas Chukwuma Makwe v Chief Obanua Nwukor* [2001] 14 NWLR (PT. 733) 356.

9 See Chapter 6, 6.2, for a more detailed analysis of the possibility of private enforcement of NOGICDA.

Like the contractual approach, the legislative approach has its merits and demerits too. First, its terms are open, accessible, binding, and applicable to all stakeholders, irrespective of whether they are local or foreign. Another merit of this approach is that because legislation is permanent until repealed, there is guarantee of continuity and certainty of the regime. Its drawback is that unlike contracts which are company specific, and as such can factor in the peculiar circumstances of each company, the legislative approach may be unduly rigid and may impede necessary changes.[10] Nonetheless, its rigidity and inflexibility may be an advantage or a disadvantage, depending on how it is viewed. It may be an advantage if it prevents petroleum firms from 'arm twisting' administrative agencies or NOCs to bend the rules for their benefit.

Viewed differently, though, legislative rigidity may impede development if it does not make room for variations which may be necessary to address factors that were unforeseen by the legislator. Such rigidity may thus serve as a disincentive to investors. For example, the rigid enforcement of Brazil's local content laws pre-2017 impeded the progress of the Brazilian Petroleum Industry (BPI) mainly because the country's domestic supply and service firms were not strong to rise to the demands of the industry. The option of infringing the country's local content laws which were contained mainly in the regulations of the National Agency for Petroleum, Natural Gas, and Biofuels (ANP), by resorting to foreign suppliers, was visited with stiff fines. The only option left was for ANP to grant waivers, but this it was reluctant to do. In the end the BPI became very unattractive to investors.[11] Again, where legislative LCRs become unduly rigid, the regulator may be forced to 'look the other way', or the requirement, if contained in a primary statute as with NOGICDA, may have to go through the costly and time consuming process of legislative amendment.

The better option for countries which desire to adopt the statutory approach, may be to insert content requirements in secondary/subsidiary regulations made by administrative agencies in pursuance to powers vested on them by the legislature. This approach will save time and address the issue of rigidity, since administrative agencies are usually vested with the power to amend their rules, without recourse to the legislature.[12] For example, Ghana's local content regulations are contained in the Petroleum (Local Content and Local Participation) Regulation, 2013 made by that country's petroleum minister in pursuance to powers conferred on him by section 22 of the Petroleum Commissions Act of 2011. Similarly, the local content laws of Brazil are contained not in Law 9478/1997 directly, but in regulations made by the ANP in pursuance to that law. Inserting these LCRs in

10 See Rutter and Knigton, 2012.

11 See World Oil, 'Cooperation between Libra Consortium Partners Reduces Project's Break-even Price' http://www.worldoil.com/news/2017/5/9/cooperation-between-libra-consortium-partners-reduces-projects-breakeven-price, accessed 21 August 2018.

12 For instance, Ghana's local content regulation is contained in the Petroleum (Local Content and Local Participation) Regulation, 2013 rather than in a substantive Act.

regulations are decidedly a better approach than that of Nigeria which is contained in a primary statute.

2.1.1 Institutional framework for local content regulation and development

After designing a legal framework for its local content, a PPC would have to erect an institutional framework to monitor compliance, further implementation, and develop local capabilities. The effectiveness of the legal framework would be largely dependent on the effectiveness of the institutional framework. In addition to designing legal and institutional frameworks, PPCs would also rely on other local content initiatives. Accordingly, they may provide funding at low interest rates for local firms, award scholarships for the training of their citizens in petroleum-related areas, or invest in research for manpower development. Nevertheless, it is important to note that an institutional framework which is suitable for country A may not be suitable for country B.

In establishing an institution to drive local content, a PPC may be largely influenced by the geopolitical or ideological divide to which it belongs. Consequently, PPCs such as Canada, Norway, the United States of America, the United Kingdom (UK), and Australia, which are inclined to open markets and globalisation, tend to rely primarily on market forces, as well as other extra-legal initiatives to drive local content, while shirking from establishing NOCs.[13] And while these countries establish formal regulators, their reluctance to stipulate local content targets means that their regulators do not usually drive local content through strict enforcement of LCRs. Rather, these PPCs may rely on banks, research institutions, and ad-hoc government policies in order to strengthen local capabilities in order to encourage their participation in their petroleum industries.

In contrast, PPCs such as Malaysia, Saudi Arabia, and Angola tend to rely almost exclusively on their NOCs to drive local content. These NOCs are often positioned to harness their closeness to petroleum firms in order to drive local content and to monitor the extent LCRs are being complied with. This approach saves funds for PPCs and dispenses with tensions that may arise if NOCs function side by side with equally vibrant regulators. The disadvantage in relying solely on NOCs is that these firms may be lackadaisical in monitoring their partners, or be complicit in violations of LCRs. Another issue is if there is the absence of functional oversight over the NOC, it may become a law unto itself, with the attendant risks for corruption and abuse of power.

But perhaps the more common approach among PPCs is to combine the efforts of formal regulatory agencies with NOCs in driving local content. For instance, although Brazil relies primarily on the ANP, the regulator in turn collaborates with Petrobras in driving local content. Similarly, Nigeria combines the efforts of

13 In fact, with the exception of Norway, and the UK until 1982, virtually all Western economies do not have NOCs. And although France and Italy have some stakes in Total and Eni, both firms have always operated like private oil companies rather than as NOCs.

the NNPC with those of the Nigerian Content Development and Monitoring Board (NCDMB) in driving local content in the NPI. By maintaining a strong presence in the upstream and downstream sectors, these NOCs are able to exercise quasi regulatory roles as far as local content is concerned. They are positioned to monitor their partners, and where necessary, insist on the patronage of local industries and the service sectors in the award of contracts related to the industry. In addition, formal regulators such as NCDMB and ANP are able to monitor compliance, and where necessary, impose sanctions on defaulting firms. One demerit with this approach, though, is that undue closeness between NOCs and regulatory agencies may increase the tendency of the latter to be 'captured' by the former and its industry partners. Should this happen, the fallout may be ineffective regulation and monitoring, undue waivers, as well as weak enforcement of local content stipulations. Secondly, NOC/regulatory agency collaboration if not properly managed, may bred in inter-agency disputes which may have negative impact on PPCs which adopt this approach. This may occur, for example, where zealous regulators attempt to enforce LCRs against NOCs or their partners.

The interplay of law, policy and institutional frameworks in driving local content, deserves greater attention at this point. And for that purpose, Brazil and Norway, two PPCs which perhaps embody the liberalised model and the protectionist model, are evaluated. While Brazil relies primarily on laws and regulations to further its local content, Norway relies almost exclusively on content initiatives. In spite of the differences in approaches, both countries have been able to build vibrant NOCs, and over time have been able to develop significant local content in their petroleum industries.

2.2 Experiences of some selected countries

2.2.1 Brazil

2.2.1.1 ANP

Brazil's central policy objective in the BPI is focused mainly on attaining and remaining self-sufficient in oil production, reducing natural gas imports, as well as increasing the contribution of petroleum to the development of its local economy.[14] The country applies a multifaceted approach to local content development, although as seen below, its LCRs are protectionist in nature. The primary driver of Brazil's local content policies is the ANP, which was established under article VII of Law 9478/1997. As principal regulator of the BPI, the agency is authorised to make local content regulations, negotiate with petroleum firms, award contracts after open and competitive bidding rounds, and protect the environment.[15]

14 See Guan, 2010.
15 See art.8 of Law 9478 generally.

Brazil utilizes the concessionary system in its onshore and non-pre salt fields, but relies mainly on PSCs in the pre-salt fields.[16] Under the concessionary system, the ANP, on behalf of the State, enters into agreements with E&P firms which invariably contain LCRs to the effect that concessionaires should give preference to Brazilian supply and service firms, provided they are competitive, with respect to price, quality, schedule, and service.[17] Furthermore, concessionaires and their supply and service counterparts are generally required to source specific percentages of their workforce, equipment, and services in Brazil.[18] So important is local content to Brazil that until its 14th bidding round which held in 2017, the ANP made local content a precondition for the award of E&P licenses. This meant that only firms which offered to utilise a high level of Brazilian content were considered for the award of oil blocks.[19]

As a means of securing compliance with its LCRs, the ANP imposes fines on defaulting firms, taking into consideration several factors such as: the contract amount, the level of local content required from each company, and the extent of compliance.[20] The ANP's fines are pragmatic. Where a firm infringes its local content obligations, the fine imposed on it by the ANP would be directly proportional to the missing value that would have been necessary to attain the minimum required local content for the project it is involved in. Over time, the agency has been known to impose significant fines on defaulters as a means of sending clear warnings to the industry that local content enforcement is given top priority in the country. For instance, in 2015, the ANP imposed a record $71 million fine on BG, an E&P partner of Petrobras, with respect to local content violations in an offshore project.[21] The ANP's regulatory reach extends to Petrobras as well. Thus

16 Under the concessionary system, the title to a country's petroleum resources are alienated in favour of the petroleum company by the PPC. The company is nonetheless required to continue to pay royalties and taxes on production. See Blades, 2011.

17 ANP, 'Resolution ANP No 36. Regulation of Local Content Certification' (2007), http://www.brasil-rounds.gov.br/arquivos/diario_oficial/Traduo_de_Resolucao_ANP36.pdf, accessed 7 January 2017.

18 EIA Report, 'Brazil' (2015) https://www.eia.gov/beta/international/analysis.cfm?iso=BRA, accessed 4 February 2017.

19 In its Libra field for instance, Brazil's LCRs stand at 37 percent for the exploration phase, 55 in the development phase, and 59 percent after 2022. Furthermore, Brazil requires petroleum firms to purchase 65 percent of their goods and services from domestic firms. Ibid. Clause 20 of its model petroleum contract which it executed with E&P companies required all firms operating in Brazil to attain an agreed percentage of locally utilised goods and services in their operations. With regards to local content, the agency has also issued the following regulations: Resolution No. 36 – Reg of local content Certification; Resolution No. 37 – Rules of Accreditation Entity for local content; Certification Resolution No. 38 – Rules of Certification Audits; and Resolution No. 39 – Reg of Local Investment Report. See ANP, 'Local Content' http://www.anp.gov.br/brasilrounds/ingles/conteudo_local.asp, accessed 3 March 2017.

20 See Adilson, 2012.

21 See BG paid the fine upfront although it benefited from a 30 percent statutory discount for accepting the fine without appeals. See ANP, 'Multas e Regularizações' http://www.anp.gov.br/wwwanp/multas-e-regularizacoes, accessed 19 June 2017; see also Valle, 2015.

in spite of Petrobras' close relationship to the Brazilian government, it is required to comply with Brazil's LCRs like other private firms.[22] Local content monitoring also requires that regulators put in place efficient measurement criteria which will enable them to effectively determine whether or not local content objectives are being achieved. As part of its regulatory roles, ANP developed a measurement methodology contained in what is known as the 'Cartilha' booklet in 2005.[23]

The ANP's LCRs are considered as being among the most stringent in the world.[24] They vary from company to company depending on factors such as field location, and stage of the operation, etc.[25] Generally, though, an assignee of a petroleum concession in Brazil is required to ensure that a minimum of 37 percent local content is attained at the exploration phase, and 65 percent at the production phase, besides satisfying the minimum LCRs in items specified in Annex 4 of the model concession contract. A progressive regime is provided for in the development phase. For instance, there is a 55 percent LCR for units which did not start production until 2016, 58 percent for those which begin between 2017 and 2019, and 65 percent for those which begin in 2020.[26]

The ANP's LCRs are not static in Brazil, though, but vary from round to round. Nonetheless, in its first four licensing rounds, local content and cash bonus were the only bidding parameters used in determining whether or not to allocate licenses to firms that bid for concessions. Subsequently, its bid evaluation criteria assigned a 40 percent weight to each cash bonus and work program, and a 20 percent weight to local content, broken down between E&P phases. In its 1999 licensing rounds, the first after Brazil liberalised its petroleum sector in 1997, the average local content target was 25 percent for the exploration phase, and 27 percent in the development phase. But the required percentages gradually increased, eventually reaching 69 and 70 percent, respectively, in the ninth licensing round held in 2007.[27]

With its vast population of over 200 million, relative capabilities in terms of vibrant domestic suppliers and service firms, advanced offshore technologies, and giant NOC, Brazil appeared poised to implement its protectionist measures in the BPI. But it has not been without its own weaknesses.[28] Its massive pre-salt fields as well as its other acreages made foreign 'support' inevitable. But that support did

22 In 2011 for instance, the firm was fined the sum of $18 million for breaching local content rules in development of 44 concessions 'ANP Slaps Petrobras with $18 million Fine' Upstream (1 September 2011) http://www.upstreamonline.com/live/article276020.ece, accessed 22 November 2017.

23 Much is said about the Cartilha booklet in Chapter 5.

24 See EIA Report 'Brazil' (n 18); see also ANP, 'The local content Reg for Concession Agreements' http://www.braziltexas.org/attachments/files/401/ANP-Marcelo.pdf, accessed 7 June 2017.

25 See Chambriard, 2011. Concessions in Brazil are awarded for fields that are not in the pre-salt area, while PSCs are used in the pre-salt in pursuance to the Production Sharing Agreement Law, 12.351 of 2010 ('PSA law'). See Blades, 2011, at pp 41–45.

26 Braga and Szklo, 2014, at p 138.

27 Tordo, Tracy and Arfaa, 2011, at p 118.

28 Adilson, 2012.

not come forth because of Brazil's protectionist LCRs, which made the BPI unattractive to foreign investors.[29] These factors as well as corruption scandals which Petrobras had to grapple with between 2014 and 2016, coupled with record low oil prices, all affected Brazil's local content policies negatively and made reform imperative. As shown in the previous chapter, the country was accordingly forced to tone down on its local content drive. For the first time since 1997, it removed local content as a bid criterion in its 14th bidding rounds held in 2017 as a means of attracting foreign investors. It also retrospectively relaxed some content requirements in licenses awarded as far back as 2005, while relaxing the penalty regime as well.[30] In addition to all that, the country contemplates a lower and more realistic minimum local content regime.[31]

As a result of these measures, Brazil's 14th bidding round was adjudged as very successful in attracting the largest signature bonus in the history of the BPI.[32] In October of the same year Brazil also auctioned off six high potential blocks in its pre-salt region, to a mix of local and foreign companies.[33] The successes of these rounds, adjudged from the enthusiasm of foreign and local players, are proof that these changes were welcomed by petroleum firms. Besides its regulatory roles, the ANP is also required by law to stimulate research and the development of new technologies for exploration, production, refining, and processing of petroleum.[34]

29 Between 2014 and 2016, Petrobras became embroiled in corruption scandals which arose out of collusion schemes between some of its executives, some politicians, and a number of its client firms. The schemes led to the fraudulent overbilling of Petrobras for construction jobs executed on its behalf. From 2004 to 2012, the scandal resulted in the payment of 3 percent of each major construction contract as kickbacks, to Petrobras' politically appointed executives and some executives of Brazil's ruling Workers' Party, and caused the loss of about $7 billion. 'Petrobras Counts Cost of Corruption Scandal as 2014 Losses Exceed $7bn' *The Guardian* (2015) http://www.theguardian.com/business/2015/apr/23/petrobras-counts-cost-of-corruption-scandal-as-2014-losses-exceed-7bn-dollars, accessed 23 April 2015.

30 Pereira, Gergio and Amorium, 2017; see also CMS Law, 'Brazil Proposes Relaxation of Local Content Requirements' (2017) http://www.cms-lawnow.com/ealerts/2017/02/brazil-proposes-relaxation-of-local-content-requirements, accessed 5 September 2017.

31 Fifty percent for onshore blocks during E&P and, for offshore blocks: 18 percent during exploration, 25 percent for well construction, 40 percent for collecting flow system, and 25 percent for stationary production units. See Pereira, Gergio and Amorium, 2017, at p 457.

32 A total of 20 companies from over eight countries participated in the bid. See ANP, 'Brazil's 14th Bidding Round had the largest signature bonus in history' (27 September 2017) http://www.anp.gov.br/wwwanp/noticias/anp-e-p/4052-brazil-s-14th-bidding-round-had-the-largest-signature-bonus-in-history, accessed 15 January 2018.

33 See ANP, 'Pre-salt Bidding Rounds Confirmed the Reestablishment of the Oil and Gas Sector in Brazil' (27 October 2017) http://www.anp.gov.br/wwwanp/noticias/anp-e-p/4115-pre-salt-bidding-rounds-confirmed-the-reestablishment-of-the-oil-and-gas-sector-in-brazil, accessed 8 January 2018; 'Factbox: Winners of Brazil's pre-salt oil Round' *Reuters* (27 October 2017) https://www.reuters.com/article/us-brazil-oil-auction-factbox/factbox-winners-of-brazils-pre-salt-oil-round-idUSKBN1CW2RA, accessed 11 January 2018.

34 Art.8x of Law 9478.

In pursuance of this mandate, it invests heavily in research, and awards scholarships related to petroleum technology.[35] These initiatives are geared towards the development of domestic capabilities in order to position domestic firms to compete for important contracts in the BPI.

2.2.1.2 Petrobras, PPSA, and other local content initiatives in the BPI

Petrobras plays a significant role in Brazil's overall petroleum industry strategy. The firm is uniquely positioned to further Brazil's local content policies because it maintains a strong hegemony over the BPI, controlling over 80 percent of crude oil production and transmission, and about 50 percent of distribution of all petroleum produced in Brazil.[36] Since the liberalisation of the BPI in 1997, Petrobras which has collaborated with IOCs as well as private players in the BPI, has been able to harness its dominant upstream position to further the Brazilian content. In that capacity the firm monitors its partners in their purchasing and contracting in its desire to ensure adequate patronage of local Brazilian firms. Petrobras was partially privatised in 2000, with the Brazilian government retaining controlling shares in it. State control has enabled Brazil's rulers to assert extensive influence over Petrobras not only in local content implementation, but also in other welfarist-related decisions. State control also implies that majority of the firm's board are appointed by the Brazilian government, who are then more amenable to its bidding. This sometimes entails giving preference to Brazilian citizens in the firm's employment, as well as in its patronage of indigenous supply and service firms. The tendency to use Petrobras to implement government policies is further bolstered by the fact that the firm has access to extensive privileges from the state.[37]

The PPSA is another institutional agent for the development of local content in the BPI as far Brazil's pre-salt fields is concerned.[38] The firm was established in

35 ANP, 'What is the ANP' (2018) https://www.google.com.ng/search?q=anp+brazil+scholarships+local+content&oq=anp&aqs=chrome.1.69i57j69i59j69i65j35i39j0.2671j0j4&client=ms-android-tecno&sourceid=chrome-mobile&ie=UTF-8, accessed 28 August 2018.

36 Anotolín and Cendrero, 2013, at p 710.

37 For instance, art.42 of Brazil's Petroleum Law 1997 had provided that bids for petroleum concessions in which Petrobras tied with other private oil companies were to be resolved in the former's favour, provided it did not bid in consortium with other firms. Similarly, Brazil's PSA law, conferred on Petrobras a minimum of 30 percent of all PSCs executed in Brazil's prolific pre-salt petroleum fields. Pursuant to arts.3, 4 and 20, the law also saddled the firm with the responsibility of operating all pre-salt PSCs. See also Blades, 2011, at p 42. On the effects of these regulatory changes on foreign investment, see Florêncio, 2016. Furthermore, Art.1 of Brazil's Onerous Assignment Law 12276 of 2010 which capitalised Petrobras in 2010, authorised the Brazilian government to directly assign to the firm, with due compensation, the activities of research and production of oil, natural gas, and other fluid hydrocarbons, in areas that contain up to five billion barrels of oil equivalent. See also Zacour, 2012.

38 By pre-salt, we refer to the giant oil fields found in the Santos Basin area, 300 kilometres off the coast of Espirito Santo, Rio de Janeiro, Sao Paulo, and Santa Catarina. The petroleum found in these fields is trapped under a layer of salt about 7 kilometres

2010 via Law 12.304/2010, perhaps in a bid to limit the pervasive powers of Petrobras. To the PPSA is awarded most of Brazil's pre-salt fields, which it enters into PSC arrangements with Petrobras, and with other E&P firms. The PPSA operates as asset manager in these arrangements and in this role it is best suited to advance local content in the BPI. Under Law 12.304/2010, it is mandated to evaluate technical and economic plans for the exploration, appraisal, development, and production of oil, natural gas, and other hydrocarbon fluids in the pre-salt, as well as to enforce contractual requirements relating to local content.[39] By virtue of articles 23 and 27 of Brazil's PSC Act, the PPSA also constitutes one half of all joint operating committees which oversee PSC operations in the pre-salt. It also has a casting vote, in the event of a tie. This positions it strategically to evaluate and sanction expenditures before they are made, and to require its PSC partners (including Petrobras) to comply with pre-arranged local content targets, as well as ANP's regulations.

Lastly, Brazil relies extensively on local content initiatives geared towards building the capacity of local industries, encouraging foreign firms to domicile their operations in-country, stimulating research, promoting collaboration between foreign and local firms, and between policy drivers and government agencies, as well. These initiatives, which complement local content regulations and laws, are flexible and adaptable to various circumstances. Perhaps the most prominent of which is the Mobilization Program of the National Petroleum Industry (PROMINP). PROMINP was established in 2003 in pursuance to Law 4925/2003 and coordinated by the Brazilian Ministry of Mines and Energy, and Petrobras.[40] There are other initiatives directed towards the provision of cheap loans for local industries which are driven by the National Bank for Economic and Social Development (BNDE), whose funding programme is aimed at the development of local industries.[41] As a means of sustaining research for the development relevant petroleum technology, Law 9478 provides that 25 percent of royalties paid by petroleum firms are to be given to its Ministry of Science and Technology.[42]

Another local content initiative recently introduced in Brazil, is the 'Incentive Programme for Supply Chain Competitiveness and the Development and Improvement of Suppliers to the Oil and Gas Sector' (PEDEFOR) in 2016 via Law 8.637/2016. PEDEFOR is a government led initiative put in place to cushion the effects of Brazil's strict local content regime. It aims at developing the Brazilian supply chain as a means of enhancing its overall competitiveness by creating incentives for the national engineering sector, and the promotion of innovation as a means to increasing the level of Brazil's local content.[43] The

under the surface of the ocean, and are estimated to contain over 50 billion barrels of crude oil, see Millard, 2011.

39 Art.4(1).

40 'About the Program' (2015) http://www.prominp.com.br/prominp/en_us/content/about-the-program.htm, accessed 2 February 2016; see Furtado, 2003.

41 Zurli, 2011; see also Olsen, 2013.

42 Art.48.

43 CMS Law-Now, 'Reforms to Brazilian Local Content Policy' (2016), http://www.cms-lawnow.com/ealerts/2016/02/reforms-to-brazilian-local-content-policy, accessed 28 October 2017.

initiative also aims at facilitating the process for E&P companies to achieve their local content commitments to the ANP through new types of investments and activities. Under PEDEFOR, petroleum firms may undertake to purchase goods, services and systems from foreign suppliers with a bid to facilitating their establishment in Brazil. They may also directly invest in the development of their suppliers' technological innovation, or acquire goods and systems in Brazil for use abroad. Compliant firms are rewarded with 'Local Content Units', which may be used by them as part of their compliance with their overall local content obligations to the ANP.[44]

2.2.2 Norway

The Norwegian approach to petroleum resource governance consists of establishing three separate institutions with responsibilities for commerce (Statoil), regulation (Norwegian Petroleum Directorate (NPD)), and policy making (Ministry of Petroleum and Energy). The Norwegian model has been touted as being ideal, perhaps because of Norway's overall successes in several critical areas in its petroleum industry such as environmental protection, effective and transparent management of its petroleum revenues, development of a globally competitive NOC, and its high local content.

As it stands, local content in Norway is adjudged as being one of the highest in the world. It ranges between 50 and 60 percent in the development of new fields, and up to 80 percent if maintenance and operations are included.[45] Norway's petroleum industry policies, which were the bedrock for the developments that occurred in the Norwegian Petroleum Industry (NoPI) were for the most part, formulated in the early 1970s, following the discovery of vast petroleum reserves at Norway's Ekofisk field.[46] As early as 1971, Norway's legislature (the 'Storting') commissioned a committee to define a policy framework for its petroleum industry. The report of the committee was published in 1971 as the so called 'ten oil commandments', and became the basis of Norway's petroleum industry policy.[47] Since then, the growth of the industry has been positively impacted by an interplay of policy, law, and efficient public administration.

From inception, Norway's policy thrust was geared towards prudent management of petroleum resources, robust regulation, and resource nationalism.[48] Its

44 See Filho et al, 2016.
45 Heum, 2008, at p 4
46 The field is located 320 kilometres southwest of Stavanger, in the Norwegian Continental Shelf (NCS).
47 Among other things, the policy aimed at Norwegian dominance of operations at the NCS, and sought to make Norway sufficient in petroleum, while taking environmental concerns into account. In pursuance of which gas flaring was prohibited from inception except during periods of testing. The policy also aimed at ensuring the involvement of the Norwegian state at all appropriate levels in contribution and coordination of Norwegian interests in the industry. In response to the policy, the Norwegian Legislature, in 1972 unanimously resolved to establish Statoil as Norway's NOC. See Gordon and Stenvoll, 2007, Lerøen, 2010, and see generally, Thurber and Istad, 2012, at p 599.
48 See NPD, 'A Controlled Success' (26 January 2012) http://www.npd.no/en/Publications/Norwegian-Continental-Shelf/No1-2012/A-controlled-success/, accessed 13 April 2017.

petroleum industry policies were spearheaded by its NOC, Statoil, and other indigenous E&P firms, working side by side with capable industry regulators administrators.[49] Norway invested in building regulatory capacity and also emphasised credible regulatory commitment. Besides, it created an investor friendly environment which made domiciling operations in Norway not only attractive, but also competitively advantageous.[50] Norway did not set specific local content targets for IOCs, but focused rather on value addition, while encouraging the development of indigenous firms.[51] A Royal Decree nevertheless obligated E&P firms to give preference to Norwegian suppliers in contract awards, provided they were competitive in terms of price, quality, and delivery reliability.[52]

Norway's regulatory policies were implemented mainly by the NPD, which acted primarily as industry regulator. The Norwegian state, however, participated directly in its petroleum industry through Statoil. One strategy the country relied on in encouraging the new firm, as remarked previously, was to give Statoil a minimum participatory right of 50 percent of all concessions awarded in the Norwegian Continental Shelf (NCS), with an option to increase to 80 percent.[53] Unlike Brazil which gave Petrobras exclusive monopoly rights over the BPI, the NoPI was opened to local and foreign firms, which for the most part, collaborated with Statoil. For example, Statoil collaborated with Phillips Petroleum Company, which had already gained a foothold in Norway's upstream and pioneered Norway's first major discovery at its Ekofisk oil field.[54] Norway also encouraged the development of its indigenous E&P firms and supported local contractors. As such, it formulated a policy of awarding concessions to two or more indigenous petroleum firms, which were thus able to pool resources together to develop their petroleum blocks,[55] while also encouraging partnerships between local and foreign firms operating in the NCS.[56]

By harnessing technology transfer arrangements with its IOC partners, Statoil was able to develop its knowledge base via technology transfer arrangements. Its position as majority partner also positioned it to promote Norway's interests by ensuring adequate accounting and repatriation of profits earned, and the promotion of local content.[57] By the early 1980s, Statoil was already established as a viable sole operator, and by the late 1980s, it had become the dominant force in the NoPI.[58] The successes of Statoil were used as a launching pad for the

49 Baines, 2009, at p 48.
50 Olsen, n.d.
51 Easo and Wallace, 2014.
52 Royal Decree of Dec. 8, 1972, § 54.
53 See Tonne, 1983.
54 Tonne, 1983, at p 734.
55 See Ryggvik, 2010.
56 Semikyina, 2010.
57 Hunter, 2014.
58 Statoil currently produces about 80 percent of the NCS's petroleum, and champions Norway's local content policies. See Thurber and Istad, 2012; see also US Energy Information Administration, 'Norway' (2012) http://www.eia.gov/countries/cab.cfm?fips=no, accessed 7 July 2018.

development of Norway's domestic petroleum services industry, which is today adjudged as being vibrant and very competitive.[59] By the mid-1980s, Norway's local content had developed rapidly as it applied its petroleum policies through Statoil and the NPD. The country was therefore positioned to liberalise its petroleum industry in 1994, when it joined the European Economic Area (EEA).

Membership of the EEA meant that Statoil lost all exclusive privileges in the NCS since Norway was prohibited from conferring privileges on Norwegian E&P firms and their service counterparts.[60] But by this time, Norwegian firms were already playing dominant roles in the industry, and as such were in a better position to stand on their own with little or no government support. Norway's membership of the EEA means that Norway can rely only on local content initiatives such as building shipyards and dockyards, vibrant service firms, and creating an enabling environment for foreign firms to domesticate their operations in Norway. In retrospect, it is doubtful if Norway would have been able to develop its local content to the extent that it is today without the special privileges it conferred on Statoil and local firms prior to its joining the EEA. That being said, one significant thing about the development of the Norwegian local content is that the country did not rely solely on laws and strict stipulations, but rather encouraged its NOC to develop over time, while making its terrain attractive to foreign investors. After becoming a member of the EEA, the Norwegian government became less involved in the workings of Statoil, which began to operate more and more like a private oil company. This prepared the firm for its eventual partial privatisation in 2001, with the Norwegian government continuing to retain controlling stake.[61]

The Norwegian and Brazilian experiences demonstrate that PPCs may rely on approaches which are suitable to them in furthering their local content and still achieve their policy objectives, if properly implemented. They also demonstrate that these strategies and approaches are not cast in stone. Flexibility and adaptability are necessary from time to time. For example, although Norway liberalised its petroleum industry, it did not deem it fit to fully privatise its NOC as was the case with the UK. Rather, it maintained an arm's length relationship with a competitive and partially privatised Statoil. Again, Brazil was ready to change when strict protectionism did not yield desired results. Its preference for strict top-down requirements rather than the bottom-up approach, as was the case with Norway, also reflects its historic and geographical influences, as was the case with Norway. Its ability to quickly adapt to changes in the petroleum industry and to 'back down' when necessary, also indicates that the country's leaders are amenable to changes and are quick to respond to feedbacks from the industry.

African PPCs, a number of which have settled for protectionism, may glean some lessons from the Norwegian and Brazilian experiences. From Norway comes

59 See Spurn, 2009.

60 See Hanne and Kaare, 2000, see also Charlemagne, 'The Norwegian Option: Those strange countries that have kept out of the European Union' (2004) 373 *Economist*, 50.

61 See Wolf and Michael, 2009.

the lesson that they should concentrate on developing vibrant supplies and service sectors. And that they may not need to jettison their NOCs, provided other vibrant regulators can be established to monitor their operations. One lesson from Brazil is that African PPCs may retain protectionism, but should be quick and ready to change. They should also be willing to combine the regulatory and contractual approaches, where necessary. As shown in this chapter, Brazil relies on contracts in concessionary contracts and PSCs, as well as regulatory stipulations published by the ANP. But beyond that, it also relies on the PPSA, ANP, and several initiatives to support its policies. Mere reliance on law to drive local content will not yield much results. Rather, there is need for a combination of law, NOCs, and where necessary, other vibrant regulators such as the ANP and NPD. In addition to all these, African PPCs should develop vibrant domestic sectors by ploughing their petroleum resources into where they are most needed: building strong research institutions, infrastructure, and vibrant domestic suppliers. All of these require comprehensive petroleum industry policies which should be reviewed from time to time, as well as the strategies put in place to drive them.

2.3 Conclusion

This chapter appraised the legal frameworks which have been adopted by PPCs for the development of local content. It was demonstrated that while some PPCs rely substantially on contracts, there is a growing tendency to rely extensively on legislative LCRs, as is the case with Nigeria, and a growing number of African PPCs. While yet other PPCs such as Norway and the UK relied, and continue to rely, on local content initiatives rather than on contractual or legislative stipulations. The chapter also assessed the institutional frameworks which exist for local content development and demonstrated that some PPCs like Brazil and Nigeria prefer to combine NOCs/regulatory agencies to drive local content, while some others rely either on regulatory institutions, or on government led initiatives. Notable among the latter are Canada, the UK, and Australia. A third category was shown to exist: PPCs such as Angola, Malaysia, and Saudi Arabia, which rely almost exclusively on NOCs to implement or drive their local content policies. Special emphasis was placed on the Brazilian approach to local content development. In that regard, the efforts of the ANP, Petrobras, PPSA, and other content initiatives were appraised, as was the Norwegian approach. In relation to Norway it was shown that the country combined the strengths of Statoil and the NPD in developing its local content prior to its joining the EEA. It was also shown that while the country was not strictly protectionist, it nevertheless benefitted from some regulatory requirements which positioned domestic Norwegian firms to develop their competencies and capabilities over time.

In laying a theoretical foundation for this book, Chapters 1 and 2 borrowed heavily from Norway and Brazil, first because of the extensive experiences these countries have had in developing local content as well as their unique approaches, which are diametrically opposite but have proved relatively efficient. The remaining chapters which follow concentrate, however, on local content oil and gas law as it relates to

African PPCs, with particular emphasis on Nigeria. A holistic assessment of Nigeria's local content policies and laws therefore engages the next five chapters, while at the same time drawing lessons from other African, and non-African PPCs where necessary. It is thus appropriate that the next chapter begins by exploring the historical context surrounding the development of local content in Nigeria. The chapter will conclude by analysing certain factors which affected the growth of local content before 2010.

Bibliography

Adilson V, 'Brazil's Local Content Policy Stirs Concerns' *E&P* (21 October 2012) http://www.epmag.com/Technology-Regulations/Brazils-Local-Content-Policy-Stirs-Concerns_109056, accessed 22 November 2017.

Anotolín MJP and Cendrero MR, 'How Important are National Companies for Oil and Gas Sector Performance? Lessons from the Bolivia and Brazil Case Studies' (2013) 61 *Energy Policy*, 707.

Baines I, 'Studies of Regulatory, Corporate and Financial Alternatives for the Exploration and Production of Oil and Gas and the Industrial Development of the Oil and Gas Production Chain in Brazil' (2009) http://www.bain.com/bainweb/images/LocalOffices/BNDES_Consolidated_Report_BNDES_eng.pdf, accessed 2 April 2018.

Blades WB, 'Production, Politics, And Pre-Salt: Transitioning to a PSC regime in Brazil' (2011) 7 *Texas Journal of Oil, Gas & Energy*, 33.

Braga LP and Szklo AZ, 'The Recent Regulatory Changes in Brazilian Petroleum Exploration and Exploitation Activities' (2014) 7(2) *Journal of World Energy Law & Business*, 120.

Chambriard M, 'Brazil's Regulatory Framework Challenges of a Rapidly Expanding Petroleum Industry' (2011) http://www.anp.gov.br/?dw=60218, accessed 13 November 2017.

Easo J and Wallace A, 'Understanding Local Content Policies in Africa's Petroleum Sector' (2014), http://www.worldlawgroup.com, accessed 28 October 2017.

Filho M et al, 'New Federal Decree seeks to improve the Brazilian O&G local content policy' *Lexology* (28 January 2016) http://www.lexology.com/library/detail.aspx?g=64829e3e-2117-4334-8206-6baf83e6ca0f, accessed 29 November 2017.

Florêncio P, 'The Brazilian 2010 oil regulatory framework and its crowding-out investment effects' (2016) 98 *Energy Policy*, 378.

Furtado TA, 'Institutional Changes and Innovation in the Brazilian Petroleum Industry' International Symposium on 'Energy Reforms and Institutional Development in Latin America' (2003) National Autonomous University of Mexico, University of Grenoble PMF Mexico City, http://www.depfe.unam.mx/p-cientifica/.../10CbAndrefurtadoenglishLtt.pd., accessed 20 November 2017.

Gordon R and Stenvoll T, 'Statoil: A Study in Political Entrepreneurship' (2007) James A. Baker III Institute for Public Policy of Rice University and Japan Petroleum Energy Center, https://www.bakerinstitute.org/media/files/page/9ffcb110/noc_statoil_gordon_stenvoll.pdf, accessed 7 July 2017.

Guan EG, 'Understanding Brazil's Oil Industry: Policy Dynamics and Self Sufficiency' (2010) 2 *Journal of Emerging Knowledge of Emerging Markets*, 80.

Hanne MN and Kaare S, 'Adaptation without EU Membership: Norway and the European Economic Area' (2000) 6(1) *The Journal of Legislative Studies*, 125.

Heum P, 'Local Content Development: Experiences From Oil and Gas Activities in Norway' (2008) *SNF Working Paper No. 02/08* https://brage.bibsys.no/xmlui/bitstream/handle/11250/166156/1/A02_08.pdf, accessed 22 November 2016.

Hunter T, 'The Role of Regulatory Frameworks and State Regulation in Optimising the Extraction of Petroleum Resources: A Study of Australia and Norway' (2014) 1 *The Extractive Industries and Society*, 55.

Lerøen BL, 'Ten Commanding Achievements' *Norwegian Petroleum Directorate* (15 December 2010) http://www.npd.no/en/Publications/Norwegian-Continental-Shelf/No2-2010/10-commanding-achievements/, accessed 1 November 2017.

Martin AT and Park JJ, 'Global Petroleum Industry Model Contracts Revisited: Higher, Faster, Stronger' (2010) 3(1) *Journal of World Energy Law & Business*, 4.

Millard P, 'Brazil Oil Fields May Hold More Than Twice Estimates' *Bloomberg* (19 January 2011) http://www.bloomberg.com/news/2011-01-19/brazil-oil-fields-may-hold-more-than-tw ice-estimated-reserves, accessed 19 January 2017.

Oguine I, 'Nigerian Content in the Nigerian Petroleum Industry: Legal and Policy Issues' (2011) 29(4) *Journal of Energy & Natural Resources Law*, 405.

Olsen WH, 'Brazil's Local Content Policy, Strategy and Ambitions' (2013) http://10.64.0.51:2111/usg/NdxICC.htm?IP=10.64.0.51&MA=20107A247174&OS=http://www.intsok.com%2Fcontent%2Fdownload%2F249%2F1809%2Fversion%2F4%2Ffile%2FBrazil_Local_Content_Strategy.pdf, accessed 7 January 2017.

Olsen WH, 'Norway-Local Content Lessons Learned' (n.d.) http://www.biee.org/wpcms/wp-content/uploads/Olsen-Norway-local-content-strategy2.pdf, accessed 17 May 2018.

Pereira EG, Gergio F and Amorium L, 'The Brazilian pre-salt case: Governmental Interference and Challenges for Potential Joint Ventures' (2017) 35(4) *Journal of Energy & Natural Resources Law*, 456.

Rutter J and Knigton W, 'Legislated Policy Targets' (2012) *Institute for Government Briefing* https://www.instituteforgovernment.org.uk/sites/default/files/publications/Legislated%20policy%20targets%20final.pdf, accessed 20 November 2017.

Ryggvik H, 'The Norwegian Oil Experience: A Toolbox for Managing Resources?' (2010) http://www.handelskampanjen.no/files/documents/The_Norwegian_Oil_Experience.pdf?, accessed 4 December 2017.

Semikyina IO, 'Managing Regional Economic Development through Local Content Requirements in Oil and Gas Industry' (2017) 13(2) *Economy of Region*, 460.

Spurn C, 'Oil Regulation in 28 Jurisdictions Worldwide: Norway' (2009) http://www.kluge.no/arch/img.aspx?file_id=9084808&ext=.pdf, accessed 15 October 2017.

Thurber MC and Istad BT, 'Norway's Evolving Champion: Statoil and the Politics of State Enterprise' in DG Victor et al (eds) *Oil and Governance State-owned Enterprises and the World Energy Supply* (Cambridge University Press, Cambridge, 2012).

Tonne T, 'Energy Policy: A Norwegian Perspective' (1983) 5(4) *North Western Journal of International Law & Business*, 738.

Tordo S, Tracy BS and Arfaa N, 'NOCs and Value Creation' (2011) *World Bank Working Paper No. 218* http://siteresources.worldbank.org/INTOGMC/Resources/9780821388310.pdf, accessed 2 January 2016.

Valle S, 'BG Pays $71 Million for Local Content Breaches in Brazil' *Bloomberg* (2015) http://www.bloomberg.com/news/articles/2015-02-03/bg-said-to-pay-71-million-local-content-fine-in-brazil, accessed 2 February 2017.

Wolf COH and Pollitt MG, 'The Welfare Implications of Oil Privatisation: A Cost-Benefit Analysis of Norway's Statoil' (2009) *Cambridge Working Paper in Economics No. 0907.*

Zacour C, et al, 'Petrobras and the New Regulatory Framework for the Exploration and Production of Oil and Natural Gas in the Brazilian Pre-salt Region' (2012) 5(2) *Journal of World Energy Law and Business*, 131.

Zurli RZ, 'Financing Oil & Gas Projects in Brazil' (2011) http://www.bndes.gov.br/SiteBNDES/export/sites/default/bndes_pt/Galerias/Arquivos/conhecimento/seminario/Brasil_Noruega_BNDES_OleoeGas_Zurli.pdf, accessed 7 January 2016.

3 An overview of the historical development of local content in the Nigerian petroleum industry

3.1 A review of historical development of local content in Nigeria's petroleum industry

Domestic participation in the petroleum industry is weak in several African petroleum producing countries (PPCs), when compared to countries such as Norway, Malaysia, or Brazil. What this means is that for the most part, these countries rely almost exclusively on international oil companies (IOCs) and their service counterparts for exploration, production, and the processing of their petroleum resources. These foreign firms also provide the finances and technical knowhow for the most part, with their African hosts acting as non-operators and managers through national oil companies (NOCs). This means that African PPCs are largely at the mercy of these foreign-based firms for the extraction and production of their petroleum resources, with little input being made from local supply and service sectors.

While excuses may be made for new entrants into the petroleum industry such as Ghana, Uganda, or Tanzania, the same may not apply to more established PPCs such as Nigeria, Angola, or Libya, which have had decades of experience in the industry. It is because of this desire to turn around the tide of an unacceptably low local content that several African PPCs, both old and new, have made local content a priority in their interactions with foreign firms operating in their terrains. One country which has been at the forefront of this current trend is Nigeria, Africa's largest petroleum producer. For although it commenced production of petroleum as far back as 1956 (long before Norway and Malaysia, and about the same period as Brazil), Nigeria's upstream sub-sector remained exclusively dominated by IOCs in the period between 1956 and 1991. During the intervening periods, Nigeria sought to participate in its petroleum industry through its NOC, the Nigerian National Petroleum Corporation (NNPC), but as seen below, the firm participated mainly as a non-operator/asset manager, a fact which did not translate into an appreciable local content.

As at 2002, estimates showed that the Nigerian content in the Nigerian petroleum industry (NPI), stood at less than 5 percent.[1] This figure was deemed to be unacceptably low. Since then there has been some slight improvement following

1 See Balouga, 2012, Heum et al, 2003, who put Nigerian content development at 25 percent in 2003, while the Nigerian Content Division put it at 20 percent in 2005. See Oguine, 2011.

the passage of the Nigerian Oil and Gas Industry Content Development Act 2010 (NOGICDA), and the implementation of some policy directives and initiatives. Even so, some industry observers still place the Nigerian content at around 12–18 percent.[2] Put into context, this means that although an appreciable number of Nigerians are currently employed in the NPI as engineers, geologists, and lawyers, etc., about 70 percent of the upstream sector of the industry remains under the dominance of IOCs, and their service and supply counterparts.[3] The midstream and downstream sub-sectors of the NPI have not fared better either, especially in the area of refining. This is due primarily to the fact that NNPC's four refineries operate at less than 20 percent of their installed refining capacity of 445,000 barrels per day. This explains why Nigeria continues to import most of its refined petroleum products.[4]

In a bid to improve domestic participation in the NPI, in 2010 Nigeria turned to NOGICDA, a protectionist local content legislation. The salient provisions of the Act are examined and analysed in the following four chapters. The first part of this chapter, however, undertakes a review of the historical development of the Nigerian content from 1956 to 2010. It therefore seeks to understand the various eras or phases of local content development in Nigeria. The second part analyses certain factors which made a strong domestic participation difficult pre-2010. This review is important in order to glean valuable lessons which can be applied by policy makers not only in Nigeria, but also for other African countries. It also enables observers and industry stakeholders to appreciate why Nigeria and several African PPCs are increasingly turning to protectionist local content measures as against the milder approach adopted by countries such as Norway and Australia. But first it is important to give a background to the NPI.

With about 37 billion barrels of crude oil and home to an estimated 192.065 trillion cubic feet deposits of natural gas, Nigeria can be said to be considerably rich in petroleum.[5] The resource is strategically important to the African giant in terms of revenues as it contributes about 10 percent of Nigeria's gross domestic product (GDP), over 70 percent of government revenues, and accounts for about 90 percent of its foreign exchange.[6] Petroleum is also important to Nigeria as source of energy, besides being considered a vital national security asset.

2 See Alike, 2012, although the NCDMB reports that the Nigerian content is around 28 percent, see NCDMB News Release 'NCDMB to Sue Offenders of Local Content Act' (6 March 2018) https://www.ncdmb.gov.ng/2018/03/ncdmb-sue-offenders-local-content-act/, accessed 6 August 2018.

3 See Adeniyi, 2013.

4 'Time to Sell off the Refineries' *Thisday* (15 September 2016) http://www.thisdaylive.com/index.php/2016/09/15/time-to-sell-off-the-refineries/, accessed 4 November 2017.

5 British Petroleum, 'BP Statistical Review of World Energy' https://www.bp.com/content/dam/bp/en/corporate/pdf/energy-economics/statistical-review-2017/bp-statistical-review-of-world-energy-2017-full-report.pdf, accessed 11 March 2018.

6 Petroleum contributes about ten percent of Nigeria's GDP, about 70 percent of government revenues, and is responsible for about 90 percent of foreign exchange for the country. See Florence, 2018.

Atop the NPI is the Minister of Petroleum Resources ('the Minister'), who is an appointee of the president of the federal republic of Nigeria. The Minister coordinates the affairs of the NNPC, the Ministry of Petroleum Resources (the 'Ministry'), the Department of Petroleum Resources (DPR), the Nigerian Content Development and Monitoring Board (NCDMB), and the National Oil Spill Detection and Regulatory Agency (NOSDRA). Similar in some ways to Norway and Brazil, there is some division of institutional responsibilities in the NPI.[7] The DPR is principal industry regulator, NCDMB is responsible for local content, while NOSDRA regulates oil spill detection and response. The Ministry formulates industry policies, while NNPC is the federal government of Nigeria's (FGN) commercial and operational arm in the NPI. Other agencies whose operations have some bearing on the NPI include the Nigerian Extractive Industries Transparency Initiative, the Central Bank of Nigeria, and the Federal Inland Revenue Services.

The NPI is partially liberalised, with indigenous E&P firms such as Monipulo, Dubri Oil, London listed Seplat, and Conoil, etc., operating side by side with established IOCs such as Shell, Chevron, Total, and Eni/Agip. In the same vein, domestic and foreign supply and service firms operate side by side in the NPI. Other Asian service firms such as Samsung and Hyundai also operate in the NPI, as well as a number of foreign NOCs such as China Petroleum and Chemical Corporation, China National Offshore Oil Corporation, Statoil of Norway, and Petrobras of Brazil. E&P firms operating in the NPI operate either through sole risk operations or in collaborations with NNPC through joint ventures (JVs), production sharing contracts (PSCs), etc. On the one hand, these firms are allowed to compete for petroleum concessions and supply and service contracts through open and competitive processes. But on the other hand, the FGN retains discretionary powers which it also uses from to time to advance and direct government policies.

Historically, local content development in Nigeria has gone through four eras or phases. The first era, 1956–1968 was characterised by a focus on generating employment for Nigerians in the NPI. Moving on from there, from 1969 to 1990, Nigeria began to directly participate in the NPI through NNPC and was thus poised to forward local content through NNPC's collaborations with IOCs. The third era (1991–2010) saw the rise of indigenous players in the NPI as well as a shift to PSCs. The fourth is the NOGICDA era, which began in 2010. The first three eras are reviewed briefly in this chapter, while the next three chapters concentrate on the NOGICDA era.

3.1.1 1956–1968: focus on employment of Nigerians

Petroleum was first discovered in Nigeria in commercial quantities in the year 1956 by Shell-BP, after decades of exploration and conducting seismic activities.[8]

7 On the so-called Norwegian model and its impact on petroleum sector performance, see Thurber et al, 2011.

8 The location of the epoch discovery was Oloibiri, in the present day Bayelsa State, in Southern Nigeria.

It is therefore safe to assert that 1956 is the year the NPI began in earnest.[9] The principal regime under which petroleum firms explored and produced petroleum during this period was the Mineral Oils Ordinance of 1914. The law, a legacy of the British Colonial Government, understandably advanced the interests of Britain and its subjects.[10] For example, it reserved concessionary rights for petroleum firms of mainly British origin. As Nigeria did not obtain its independence until 1960, the British government took advantage of its administrative dominance of the country to entrench the interests of Shell-BP over the NPI. Eventually, though, Shell-BP was joined by other IOCs from Europe and America.[11]

The role of the Nigerian government in the NPI in this period was largely limited to minor regulation and collection of taxes from IOCs. For example, IOCs were required to pay petroleum profits tax, which at the time, was administered by the Federal Ministry of Finance on behalf of the FGN. Regulatory responsibilities were left to the Ministry of Lagos Affairs from 1959 to 1963, and thereafter by the Federal Ministry of Mines and Power in 1963.[12] During this period, the fledgling country did not formulate policies aimed at enabling a strong local participation in the NPI, nor was there any strategy for the development of indigenous petroleum firms or vibrant supply and service firms. Also noticeably absent was the fact that the FGN did not establish an NOC nor did it mandate IOCs to patronise locally produced goods or services. The IOCs and service firms operating in the NPI were also not required to domesticate their operations in-country, or to utilise locally produced goods in their operations in the NPI.

Several reasons may have been responsible for the absence of a discernible and properly articulated local content policy in Nigeria at this early stage. The first is perhaps due to the fact that Nigeria, as a newly independent state, lacked the political and administrative experience as well as the in-depth expertise required to negotiate and interact efficiently with IOCs. It was therefore hardly in a position to require these firms to consider local content in their operations.[13] On the heels of that is the fact that the country, at this time, lacked skilled personnel with expertise in petroleum related fields such as engineering, geology, and geophysics. It also lacked budding manufacturing

9 The industry's development, however, predates the First World War as efforts by the German Bitumen company were already in top gear to discover oil in Nigeria. See Steyn, 2009.

10 The Mineral Oils (Amendment) Act, 1962, however, abrogated the exclusive rights of British-registered companies to the NPI, and in essence opened it up for non-British actors.

11 And in fact Shell was granted complete dominion over the whole of Nigeria, although it eventually relinquished some of its concession to new entrants to the NPI such as Mobil, and Chevron, etc. Etikenrentse, 2004, at p 266.

12 Nwokeji, 2007.

13 Nigeria became independent from Britain on 1 October 1960. The British monarch, however, continued to act as the constitutional Head of State until 1963, when Nigeria became a republic.

and service industries, and its infrastructure was generally underdeveloped. As such, requiring petroleum firms to patronise local industries would have seemed untenable at the time. It is also likely that Nigeria's rulers were contented with the negligible tax remittances paid by IOCs, at a time when the economy was driven mainly by agriculture.

Some minor local content requirements (LCRs) were nevertheless inserted in oil mining leases (OMLs) awarded to IOCs, aimed at securing non-skilled employment for Nigerians in the NPI. Concessionaires were, for example, required to commence and initiate schemes for the technical training of suitable Nigerians in order to prepare them to work as tradesmen and craftsmen in the industry. These firms were also expected to train Nigerians to carry out supervisory roles in their operations, as well as to prepare Nigerian professionals in their employment, with the aim of paving senior managerial roles for them in the future.[14]

The nationalistic fervour which resonated in the 1950s and 1960s among developing countries of South America, the Middle East, and Africa, gave impetus for some changes in the interactions between PPCs and IOCs. It saw newly independent countries, which were eager to play more active roles in the management of their natural resources, take the bold initiative to both nationalise and convert the assets of IOCs to NOCs,[15] or establish NOCs from the start.[16] Some of these PPCs also renegotiated with IOCs in order to address perceived unfairness in the terms under which they had operated – terms which were deemed as largely unfavourable and skewed in favour of IOCs. And Nigeria was not left out. From 1969 onwards it began to assert greater authority over its petroleum resources. First it enacted the Petroleum Act in the same year, and began to participate directly in the NPI through the Nigerian National Oil Corporation (NNOC). Some of these developments, and the extent to which they impacted the growth of the Nigerian content, are now assessed.

3.1.2 1969–1990: the Petroleum Act, DPR, and NNPC

In 1969, Nigeria was headed by a military junta. It was also in the third year of a bloody civil war. Its economy was weak, and much of its infrastructure was devastated as a result of the war. Desperately in need of funds to reinvent itself, the

14 See for instance, Clause 17(1) of OML 92, see also Oguine, 2011, at p 406.

15 For instance, Mexico established Pemex by nationalising and expropriating the assets of Anglo-Dutch and US companies operating in Mexico in 1938, while in the 1970s, Libya expropriated and nationalised concessions operated by Conoco-Phillips, BP, and Amoco. Similarly, the Saudi government acquired the assets of the Arabian American Oil Co and renamed it Saudi Aramco. See Kultgen, 2014. Similarly, in 1975 Venezuela passed the Organic Law Reserving to the State Industry and Trade of Hydrocarbons, through it terminated all outstanding IOCs' concessions, expropriated all their assets, and granted the state a monopoly over the Petroleum industry. See Cuervo, 2010, at pp 644–645.

16 Today, most PPCs have established NOCs which play varying degrees in their petroleum industries. They include Kuwait, Saudi Arabia, Nigeria, Mexico, Brazil, Venezuela, Algeria, Norway, Russia, Iran, Iraq, and Qatar.

country turned to its burgeoning petroleum industry. Dissatisfied with the conditions under which IOCs operated at the time, and desirous of playing a more active role in the NPI, Nigeria turned to legislation. First it enacted the Petroleum Act of 1969. Through this law it repealed the Minerals Oils Ordinance of 1914, and established a new framework which gave the Nigerian state greater powers over its petroleum resources.[17] Section 2 of the Petroleum Act conferred on the Minister the right to grant concessions in the form of OMLs, oil prospecting licenses (OPLs), and oil exploration licenses, to petroleum companies.[18] The Minister was also authorised to make regulations for the governance of the industry.[19] The Act also reserved for the Nigerian state, the right or option to participate directly in concessions awarded to petroleum firms.[20] And in order to whittle down the powers of IOCs, it reduced the tenure of post-1969 OMLs from the 30 or 40 years which had been the norm under the previous regime, to a maximum of 20 years. Furthermore, holders of OMLs were to relinquish one half of their concessions after an initial 10-year period.[21]

Although the Petroleum Act did not operate retrospectively to pre-1969 concessions, its impact was appreciable. Notably, it created a framework for greater government participation in the NPI, and by so doing, limited the powers of IOCs to some extent.[22] But while the reservation of participatory rights in the Nigerian government thus created opportunities which could have been used to further the Nigerian content, the Petroleum Act appeared to have had a limited local content focus. Similar to the requirements contained in pre-1969 OMLs, LCRs were limited to securing employment and training of Nigerians in the NPI. Paragraph 38(a)i of the first schedule to the Act for instance, required grantees of OMLs to attain a 75 percent Nigerian content in managerial, professional, and supervisory grades in connection with their concessions. Under paragraph 38(a)ii of the same schedule, Nigerians in the employ of concessionaires in any particular job group, were not to be less than 60 percent of the total number of employees. And under paragraph 38(b), all skilled, semi-skilled, and unskilled workers were to be Nigerians. In addition, some slight local content provisions were also contained in the Petroleum (Drilling and Production) Regulations 1969, which was made under the Petroleum Act. For example, regulation 26 required holders of OPLs to submit detailed programmes for the recruitment and training of Nigerians which

17 S.14(1) and para.42 of the third schedule to the Act.
18 S.2.
19 S.8.
20 Para.35 of the first schedule to the Act. Nigeria's first opportunity to participate in the oil industry was in 1962 when Agip and its partner Phillips Oil offered Nigeria the option to acquire 33 percent of its equity. This option was not taken up. See Etikenrentse, 2004, at p 23.
21 See para.12(1) of the first schedule to the Act.
22 Para.35 of the first schedule to the Petroleum Act authorises the Minister, in the public interest, to impose special terms on concessions as he deems necessary which would, among other things, entitle the Nigerian government to participate in ventures to which the concessions relate, on terms to be negotiated between the Minister and the concessionaires.

were to be approved by the Minister, within 12 months of the grant of their concessions. Another drawback to the Petroleum Act was that it did not also establish any institutional framework for the implementation of its provisions, although it authorised the Minister to delegate his powers, where necessary.[23]

At the institutional level, the FGN which was keen to strengthen the regulation of the NPI, established the DPR in 1970, and saddled it with the mandate of regulating the industry. In addition, the government established the NNOC in 1971 in pursuance to Decree No. 18 of the same year. Together, these institutions became the primary government agencies in the NPI, which were responsible for driving government policy. Functionally, DPR partnered with the NNOC in advancing government related policies in the NPI, with the former acting as regulator, and the latter as Nigeria's commercial agent in the industry. NNOC's responsibilities included mining and marketing petroleum resources, and engaging in all other activities related with the petroleum industry.

Through the NNOC, Nigeria began to acquire participatory stakes in acreages operated by IOCs, although it did not acquire equity in these firms. In most of these arrangements, the firm became the majority non-operating partner, while IOCs, as minority partners functioned as operators and providers of technical expertise. NNOC later merged with the Ministry of Petroleum Resources in 1977 and was renamed the NNPC.[24] Through NNPC, the FGN continues to participate directly in the NPI via collaborations with IOCs primarily through JVs,[25] and lately via PSCs.[26] Despite the passage of the Petroleum Act, the establishment of

23 See ss 4(5) and 12 of the Petroleum Act.

24 In 1975, the DPR was upgraded to a Ministry of Petroleum Resources.

25 Similar in many ways to a partnership, a JV is an association of two or more parties who engage in a business enterprise for profit. In some instances, the venture partners may incorporate a company, and use same as a vehicle for achieving their aims. In a typical JV arrangement between NNPC and an IOC, both parties are made joint owners of oil concessions. Petroleum found in the block belongs to both parties. The parties participate from the profits of the venture in proportion to their percentage in the venture, while funding responsibilities and risks are shared or borne in proportion to the holdings of each of the parties. Where there is more than one IOC party in the venture, one of them may be appointed as the operator of the concession. A memorandum of understanding is usually executed among the parties, which outlines the profit sharing formula, responsibilities, and addresses issues such as taxes, and royalties etc. Furthermore, a participatory agreement and a joint operating agreement will be executed in order to provide a framework to regulate the operation of the venture. See Martin and Park, 2010. S.24 of the PPTA recognises partnerships between companies, JVs or schemes of arrangements for the purposes of exploration of oil, and empowers the Minister to make rules which may modify the PPTA for the purposes of taxation.

26 Nigeria shifted towards PSCs due to its inability to meet its cash call obligations under the various JVs it was involved int. Its constant default 'forced' IOCs to rely on syndicated loans to finance their operations which came at a higher cost, as interests were imposed on such loans. Keen to utilize a less onerous and risky arrangement, the Nigerian government began increasingly rely on the PSC model from the early 1990s. The PSC is discussed in more detail in the course of this book. See Ameh, 2007; Adepetun, 1995, and Etikerentse, 2004, at pp 31, and 41–43. Since 2017, the FGN began to employ an alternative funding mechanism for its JVs. Under this

DPR, and NNOC's direct participation in the NPI, the Nigerian content remained largely marginal.

The preceding chapter demonstrated that Brazil and Norway were keen on developing the competencies and operational capabilities of Statoil and Petrobras from the inception of their petroleum industries. Over time, these NOCs were used to further the petroleum industry policies of their host states through their active operational involvement in exploration and production. Unlike these countries, Nigeria appeared to have been content to use NNPC primarily as sector administrator and 'profit' collector during the period under review. This accounts for why it did not strategically position the firm to develop into a viable upstream operator. The government's attitude towards the firm in this regard may have been due to an acute lack of trust in its ability to effectively handle challenging upstream projects. The consequence was that NNPC, for the most part, lapsed into the role of an asset manager, rather than a viable sole operator.

Several positives can, nonetheless, be extricated from some of the developments that occurred in the period under review. For one, NNPC's direct participation primarily through JVs, positioned it to monitor the expenditure and operations of its IOC partners. Whether it utilised this position effectively is a different thing altogether. Be that as it may, the establishment of DPR, and its eventual merger into NNPC, also gave the Nigerian government stronger regulatory roles which it used to advance some policies of the state in the NPI. Thus even though Nigeria did not have indigenous E&P firms or through indigenous supply and service firms (ISSFs), the number of Nigerians employed in the NPI continued to grow. This growth was bolstered by the establishment of the Petroleum Trust Development Fund (PTDF) via Decree No. 25 of 1973. The objective of the PTDF was to develop human capacity in order to enable Nigerians play more active roles in the NPI.[27] The Fund began almost immediately to grant scholarships to thousands of Nigerians to study within and outside the country in petroleum related subjects such as engineering, and geology, besides providing funding to Nigerian research institutions.[28] Many of these graduates returned to Nigeria to play active roles in the NPI either as employees of IOCs and service firms, or as administrators and regulators. Beyond these developments, the Nigerian content in the

arrangement, which had already been used between NNPC and Chevron Nigeria Ltd, the JV business finances itself by retaining its operating costs and capital allowances for the sustenance of the business. It is also able to source for its own funding, and by so doing, relieves the government of the burden of meeting its yearly cash calls. See Okere, 2016. Alternative funding arrangements now account for about 13.42 percent of Nigeria's crude oil production in 2017. NNPC Report for January 2018 http://nnpcgroup.com/Portals/0/Monthly%20Financial%20and%20Operations%20Data/Full%20Reports/NNPC%20Monthly%20Financial%20%20Operations%20Report%20for%20the%20Month%20of%20January%202018.pdf, accessed 16 May 2018.

27 Ch. P.14 LFN 2004, see PTDF, 'History' (2012) http://www.ptdf.gov.ng/index.php?option=com_content&view=article&id=40&Itemid=54, accessed 13 November 2012.

28 PTDF, 'Local and Overseas Scholarship Scheme' (2013) http://www.ptdf.gov.ng/index.php?option=com_content&view=article&id=105, accessed 18 March 2013.

upstream aspects of the NPI did not extend beyond NNPC's minor upstream activities. At the downstream, however, the firm was involved in the refining, transportation, and retailing of petroleum products.

3.1.3 1990–2010: discretionary awards of OPLs, marginal oil fields, and the birth of indigenous petroleum firms

As Nigeria approached the end of the 1980s, there was growing discontent with the virtual absence of indigenous Nigerian firms in the upstream sector of the NPI, perhaps other than in the employment of IOCs. It was considered unacceptable that a country as large as Nigeria which had enormous human capital, had practically no direct input in the NPI in the form of a vibrant operator NOC, competitive indigenous E&P firms, or ISSFs. This concern gave rise to action when the Ibrahim Babangida administration (1985–1993) formulated a policy of awarding OPLs to indigenous upstream firms discretionarily, on terms which were relatively favourable and liberal.[29] That strategy, as well as other developments in this period, came to impact the Nigerian content in no small measure. The indigenous E&P firms to which upstream concessions were awarded operated mainly under sole risk arrangements, in contrast to IOCs which collaborated with NNPC. The cornerstone of a sole risk operation is that the petroleum firm bears all the risks associated with its petroleum related activities, and is also entitled to all the profits it makes after paying taxes, royalties, and a signature bonus to the FGN.[30]

In addition to awarding OPLs discretionarily, the FGN also decided resolutely to farm-out marginal oil fields and award same to indigenous E&P firms in order to give the opportunity to smaller indigenous firms to participate in the NPI. Marginal fields refer to portions of concession areas already awarded to NNPC/IOCs, which have been left unattended for a period of not less than ten years from the date of the first discovery of crude oil in those fields.[31] Holders of OMLs were also entitled to farm-out producing marginal fields to smaller E&P firms. They could only do this, however, if they first obtained the consent of the president of Nigeria. In granting his consent, the president must first be satisfied that it is in the interest of the public to so, and that the proposed assignee of a marginal field is acceptable to the FGN. Non-producing marginal fields may also be farmed-out if they had been left unattended for at least a period of ten years.

This policy of awarding upstream licenses to indigenous E&P firms discretionarily, despite its advantage in shoring up domestic firms, had some demerits as well. First, by not requiring indigenous firms to bid for oil blocks under a competitive system, it created opportunities for rent seeking, patronage, corruption, and self-dealing, since due process was hardly followed in the award of these concessions.[32] Another

29 Etikerentse, 2004.

30 See generally, Omorogbe, 1997.

31 See para.16A of the first schedule to the Petroleum Act. For a more detailed analysis, see Oke, 2011; see also Omorogbe, 1999, and Atsegbua, 2005.

32 See Wangelow, 2018.

limitation with the policy as far as local content was concerned, was that the FGN appeared to have focused only on giving indigenous E&P firms a 'bite' in the upstream business, but did not give the same attention to developing ISSFs. The effect was that while it led to the growth of Indigenous E&P firms, the reliance on foreign firms for technical support, and for the supply of equipment and materials, continued. Again, because some of the awardees lacked the requisite expertise and capacity to develop their concessions, they failed to embark on petroleum operations, choosing rather to quickly resell them to foreign firms-making quick profits in the process, but in effect defeating the Nigerianisation objective.[33]

The above constraints notwithstanding, developing indigenous E&P firms through the discretionary regime was one of the best things to have happened to Nigeria in the area of indigenous participation, up to that time. In fact, had the policy been initiated in the 1970s, in all probability, it would have translated much earlier into the development of vibrant indigenous E&P firms, which would have also have impacted the Nigerian local content meaningfully. The discretionary policy heralded the birth and rise of firms such as Conoil, Monipulo, New Nigeria Development Company, and Dubri Oil, some of which are becoming a force in the NPI. The firms which developed as a result of these policies have created jobs for quite a number of Nigerians in the NPI, besides paying taxes, and executing corporate social responsibilities in their areas of operations.

The discretionary policy also enabled fledgling Nigerian firms to develop relevant expertise in the NPI by being exposed to challenging projects. Today, some of these firms are able to collaborate with NNPC through PSC arrangements,[34]

33 A case in hand is the Malabu Oil deal, whose reverberations continue to impact the NPI. Malabu Oil and Gas Ltd was incorporated by the former minister for petroleum, Chief Dan Etete. In 1998, when the firm was only about nine days old it was awarded OPL 245 by the Abacha regime. The block is very prolific and contains an estimated nine billion barrels of crude oil. The controversy and scandals surrounding the block are chequered. First it was alleged that the block was awarded to Malabu without following due process. It was later cancelled by the Obasanjo regime in 2001 and after a series of litigations, the matter was amicably settled out of court between Malabu and the FGN for the sum of $1.1 billion under an arrangement under which Shell and Eni were to pay Malabu the said sum, in exchange for the block. It has been alleged that the funds were paid to Malabu via an account domiciled in England, and was subsequently distributed to some persons with close ties to the Nigerian government. Currently, Nigeria and Italy are probing the involvement of a number of prominent Nigerians, including the former minister of petroleum, Diezani Madueke, Nigeria's former President, Goodluck Jonathan, Shell, Eni, Dan Etete (managing director of Malabu), Mohammed Adoke, Nigeria's former minister for justice; see 'Malabu $1.1 billion scandal: Italian prosecutors request trial of Etete, Shell, Eni, others' *Premium Times* (9 February 2017) http://www.premiumtimesng.com/news/top-news/223048-malabu-1-1-billion-scandal-italian-prosecutors-request-trial-etete-shell-eni-others.html, accessed 8 July 2017; see also L Faull et al, 'The Oil Deal, the Disgraced Former Minister, and $800m paid via a UK Bank' *The Guardian* (5 March 2017) https://www.theguardian.com/business/2017/mar/05/the-oil-deal-the-disgraced-minister-and-800m-paid-via-a-uk-bank, accessed 8 July 2017.

34 Some indigenous firms which collaborate with NNPC include Conoil, Monipulo, and New Nigeria Development Company Ltd, etc. See DPR, '2016 Oil and Gas Annual

while others now operate offshore concessions in areas which were hitherto reserved for IOCs.[35] Beyond that, some Nigerian upstream firms have also been able to export their expertise to other African countries such as South Sudan and Equatorial Guinea.[36] Two other developments which bordered somewhat on local content development in the period under review are worthy of mention. The first is Nigeria's increasing utilisation of PSCs in its interactions with E&P firms. The second was the publication of the Oil and Gas Pipelines Regulation of 1995.

In the early 1990s the FGN began to increasingly favour the PSC approach in its interactions and collaborations with IOCs. It also began to rely less on JVs, which had been its dominant approach from the early 1970s. The reason for this shift was due largely to NNPC's inability to meet its cash call obligations to its JV partners. These PSCs contained LCRs over and beyond what was contained in the Petroleum Act regime. Furthermore, they positioned NNPC to advance the Nigerian content in the NPI, through its membership of management committees. Then there was the Oil and Gas Pipelines Regulation which was made in 1995 in pursuance to the Oil Pipelines Act. Under regulation 2(3) thereof, DPR was authorised to approve firms which could bid for contracts to construct oil and gas pipelines in Nigeria. In essence, the regulator was empowered to approve or disapprove non-Nigerian firms from bidding for such contracts.[37]

In spite of these developments and measures, the Nigerian content during this period remained significantly weak. As shown in earlier in this chapter, it was estimated that the Nigerian content in the NPI was around 5 percent by the year 2000. Firms operating in the NPI continued to import most of their equipment. Fabrication, engineering, and in some cases, welding jobs, were outsourced to foreign service firms. Expatriate quotas were flaunted serially by IOCs, while Nigerians were routinely passed over in the contracting of E&P firms operating in the sector. Clearly, something more was needed to be done urgently in order to improve the Nigerian content. Whether in the form of legislation, contracts, or local content initiatives, it was obvious to Nigerians that their virtual absence in petroleum contracting was depriving the country of billions of dollars.

Report' (2016) https://dpr.gov.ng/index/wp-content/uploads/2016/01/2016-Oil-Gas-Industry-Annual-Report.pdf, accessed 4 July 2018, at p 31.

35 Some Nigerian firms that operate offshore include NPDC, Monipulo, Conoil, and Oando. See DPR, '2016 Oil and Gas Annual Report' ibid.

36 For example, Sahara Energy has a visible presence in Africa, the Caribbean, Asia, and Europe. Sahara Energy, 'About Us' http://www.sahara-group.com/about_us.html, accessed 29 January 2018. Televeras, another Nigerian firm, also has operations in Equatorial Guinea, and Ivory Coast. See Nsehe, 2017. Similarly, Atlas-Oranto Petroleum has operations in Equatorial Guinea, Ghana, South Sudan, Benin, Senegal, Sao Tome, and Uganda. See Oranto Petroleum, 'Portfolio' http://atlas-oranto.com/portfolio/, accessed 29 January 2018. See also S Obasi, 'Nigerian Oil Firm, Oranto Invests $500mn in South Sudan Oil Bloc'.

37 C Okafor, 'FG Insists on Nigerian Content for Oil Bid Rounds, Licences' *Thisday* (Abuja, 25 June 2012) http://www.thisdaylive.com/articles/fg-insists-on-nigerian-content-for-oil-bid-rounds-licences/118677/, accessed 19 November 2017.

Incidentally, during this period, Nigeria transitioned from military rule to civilian rule in 1999. Following this, the FGN commissioned two studies on its local content, tabled a Nigerian content Bill before its central legislature in 2003, established a Nigerian Content Division in 2003, and published Nigerian content guidelines in 2006. These developments culminated in the passage of NOGICDA in 2010, which is the focus of Chapters 4, 5, 6, and 7. It is sufficient for now to investigate the factors responsible for Nigeria's weak local content during the phases examined above. First there is the colonial factor which, as noted above, laid the foundation for the domination of foreign interests over Nigeria's petroleum resources. In addition to this factor, however, other factors that contributed to the weak Nigerian content included the absence of a discernible local content policy, insufficient regulation/monitoring, funding, inadequate technical know-how, poor infrastructure, and weak human capacity. Incidentally, some of these factors continue to pose challenges to the development of the local content in Nigeria, even though some of them have been or are being addressed, to some extent. Because their tendency to negate the success of Nigeria's current local content policy as embodied in NOGICDA, these factors require further analysis.

3.2 Analysis of some factors responsible for the weak Nigerian content in the petroleum industry pre-2010

Perhaps the most significant hindrance to the development of the Nigerian content during the pre-NOGICDA era was the absence of a discernible and forward looking local content policy. It is safe to assert that a properly designed and articulated local content policy is the starting point for any PPC which desires to develop its local content. A local content policy must be deliberate and realisable, within specific time frames and phases. For example, the local content policies of Norway and Brazil which eventually translated to the dominance of Statoil and Petrobras, and also laid the foundation for the development of viable local service and supply firms in those countries, were deliberate and focused.[38] In contrast, Nigeria's policy makers appeared not to have foreseen a time when local firms would play active roles in the NPI, and therefore did not take steps to lay a proper groundwork for such to occur. This probably accounts for why the country's earliest approach to local content was concentrated on securing junior and mid-level jobs for Nigerians in the NPI, rather than creating platforms for local firms to bud, develop, and participate in the NPI. In addition, this lack of policy focus meant that even when Nigeria began to participate directly in the NPI after the passage of the Petroleum Act, it concentrated mainly on increasing the government take from JVs, rather than harnessing the opportunities which arose from its participation, for the furtherance of the Nigerian content, as was the case with Norway.

38 For example, it is estimated that Norway has over 1,000 service and related companies with an annual turnover of $60 billion. See Aramco, 'In-Kingdom Total Value Add (IKTVA) Program Launch' (1 December 2015) http://www.saudiaramco.com/en/home/news-media/speeches/IKTVA-Launch.html, accessed 10 May 2018.

This absence of a local content policy came to eventually impact every aspect of the NPI. First, it meant that Nigeria did not see the need to 'aggressively' invest in research for the purpose of developing indigenous technology, other than granting scholarships to some Nigerians to study abroad through the PTDF scheme. For laudable as that scheme was, it did not go far enough. It also manifested in the absence of programmes/initiatives to strengthen budding local entrepreneurs such as the provision of loans on favourable terms, etc. And even when petroleum concessions were awarded to Nigerians in the 1990s, they did not necessarily translate into a strong local content, but rather to 'local ownership', which meant that indigenous petroleum firms continued to rely almost entirely on foreign-based service and supply firms.

Another manifestation of the absence of a properly articulated local content policy was the FGN's lackadaisical attitude towards developing NNOC and later NNPC into a viable operator in the NPI. Had such a policy been in place, the government would have required the NOC to operate some of the fields in which it collaborated with IOCs, given that NNPC had shown some upstream promise from inception.[39] A viable operator NOC in the mould of Statoil and Petrobras would have thus been positioned to exercise stronger control over the NPI, and would have also been used as a spring board to develop local industries, since its experiences and expertise would have been translated to other indigenous firms.

Another factor that contributed to, or flows from, the absence of a discernible local content policy, was the absence of an independent and capable local content monitor/regulator. Prior to NOGICDA, Nigeria relied mainly on the DPR and NNPC for the regulation and monitoring of local content. DPR administers the Petroleum Act and the Drilling and Production Regulations of 1969, and was therefore responsible for enforcing the local content provisions contained in those regimes. As the body responsible for negotiating and awarding E&P contracts to petroleum firms, DPR routinely made local content a pre-condition for the award of petroleum concessions in its bidding rounds.[40]

DPR's major weakness was in the area of monitoring and enforcement. Its efforts in this area could be described to be at best, lame and ineffective.[41] First DPR struggled with capacity. It lacked and still lacks independence as well, due primarily to its undue closeness to NNPC which is brought about by the fact that both agencies are answerable to the Minister, and ultimately to the Nigerian president. The issue is that NNPC is the majority partner in most of the concessions operated by IOCs, which means that any stringent regulation of IOCs by DPR may translate in it regulating NNPC and, by extension, the Minister, who chairs the NOC's board. This closeness between the regulator and the industry has,

39 Nwokeji observes that, in the past, even where NNPC's minor upstream exploratory activities resulted in discovery of crude oil, its concessions were immediately turned over to IOCs for development: Nwokeji, 2007, at p 36.

40 See S Wabote, 'Eight Years of Local Content Act' *The Nation* (23 April 2018) http://thenationonlineng.net/eight-years-of-local-content-act/, accessed 8 August 2018; Edward, 2000; see also Okafor, 2012.

41 Amanze-Nwachukwu, 2012.

naturally, weakened DPR's capacity to regulate the NPI effectively and dispassionately. The regulator also struggles with legitimacy issues. This is because DPR is, surprisingly, not a creation of any statute. Rather, it is a carryover from NNPC's Petroleum Inspectorate, which was established by section 10 of the NNPC Act of 1977. This means that in contrast to the Norwegian Petroleum Directorate or the National Agency for Petroleum, Natural Gas, and Biofuels of Brazil, DPR which regulates so important an industry, does not operate under any comprehensive legal framework which outlines its powers to enforce breaches of the Petroleum Act, its regulations, or the terms under which concessions are awarded to petroleum firms. The absence of a comprehensive legislative framework understandably contributed to the DPR's weak enforcement of the minor local content provisions contained in the Petroleum Act.

The absence of an articulated local content policy also meant that NNPC's subsidiary, the National Petroleum Investment Management Services (NAPIMS), which was saddled with the responsibility of protecting Nigeria's interests in its collaborations with petroleum firms, did not prioritise local content. Through its membership of operating committees, NNPC/NAPIMS was positioned to vet and approve the budgets, expenditures, and work programmes of its operator-partners, in order to ensure that, among other things, an appreciable Nigerian content was accommodated by its partners. In principle, NAPIMS could have utilised its powers to propose or insist on the inclusion of Nigerian firms on the list of bidders for more substantial contracts. In addition, it could have used its membership of bid committees to ensure that, where practicable, the local aspect of certain jobs be performed by the local subsidiaries of its partners or by indigenously owned firms.[42] But like DPR, NAPIMS was largely unable to restrain its partners from outsourcing relevant jobs abroad in violation of their contractual obligations under PSCs/JVs, etc.[43]

In fact, besides its inability to rein in its E&P partners, it is actually doubtful whether NNPC/NAPIMS was actually committed to the development of the Nigerian content. It has been alleged that some violations of the Nigerian content in the pre-NOGICDA era were largely done with NNPC's knowledge or tacit consent.[44] Even in the current era there have been allegations that the firm has violated NOGICDA in its contracting.[45] During the pre-NOGICDA days when advancement of the Nigerian content in JV/PSC contracting was all but left for

42 Oguine, 2011, at p 409.

43 See Balouga, 2012.

44 Nwaokoro, 2011.

45 Nwaokoro, 2011, at p 152. In 2014, for instance, an action was instituted at the Federal High Court against NNPC, Nigeria's Finance Minister, and accounting giant PricewaterhouseCoopers, by three accountants. The claimants, Messrs Robert Ade-Odiachi, Ladi Smith, and Ituah Ighodalo, alleged that the appointment of PricewaterhouseCoopers to audit NNPC was in gross violation of ss 10, 11 and 15 of the Act. They also claimed that the contract was awarded without any bidding by the local industry or from any Nigerian accounting firm. See 'Missing $20bn: Okonjo-Iweala Disowns Pricewaterhousecoopers, says she didn't hire firm' *Premium Times* (30 April 2015), https://www.premiumtimesng.com/news/headlines/182286-missing-20-billion-okonjo-iweala-denies-appointing-pricewaterhousecoopers.html, accessed 6 March 2018. See also Opeisetain, 2014.

NNPC/NAPIMS, Ike Oguine pointed out that policy makers, businessmen, and commentators felt that very little was being achieved in that regard, particularly in relation to employment and utilisation of locally supplied goods and services in the NPI.[46]

An in-depth assessment of the position may reveal that while NAPIMS remained majority partner in most of its collaborations with IOCs, it was in reality the weaker party in its interactions with IOCs, and was often 'forced' to rely on them for funding, as well as for the supply of information, and technology. NNPC/NAPIMS' consistent cash call defaults naturally weakened its capacity and its justification to insist on the patronage of Nigeria's goods and services, particularly in its JVs operations. In fact, it is arguable that the regulatory/monitoring inefficiency of DPR/NAPIMS in the area of local content may have necessitated or justified the establishment of the NCDMB (about which much is said in the next chapter), to function as a separate and independent regulator.

Added to the above factors was the fact that the IOCs and their service counterparts, which dominated the NPI pre-2010, did not take significant steps to strengthen local industries or to further local content. These firms which had made measurable inroads in the NPI could have formulated policies aimed at bolstering local industries by providing funds for local contractors, domesticating their operations in the country, or partnering with domestic firms. These efforts which would have contributed to the growth of the Nigerian content one way or another would have ultimately benefitted the IOCs and their service counterparts in the long run, and saved them huge costs of importing a significant percentage of the goods and services they require for their operations. For the most part, however, these IOCs focused on minor social initiatives such as granting scholarships, and building cottage hospitals and link roads in their areas of operations, but shirked largely from taking steps to develop local capabilities.

The Nigerian content was also affected by Nigeria's weak manufacturing sector and the absence of industrialisation.[47] The technology intensive nature of the petroleum industry requires a strong manufacturing and industrial base for the development of vibrant service and supply firms which would be able to execute petroleum related contracts such as fabrication, construction, and integration of steel pipes, etc. In effect, developing a strong local content may be largely dependent on the degree to how strong a country is in terms of manufacturing, infrastructure, and construction. But Nigeria is not a manufacturing giant, nor is it industrialised. As at 2003, manufacturing accounted for less than 5 percent of Nigeria's exports.[48] And as at 2017, it still accounted for less than 10 percent of Nigeria's GDP.[49] Despite its over 170 million inhabitants, Nigeria's per capita

46 Oguine, 2011, at p 409; see also Ihua et al, 2009, at p 165.
47 See Okonji, 2014.
48 See Heum et al, 2003, at p 11.
49 National Bureau of Statistics, 'Nigerian Gross Domestic Report Quarter Three' (2017), http://www.nigerianstat.gov.ng, accessed 29 October 2018.

industrial steel consumption is still within the range of 10 kilogrammes, which is far below the world average of 150 kilogrammes.[50]

In practical terms, this means that while some Nigerian firms may have attained some strides in fabrication, they are still unable to develop floating, production, storage, and offloading facilities (FPSOs) for Nigeria's deep-water oil fields. To put things in perspective, it is noteworthy that while a typical FPSO for Nigeria's deep water oil fields weighs about 110,000 tonnes, only about 8,000 tonnes of steel are currently fabricated by Nigerian firms. And even where steel is fabricated in Nigeria, its integration into FPSOs is done outside Nigeria and re-imported back to the country.[51] The absence of industrialisation accounts for why Nigerian firms continue to rely on their foreign partners for the provision of subsea systems engineering, project management, subsea Christmas trees, production and intervention control systems, manifolds, flow line connection systems, installation support, and associated spares.[52]

Closely allied to weak manufacturing was Nigeria's weak infrastructural base. Nigeria's road, rail, and water transport systems are all in dire need of refurbishment. These limitations have invariably impacted Nigeria's local content, since adequate infrastructure is the base upon which indigenous petroleum firms can develop. The country continues to struggle with the non-availability of constant power supply, which is an integral component for the development of a vibrant manufacturing sector.[53] To place the Nigerian situation in perspective, it is noteworthy that although home to about 50 million inhabitants, South Africa's electricity generation is estimated at being about 55 percent more that of Nigeria, which has over 170 million inhabitants.[54]

Lastly, there was the human capacity factor. After over five decades as a PPC, coupled with its huge population, Nigeria can boast of having an appreciable number of highly trained engineers, geologist, geophysicists, lab scientists, bankers, and lawyers, some of whom were trained in the best institutions in the world and are thus able to play critical roles in the NPI.[55] It is also a fact that quite a

50 Nastha, 2012.

51 '4 Years of Nigerian Content: Challenges Abound despite Relative Successes' *Energymix* (14 September 2014) http://energymixreport.com/4-years-nigerian-content-challenges-abound-despite-relative-successes/, accessed 9 November 2017.

52 In 2016, however, a logistics firm, LADOL, for the first time was able to construct a $300 million fabrication and integration yard in Lagos State for the NPI, ahead of a March 2017 schedule. The yard was constructed for the integration of Total's Upstream Floating Production Storage Offloading vessel for the $16 billion Egina deep water field ahead of the arrival of Total's $3.3 billion FPSO from South Korea. See 'Jadesimi: LADOL's Integration Facility for Egina FPSO is Ready' *Thisday* (25 July 2016) http://www.thisdaylive.com/index.php/2016/07/25/jadesimi-ladols-integration-facility-for-egina-fpso-is-ready/, accessed 9 November 2017.

53 Roads, water, and rail are all moribund. See Vivien and Pushak, 2011. See also Familoni, 2006.

54 For more information on Nigeria's electricity challenge and the steps being taken to address it, see Elo, 2018.

55 The PTDF fund sponsors Nigerians to study within and outside Nigeria in strategic areas relative to the needs of the petroleum industry. In 2007, the Petroleum Training

number of Nigerians work as expatriates in Angola, Gabon, Equatorial Guinea, Britain, Saudi Arabia, the USA, etc. That notwithstanding, the NPI continues to struggle with a shortage of skilled and capable manpower. One reason for this is because Nigeria grapples with constant brain drain which has seen some of its best brains emigrate to PPCs all over the world. The effect of which is that the country was, and still is, constantly in need of qualified and highly skilled workforce. Another factor that resulted in skills shortages in the NPI is the fact that Nigeria's tertiary institutions, which are primary sources for human capacity development, are often ill equipped, poorly funded, and suffer from frequent strikes. These institutions therefore struggle to train and churn out suitably qualified graduates to meet the practical demands of the petroleum industry.[56] A shortage in skills was and is still cited in justification of the continued use of expatriates by petroleum firms, as graduates from Nigerian institutions are said to be unemployable, with many struggling to meet basic entry requirements into the petroleum industry.[57]

3.3 Conclusion

This chapter analysed local content development in the NPI from a historical perspective. It also analysed certain factors which contributed to the weak Nigerian content pre-2010. The first part traced the development of local content in the NPI from the inception of the NPI to the current dispensation as embodied in NOGICDA. The second part analysed certain factors that were responsible for the weak Nigerian content pre-NOGICDA. Incidentally, most of the factors highlighted above can be found in several African countries in varying degrees. Some of these countries struggle with poor infrastructure, weak NOCs, weak regulatory agencies, as well the absence of discernible local content policies.

Some of the new entrants such as Ghana, Tanzania, and Uganda have the advantage which Nigeria did not have. With the benefit of hindsight and history on their side, they have developed policies geared towards strengthening local content, the issue is that most of these new entrants also struggle with weak in-country capacity in terms of technology, funding, and expertise. All of these challenges will require concerted efforts by African PPCs to address them, in order to ensure that local content policies are actualised to the benefit of their people.

Institute was upgraded to the Federal University of Petroleum Resources, with the vision of training capable Nigerians to play significant roles in the industry. The university is in its fledgling stage. See Ihua, 2010.

56 In the 2016/2017 world ranking of universities, no Nigerian university was among the top 400 in the world. The University of Ibadan, which is the highest ranking university, is 801 out of 1,000 in the Times Higher Education Ranking. See 'The World University Ranking' *Times Higher Education* http://www.timeshighereducation.co.uk/world-university-rankings/2016-17/world-ranking, accessed 17 March 2018, see also 'Study in Nigeria' https://www.timeshighereducation.com/student/where-to-study/study-in-nigeria, accessed 15 July 2018.

57 Edukugho, 2012.

Keen to shore up its local content, the Nigerian government turned to a more aggressive approach to the development of its local content when it enacted NOGICDA in 2010. The Act moved local content from the realm of contract to that of statute, and brought it to the national discourse. It also served as a template for several African countries to emulate in the advancement of local content. The provisions of NOGICDA are considered in detail in the next four chapters.

Bibliography

Adeniyi S, 'Real Ownership of Oil Blocks Revealed' *Thisday* (14 March 2013) http://www.thisdaylive.com/articles/real-ownership-of-indigenous-oil-blocks-revealed/142113/, accessed 14 March 2016.

Adepetun S, 'Production Sharing Contracts – The Nigerian Experience' (1995) 12 *Journal of Energy & Natural Resources Law*, 21.

Alike E, 'Nwapa: Nigerian Content in Oil Industry Hovers around 18% 5 June 2012' *Thisday* (5 June 2012) https://www.thisdaylive.com/?s=%E2%80%98Nwapa%3A+Nigerian+Content+in+Oil+Industry+Hovers+around+18%25+5+June+2012%E2%80%99+Thisday, accessed 15 November 2016.

Amanze-Nwachukwu C, 'Why DPR Can't Efficiently Regulate Oil Sector' *Thisday* (13 December 2012) http://www.thisdaylive.com/articles/why-dpr-can-t-efficiently-regulate-oil-sector/104909/, accessed 9 September 2017.

Ameh OM, 'The Shift from Joint Operating Agreements to Production Sharing Contracts in the Nigerian Oil Industry's: Any Benefit for the Players?' (2007) The Centre for Energy and, Petroleum and Mineral Law and Policy Annual Review, 27.

Atsegbua L, 'Issues in the Development of Marginal Oilfields in Nigeria' (2005) 25(3) *Journal of Energy & Natural Resources Law*, 323.

Atsegbua LA, 'The Nigerian Oil and Gas Industry Content Development Act 2010: an examination of its Regulatory Framework' (2012) 36(4) *OPEC Energy Review*, 479.

Balouga J, 'Nigerian Local Content: Challenges and Prospects' (2012) (Third Quarter) *International Association of Energy Economics*, 23 http://www.iaee.org/en/publications/newsletterdl.aspx?id=176, accessed 11 November 2012.

Cuervo C, 'The Uncertain Fate of Venezuela's Black Pearl: The Petro State and its Ambiguous Oil and Gas Legislation' (2010) *Houston Journal of International Law*, 637.

Edukugho E, 'Challenge of Producing Unemployable Graduates', *Vanguard* (21 July 2012) http://www.vanguardngr.com/2012/07/challenge-of-producing-unemployable-graduates/, accessed 17 March 2016.

Edward V, 'Nigeria Licensing: Notes for Prospective Bidders' (2000) 18(3) *Journal of Energy & Natural Resources Law*, 301.

Elo A, 'Democratisation of Electricity in Nigeria' (2018) 3(2) *The Electricity Journal*, 106.

Etikerentse G, *Nigerian Petroleum Law* (2nd edn, Drewdrew, Nigeria, 2004).

Familoni KA, 'The Role of Economic and Social Infrastructure in Economic Development: A global View' (2006) 6(4) *Journal of Economic Perspectives*, 11.

Florence D, 'Fuelled Power: Oil, Financiers and Central Bank Policy in Nigeria' (2018) *New Political Economy*, 1.

Heum P et al, 'Enhancement of Local Content in the Upstream Oil and Gas Industry in Nigeria: A comprehensive and Viable Policy Approach' (2003) *SNF Report No. 25/03*, SNF: Institute for Research in Economics and Business Administration http://extrayen

dotransparencia.grupofaro.org/wp-content/uploads/2014/12/Enhancement-of-LC-in-the-upstream-oil-and-gas-industry-in-Nigeria.pdf, accessed 12 November 2016.

Ihua UB et al, 'Nigerian Content Policy in the Oil and Gas Industry: Implications for Small to Medium-Sized Oil-Service Companies', in *Proceedings of the 10th Annual Conference of the International Academy of African Business and Development* (IAABD, 2009).

Ihua UB, 'Local content Policy and SMEs Sector Promotion: The Nigerian Oil Industry Experience' (2010) 5(5) *International Journal of Business and Management*, 3.

Kultgen DB, 'Saudi Aramco: A Look Ahead' (2014) 7(2) *Journal of World Energy Law and Business*, 153.

Martin AT and Park JJ, 'Global Petroleum Industry Model Contracts Revisited: Higher, Faster, Stronger' (2010) 3(1) *Journal of World Energy Law & Business*, 4.

Nastha RT, 'Poor Funding, Bane of Steel Sector's Growth' *The Nation* (6 October 2012) http://www.leadership.ng/nga/articles/36663/2012/10/06/poor_funding_bane_steel_sectors_growth.html?quicktabs_3=1, accessed 20 November 2017.

Nsehe M, 'Nigerian Energy Group Televeras and ExxonMobil Win Oil Blocks in Equatorial Guinea' *Forbes* (7 June 2017) https://www.forbes.com/sites/mfonobongnsehe/2017/06/07/nigerian-energy-group-taleveras-and-exxonmobil-win-oil-blocks-in-equatorial-guinea/, accessed 29 January 2018.

Nwaokoro JE, 'Nigeria's National Content Bill: The Hype, the Hope and the Reality' (2011) 55(1) *Journal of African Law*, 128.

Nwokeji U, 'The NNPC and the Development of the Nigerian Oil and Gas Industry: History, Strategies and Current Directions' (2007) James A Baker III Institute for Public Policy of Rice University and Japan Petroleum Energy Center, https://www.bakerinstitute.org/media/files/page/9b067dc6/noc_nnpc_ugo.pdf, accessed 4 November 2017.

Oguine I, 'Nigerian Content in the Nigerian Petroleum Industry: Legal and Policy Issues' (2011) 29(4) *Journal of Energy & Natural Resources Law*, 405.

Okafor C, 'FG Insists on Nigerian Content for Oil Bid Rounds, Licences', *Thisday* (25 June 2012) http://www.thisdaylive.com/articles/fg-insists-on-nigerian-content-for-oil-bid-rounds-licences/118677/, accessed 19 November 2017.

Oke Y, 'Marginal Fields in Nigeria: who owns the Fields' *Business Day* (12 March 2011) http://businessdayonline.com/NG/index.php/law/cover/21306-marginal-fileds-in-nigeria-who-owns-the-field, accessed 9 July 2017.

Okere R, 'NNPC Sets January 1 Deadline to End $9 Billion JV Funding' *Guardian* (16 November 2016) https://guardian.ng/energy/nnpc-sets-january-1-deadline-to-end-9-billion-jv-funding/, accessed 6 March 2017.

Okonji C, 'Local Content: Nigeria Records $2.8b Investment Inflow' *Nigerian Compass* (3 September 2012) http://www.compassnewspaper.org/index.php/special-desk/maritime/7218-local-content-nigeria-records-28b-investment-inflow, accessed 2 September 2017.

Okonji E, 'Nigerian Local Content Development Attracts Foreign Interests' *Thisday* (24 February 2014) http://www.thisdaylive.com/articles/nigerian-local-content-development-attracts-foreign-interests/172252/, accessed 31 March 2014.

Omorogbe Y, 'Fundamental Issues Relating to the Development of Marginal Oil Fields in Nigeria' (1999) *Modern Practice Journal of Finance and Investment Law*, 737.

Omorogbe Y, *Oil and Gas Industry: Exploration and Production Contracts* (Malthouse Press, Nigeria, 1997).

Opeisetain T, 'Examining Local Content Legal Framework' *Daily Independent* (27 August 2014) http://uncova.com/examining-local-content-legal-framework, accessed 8 August 2017.

Steyn P, 'Oil Exploration in Colonial Nigeria' (2009) 37, *Journal of Imperial and Commonwealth History*, 250.
Thurber MC, et al, 'Exporting the Norwegian Model: the Effect Administrative Design on Oil Sector Performance' (2011) 8 *Energy Policy*, 8.
Vera-Cruz E, 'Nigeria Licensing: Notes for Prospective Bidders' (2000) 18(3) *Journal of Energy & Natural Resources Law*, 301.
Vivien F and Pushak N, 'Nigeria's Infrastructure: A Continental Perspective' (2011) https://openknowledge.worldbank.org/handle/10986/27257, accessed 16 July 2018.
Wangelow VP, 'Petroleum licensing in the European Union: the allocation of E&P rights in Denmark' (2018) 11(2) *Journal of World Energy Law & Business*, 32.

4 An overview of the provisions of the Nigerian Oil and Gas Industry Content Development Act 2010

4.1 Introduction

Nigeria returned to civilian rule in 1999 after about 25 years of military rule. Under the administration of President Olusegun Obasanjo (1999–2007), several economic reforms were introduced. Several moribund state owned enterprises were privatised, while some sectors were liberalised. In addition, there was an entrenched 'war' against corruption through legislation and the creation of specialised institutions. While it can be said that on a general note, the Obasanjo reforms did not impact the Nigerian Petroleum Industry (NPI), one thing that can be said for it is that the administration laid the foundation for an aggressive and focused local content agenda for the NPI.

Almost immediately, the administration began to put in place series of measures directed towards the development of local content in the NPI. In 2001 it commissioned a study to determine the extent of local content in the NPI. Another study was undertaken by a Norwegian firm, INTSOK, in 2003. The recommendations from both studies formed the basis of Nigeria's local content policy which was first embodied in the Nigerian Content Development Bill 2003. Pending the enactment of the Bill, the Nigerian National Petroleum Corporation (NNPC) took the initiative by establishing a Nigerian Content Division (NCD) which published local content guidelines in 2006, and sought to monitor compliance by its joint ventures (JVs)/production sharing contract (PSC) partners.[58]

Among its achievements in its few years of existence, the NCD published extensive local content guidelines which its IOC partners and their subcontractors were required to comply with. It aimed at achieving a 70 per cent local content by 2010 and introduced capacity building initiatives to strengthen local businesses to play more important roles in the NPI.[1] The NCD regime was, however, weak on

1 The directives required the domestication of engineering designs, project management, fabrication, and integration of fixed platforms weighing up to 10,000 tons, fabrication of all piles, decks, anchors, buoys, and jackets. Some of the guidelines include: Crude Oil Lifting and Other Petroleum Products' Contracts, Equipment Component Manufacturing Initiative and Certification Process, Expatriate Quotas, Fabrication And Welding: Education, Training, Qualification And Certification Services, Free Trade & Export Processing Zones, Human Capital Development, Information Systems/

three fronts. First, its scope was limited to NNPC's JV/PSC/risk service contract (RSC) partners and to their subcontractors, but did not extend to indigenous exploration and production (E&P) firms which operated under sole risks arrangements. Secondly, it suffered from an absence of independent enforcement as it could not operate independently from NNPC, and by extension its IOC partners. Thirdly, its guidelines did not have the force of law or sanctions.[2] Despite these limitations, the NCD guidelines represented the first properly articulated policy focus for the development of the Nigerian content, and became a precursor to NOGICDA. In addition, the NCD laid a strong foundation for the establishment of the Nigerian Content Development Monitoring Board (NCDMB). In order to put things in clearer perspective and address some of the weaknesses of the era under review, the Goodluck Jonathan administration (2010–2015) passed NOGICDA into law in 2010. The prospects of these measures, and the degree to which they have translated into a higher Nigerian content, are now analysed in detail in this chapter and the next three chapters.

4.2 The Nigerian Oil and Gas Industry Content Development Act 2010 (NOGICDA)

NOGICDA was enacted in 2010 in order to provide a legislative and institutional template for local content development and regulation in the NPI. The Act has 107 sections and a single Schedule.[3] It is divided into three material parts. The first part deals with Nigerian content in the NPI, while the second and third parts deal with the NCDMB, and financial provisions, respectively. As far as the Nigerian content is concerned, the Act has priority over any other petroleum related legislation previously enacted by the National Assembly.[4] Among other things, it stipulates a minimum Nigerian content for every project executed in the NPI, mandates the NCDMB to monitor, coordinate and implement its provisions,[5] and penalises local content violations.[6]

In order to demonstrate the importance attached to local content, compliance with the provisions of NOGICDA is a major criterion for award of licences, permits and any other interest in bidding for oil exploration, production, transportation, and development, or any other operations in the

Information Technology/Communications Services, Legal Services, Financial Services, Nigerian Content Compliance Certificate (NCCC), Nigerian Content Plan.

2 Atsegbua, however, points out that this notwithstanding, they had some impact on the NPI. Atsegbua, 2012, at p 494.

3 By virtue of s.1 of NOGICDA, the Act supersedes all prior legal provisions relating to local content in the petroleum industry. See also Oni, 2012.

4 S.1.

5 S.4. The functions of the NCDMB include the implementation of NOGICDA for local content enhancement

6 Under s.68, an 'operator, contractor or subcontractor who carries out any project contrary to the provisions of this Act, commits an offence and is liable upon conviction to a fine of five percent of the project sum for each project in which the offence is committed or cancellation of the project'.

NPI.[7] Thus firms which serially infringe on NOGICDA's requirements may not be considered in future bidding rounds, while their compliant counterparts would ordinarily stand a better chance in that respect.

4.2.1 Institutional framework for local content regulation and development in Nigeria

It has been demonstrated that prior to 2010, NNPC, as representative of the Nigerian state in JV/PSC collaborations, did not effectively insist on the patronage of Nigeria's supply and services firms by its international oil company (IOC) partners, and that the Department of Petroleum Resources (DPR) struggled with weak regulatory capacity besides not operating under an enabling legal framework. It was left to the Nigerian state to address these challenges through reforms. Ordinarily, several options exist for governments whose agencies or national oil companies (NOCs) consistently fail to protect public interests or advance government policies. Such firms or agencies may be reorganised, privatised, liquidated, or their powers and responsibilities may be transferred to other institutions.[8] Nigeria chose the latter approach in relation to local content.

First, it established the NCDMB via NOGICDA, and conferred it with exclusive responsibilities for the regulation and development of the Nigerian content. The Board therefore assumed all powers and responsibilities previously conferred on DPR, NNPC, and other agencies of the Federal Government of Nigeria (FGN) as far as local content in the NPI is concerned.[9] The NCDMB is, to the author's knowledge, perhaps the only legislatively established institution in the world that is vested with the singular objective of advancing local content in the petroleum industry.[10] Thus while a number of petroleum producing countries (PPCs) rely on either their NOCs or regulatory agencies to advance local content, Nigeria retains NNPC/DPR as commercial arm/regulator for the NPI, but goes

7 S.3(3).

8 When the Norwegian government deemed it necessary to reduce Statoil's influence in the Norwegian Continental Shelf, it transferred some of the firm's upstream interests to a state owned investment entity called the State's Direct Financial Interest (SDFI). The SDFI was established in 1984 in pursuance of a parliamentary resolution in 1984 to operate as a cash flow-system under which the Norwegian government will hold shares directly in the petroleum industry and not through Statoil. See Ministry of Petroleum and Energy, 'The State Direct Financial Interest' (2014) http://www.regjeringen.no/en/dep/oed/Subject/state-participation-in-the-petroleum-sec/the-states-direct-financial-interest-sdf.html?id=445748, accessed 22 March 2017.

9 S.103. Note that in practice DPR and NNPC continue to exercise some form of local content responsibilities. For instance in the area of contracting, NAPIMS may still insists that IOCs comply with its local content directives. In the same vein, DPR which allocates oil blocks to petroleum firms, may insist that the Nigerian content be complied with by a proposed operator before the contract can be awarded to it.

10 Since then, Ghana has established a local content committee, while Tanzania also has a local content committee. The NCDMB is, however, more comprehensive in scope, functions, and abilities than the Ghanaian or Tanzanian approaches. See Olawuyi, 2017; see also See Lange and Kinyondo, 2016.

forward to establish a third institution with exclusive focus on local content development.

This approach has its merits and demerits. First, unlike DPR/NNPC which have several responsibilities in the NPI, the NCDMB has a sole mandate on which it can focus.[11] Secondly, it is able to exercise extensive monitoring roles over the entire NPI. This means that in the administration of NOGICDA, the NCDMB's oversight reach extends to the upstream and downstream subsectors of the NPI. Thus all firms operating in the industry (NNPC, IOCs) as well as indigenous E&P firms and indigenous supply and service firms (ISSFs) are bound by the provisions of the Act. The establishment of the NCDMB, however, has led to a multiplicity of regulatory agencies which petroleum firms have to deal with. This may lead to over-regulation, and make the NPI unattractive to investors. From the perspective of the government, there are also financial implications in staff employment acquisition of equipment, assets, etc. The establishment of the NCDMB in an industry that already has DRP and NNPC, may also lead to conflict of regulatory roles, if the relationships existing among them are not properly managed. Because of its important roles and the unique approach it embodies, the NCDMB requires closer scrutiny.

That the NCDMB has its roots in the NCD of NNPC was discussed above. Unlike the NCD however, the NCDMB is a typical corporate entity established by law, and as such is conferred with perpetual succession, a common seal, and ability to sue and be sued in its name.[12] Its top employee is an executive secretary, who is supported by four directors overseeing the directorates of finance and personnel management, planning, research and statistics, monitoring and evaluation, and legal services.[13] The NCDMB is mandated to monitor the implementation of NOGICDA, and regulations made under it by the Minister of petroleum resources.[14] It is also responsible for supervising, coordinating, administering, monitoring, and managing the development of the Nigerian content in pursuance to the Act and as specified in its Schedule.[15] The Board's other responsibilities include the administration and operation of an e-marketplace, a Joint Qualification System (JQS), and the provision of support for indigenous firms in their bid to develop their competencies within the NPI.[16]

11 Brazil's local content regulator, the National Agency for Petroleum, Natural Gas, and Biofuels (ANP), has been known to impose sanctions not only on privately owned petroleum firms operating in the BPI, but also on Petrobras. In 2012, for example, it imposed significant fines on Petrobras for breaching Brazil's local content regulations at the time. See 'ANP Slaps Petrobras with $18 million Fine' Upstream (1 September 2011) http://www.upstreamonline.com/live/article276020.ece, accessed 22 November 2017.

12 S.69.

13 The Council of the NCDMB may, however, establish any other directorate for the purposes of the Act. S.88.

14 Ss 59 and 70(e).

15 See generally s.70 for the functions of the Board.

16 S.54.

NOGICDA envisages a multi-faceted functionary approach for the NCDMB. Thus the Board functions as a regulator, assessor, monitor, and content developer. In fulfilment of its mandate, it is required to undertake regular appraisals of the operations of firms operating in the NPI, and issue directives/guidelines. It is also responsible for reviewing plans and reports, conducting site visits of dockyards and fabrication yards, as well as granting approvals and certifications to petroleum companies.[17]

The NCDMB is required to issue directives to operators, contractors, and other entities or persons in order to develop a process for the facilitation of reporting of activities relating to any aspect of the Act.[18] It publishes local content procedures and guidelines,[19] and monitors and coordinates the Nigerian content performance of all operators. It is also required to publish auditing procedures and to conduct regular audits for the purpose of monitoring and implementing compliance.[20] It also defines and measures the Nigerian content, organises conferences, workshops, seminars, symposia, trainings, road shows, and provides public education for the purpose of developing the Nigerian content.[21] The Act authorises the NCDMB to delegate any of its functions to agents or operatives appointed by its governing council, and to do anything legally necessary to facilitate the execution of its responsibilities.[22]

Overseeing the NCDMB is a council whose head office is required to be located in one of the petroleum producing states of Nigeria.[23] The council makes rules and regulations for the proper functioning of the NCDMB, employs and pays its staff, and enters into negotiations and contractual relationships as may be necessary for the performance of its responsibilities.[24] The council is constituted by: the Minister of petroleum resources who also doubles as its chairman, one representative each from NNPC, DPR, the Ministry of Petroleum, and the Petroleum Technology Association of Nigeria.[25] Representatives are also drawn from the Nigerian Content Consultative Forum (NCCF), the Council of Registered Engineers of Nigeria, and the National Insurance Commission. Then there is the

17 Ss 8 and 70(f).
18 S.63.
19 Ss 4 and 70i and l.
20 S.70(k).
21 Ss 67 and 70(n).
22 See s.70 generally.
23 S.71. Currently, the firm's headquarters is located at Bayelsa State. Branches may be located in other petroleum producing states of Nigeria as well.
24 S.75. See also ss 76–84 for the tenure, remuneration, appointment, cessation of office of members of the Council. See also ss 86, 87, 88, 89, 90, 91, 92, 93, 94, 95, 96, 97, 98, 99, 100 and 101 for provisions relating to other employees of the Board, terms of service, transfer of service and secondment, its directorates, funding, budgets and estimates, gifts, expenditure and account, audit, and legal proceedings, indemnity of officers, service of documents on it, etc.
25 The membership of NNPC on the Council may, however, impact on its independence. This is because it may be difficult for the NCDMB to dispassionately regulate NNPC, being its governing Council member. These concerns have also been voiced elsewhere. See Nwaokoro, 2012.

executive secretary of the NCDMB, who also doubles as the secretary to the council.[26] The chairman and members of the council are all appointees of the president of the FGN and are expected to be persons of integrity and ability, and with the exception of the Executive Secretary, are all engaged on a part-time basis.[27]

The NCDMB is involved in every phase of the NPI: pre-contract, execution, and post-execution. For example, before contracts in the NPI are awarded by petroleum companies, they are obligated to submit a number of local content related documents such as plans and reports to the NCDMB, for its approval. In keeping with its overall mandate, the NCDMB is required to regularly assess and verify the plans.[28] These plans must contain details of projections and strategies related to local content, through which operators demonstrate their knowledge of their local content obligations. In addition to the plans, firms are also required to submit reports at regular intervals containing details of the extent to which they have implemented their plans. Because the submission of plans is a precondition for bidding for licenses, and obtaining permits, interests, or the execution of contracts or projects in NPI, it constitutes an important regulatory mechanism for the development of local content.[29]

Some of the documents petroleum firms are obligated to submit to the NCDMB include: a Nigerian content plan, an employment and training (E&T) plan, a research and development (R&D) plan, a technology transfer plan, a legal services plan, and a financial services plan. Petroleum firms are also required to submit quarterly reports on procurement, employment, R&D,[30] technology transfer,[31] insurance covers,[32] legal services,[33] and a Nigerian content performance report (NCPR).[34] By requiring petroleum firms to submit local content related documents, the FGN has placed local content on the front burner of the NPI, and has also given to the regulator viable mechanisms for assessing the performance of petroleum firms as far as local content is concerned. In so doing, it also has imposed on petroleum firms the burden of factoring local content into their overall programmes and policies. Some of these plans and reports require further consideration.

4.2.2 Regulation and monitoring of the Nigerian content: plans and reports

4.2.2.1 The Nigerian content plan

Submission of a Nigerian content plan to the NCDMB is a pre-condition for the award of contracts in the NPI.[35] The plan ensures that work programmes of

26 S.72.
27 Ss 73 and 74.
28 See for instance s.8.
29 S.7.
30 Ss 24, 29(c) and 39.
31 S.46.
32 S.49.
33 S.51(2).
34 S.60.
35 Ss 8 and 69.

petroleum firms give consideration to local industries in E&T, as well as in goods and services which they use in their operations.[36] Also mandated to be submitted to the NCDMB are collective agreements executed between with any association of employees which contains terms and conditions of employment that are consistent with the NOGICDA.[37] The plan is also required to contain a strategy on how operators and their contractors intend to give first consideration to Nigerian goods and services in their evaluation of bids for the supply of goods and services required for specific projects.[38] It must also outline in detail plans on how operators intend to ensure the utilisation of locally manufactured goods which meet industry specifications.[39]

Nigerian content plans are subjected to regular reviews and assessment by the NCDMB, and must demonstrate compliance with the Nigerian content requirements as contained in NOGICDA.[40] If the NCDMB is satisfied with the Nigerian content plan of a petroleum firm, it will issue a certificate of authorisation to the firm in relation to the project in question.[41] A public review of the plan may also be conducted in relation to the exercise of any of the NCDMB's functions under the Act. In order to prevent undue delays, the Act provides that reviews or assessments and the issuance or denial of the certificate of authorisation must be completed within 30 days from the date of its commencement.[42]

4.2.2.2 The NCPR

In order to provide a basis for the assessment of local content compliance, NOGICDA mandates all operators in the NPI to submit an annual NCPR to the NCDMB within 60 days of the beginning of each year. The report covers all projects and activities of an operator for the year under review.[43] It is required to set out the Nigerian content utilised in the project in question, on both a current and a cumulative cost basis, as well as employment targets achieved in terms of hours or days worked by Nigerian and foreign workers, and the respective status of these employees. Furthermore, the NCPR must contain details on procurement achievement in terms of quantity, tonnage of locally manufactured materials, and materials of foreign origin.[44]

As shown above, the NCDMB is mandated to regularly assess and verify performance reports submitted in order to ensure that there is adequate compliance.[45] For that purpose, all operators and contractors are required to grant to

36 S.10(1).
37 S.10(2).
38 S.12.
39 S.13.
40 S.7.
41 S.8.
42 S.9.
43 S.60.
44 S.61.
45 S.62.

the NCDMB, or its designated agents, access to their facilities, and to ensure that they provide all documentation and information required for substantiating the veracity of the report.[46] Operators are also obligated to extract Nigerian content information from their partners, contractors, and subcontractors, and on request submit same to the NCDMB.

4.3 Authorisations and certifications: the Nigerian Content Compliance Certificate (NCCC)

Under NOGICDA, projects in the NPI in excess of one million dollars can only commence if contractors and operators obtain the authorisation of the NCDMB in the form of an NCCC. Before issuing the certification, the NCDMB must be satisfied that there is sufficient compliance with the provisions of sections 17–22 of NOGICDA.[47] Also, under section 17 the NCDMB is expressly authorised to approve all advertisements, pre-qualification criteria, technical bid documents, technical evaluation criteria, and the proposed bidders list for all projects in excess of $1million.[48] As a pre-condition for the approval, operators are required to submit sufficient information and notifications to enable the NCDMB to satisfactorily assess the subject matter in order to ensure that Nigerian content requirements are complied with.[49]

Operators are also required to submit to the Board at least 30 days prior to the first day of each quarter, a list of all contracts, subcontracts and purchase orders in excess of $1 million to be bid or executed in the upcoming quarter.[50] For each such contract, subcontracts, and purchase orders, the list will provide a description of the service or item to be contracted or purchased, its estimated value, and an invitation to tender (ITT). It will also state the issuance, closure, and award dates, and any other information requested by the Board for the purpose of implementing the provisions of the Act.[51] In exercise of its powers of review, the NCDMB is required, subject to section 7 of the Act, to advise the operator by the first day of each quarter on which contracts and subcontracts it has designated for review. It shall also advise the operator on the outcome of the review.[52]

Prior to issuing any adverts or pre-qualification notifications to prospective bidders, operators are required to submit for review and approval by the NCDMB, a description of the scope of work, and a copy of all pre-qualification notifications with respect to that project. Other items requiring approval include a list of companies indicating locations of head offices, and persons to whom questionnaires shall be issued. Other details to be submitted include: anticipated dates

46 S.64.
47 See NCDMB, 'Operational Guidelines' http://www.ncdmb.gov.ng/index.php/nc-guidelines, accessed 16 June 2018.
48 S.17(1).
49 S.17(2).
50 S.18(1).
51 S.18(2).
52 S.19.

for closure of prequalification, the commencement of technical evaluations, and the issuance of an ITT.[53]

For every project they intend to execute, petroleum firms are required to submit to the NCDMB, prior to issuing an ITT, a list of bidders and a copy of the ITT. They are also required to submit a description of corporate ownership (main shareholders by percentage) of the bidders as well as information regarding the location of their Nigerian-based offices, plants, or facilities. In addition, they are to notify the NCDMB of anticipated dates for closure of bids and award of contracts or purchase orders, and any other information requested by the Board.[54] Before awarding any contracts, subcontracts, and purchase orders, to a selected bidder, the name of the selected contractor or vendor and a list of proposed subsuppliers (where applicable) are to be submitted to the NCDMB. In addition, where the job is a construction or service contract, they must submit information detailing the estimated Nigerian employment (in person-hours) with regards to that project. NOGICDA also requires the submission of information on the commencement and completion dates for the contract or purchase order. An award notification form signed by an appropriate official of the operator, and a statement of award rationale are also to be submitted.[55] The NCDMB is required to assess the documentation and advise the operator within ten days on which contracts, subcontracts, and purchase orders it has designated for review, and shall thereafter review same to its satisfaction.[56]

In addition to the above details which petroleum firms are required to submit, they are to submit quarterly procurement reports to the NCDMB within 30 days at the end of each quarter. The quarterly reports will contain a list of all contracts, subcontracts, and purchase orders in excess of $1 million or such other limit as the NCDMB may determine.[57] The list will also specify all items and services, the value of the contract or purchase order, the name of successful contractors or vendors, the primary work location, estimates of Nigerian content, commencement and completion dates, and other information required by the NCDMB.[58]

4.4 Other salient local content provisions contained in NOGICDA

4.4.1 Contract awards

NOGICDA requires regulatory authorities and petroleum firms involved in any project, operation, activity, or transaction in the NPI to consider the Nigerian content as an important element in their overall project development and management philosophy.[59] The Schedule to the Act details a minimum Nigerian

53 S.20.
54 S.21.
55 S.22.
56 S.23.
57 S.24(1).
58 S.24(2).
59 S.2.

content covering over 280 items which must be met by operators in the NPI.[60] All petroleum firms are required to give first consideration to Nigerian firms in the award of all contracts relating to the NPI.[61] Where Nigerians and non-Nigerians bid for a contract, the Act provides that Nigerians should be selected if their bids do not exceed the lowest bid price of non-Nigerians, by ten percent.[62] In essence, petroleum related contracts in Nigeria are not to be awarded solely based on the principle of lowest bidder. This provisions is to ensure that Nigerian firms which have capacity to execute jobs are not disqualified solely on the basis that they are not the lowest bidders. Arguably, this requirement may increase the cost of operations for petroleum firms operating in the NPI, it may also have long-term benefits if it succeeds in building and strengthening local firms, in the form of jobs, capacity building, and experience gained.

The local content agenda of NOGICDA is targeted not only at operators and their contracting processes, but also at the administrators of Nigeria's petroleum resources. In that regard, the Act seeks to encourage Nigerians who demonstrate competence and operate in accordance with best practices in the global petroleum industry and, as such NOGICDA provides that Nigerian independent operators are to be given first consideration in the award of oil blocks, oil field licenses, oil lifting licenses, and in all projects for which contracts are to be awarded in the NPI subject to the fulfilment of such conditions as may be specified by the Minister.[63] In the award of contracts and services on land and swamp areas on the matters contained in the Schedule to the Act, exclusive consideration is to be given to Nigerian indigenous service companies which demonstrate ownership of equipment, Nigeria personnel, and capacity to execute such jobs.[64]

Under section 14 of the Act, all operators and project promoters are required to consider Nigerian content when evaluating any bid, where the bids are within 1 percent of each other at commercial stage. And the bid containing the highest level of Nigerian content shall be selected provided the Nigerian content in the selected bid is at least 5 percent higher than its closest competitor. All operators are also required to maintain bidding processes for acquiring goods and services

60 S.11(1) and (3). Under s.102 of the Act, the Board is mandated to conduct a review of the Schedule to the Act at such intervals as it may determine subject to the approval of the Minister, but not later than every two years, with a view to ensuring a measurable and continuous growth in Nigerian content in all projects, operations, activities, and transactions in the Nigerian oil and gas industry for onward transmission to the National Assembly.

61 See ss 3, 12, 10 and 28.

62 S.16. Although the Act does not define what is meant by a foreign company, it defines a Nigerian companies from the perspective of registration and from that of equity. Hence for a firm to qualify as a Nigerian company for purposes of the Act, it must have been formed and registered in Nigeria in accordance with the provision of Companies and Allied Matters Act. Secondly, Nigerians must hold not less than 51 percent equity of the shares of such company.

63 S.3(3).

64 S.3(2).

which give full and fair opportunity to Nigerian indigenous contractors and companies.[65]

4.4.2 E&T

The highly technological nature of the petroleum industry has meant that PPCs, more often than not, rely to some degree on expatriates who bring technical expertise to bear and, in so doing, fill up gaps in human resources which such countries may lack. These expatriates are sourced from all over the world to work as geologists, engineers, scientists, and geophysicists, etc. In the absence of proper regulation, however, there is the tendency for some petroleum firms to employ expatriates to perform tasks which can be executed by citizens of the country in which they operate. This tends to deprive PPCs of foreign exchange since most expatriates are paid in foreign currency. In order to curtail some of these abuses and protect local industries, it is customary practice for countries all over the world to regulate the extent to which foreigners may work within their terrains.

The tensions that may arise between locals and expatriates, where the former are of the view that the latter are taking their jobs and their livelihood, can be a very testy issue. Nationalists routinely incite public sentiments by arguing that foreigners are taking jobs meant for locals, and where not handled properly, it may result in violence. The xenophobic attacks in South Africa which have claimed the lives and property of many African nationals seeking a livelihood in that country is indicative of these tensions.[66] Developed countries are not left out either. In fact, the need to secure employment was one of the primary reasons the United Kingdom (UK) voted to leave the European Union (EU). Those who called for the 'leave vote' argued, among other things, that the UK's membership of the EU resulted in loss of jobs to mainly Eastern Europeans, jobs which would otherwise have been performed by UK nationals.[67] Similarly, the immigration policies of the administration of the US President Donald Trump are not unconnected with the desire to secure jobs for the American people.[68]

The contradictions created by the use of expatriates is pronounced in the petroleum sectors of many developing countries, which because of the highly technological nature of the industry, rely more extensively on foreign petroleum firms. This proclivity for relying extensively on expatriates is stronger where petroleum firms operate in foreign terrains. Such firms will, inevitably, require personnel, and in that regard there is a natural tendency for them to prefer employees who already work for them at home. There are several reasons for this. First, such employees may have been trained by these firms and acquired required experience and competence over time, besides they would be conversant with the procedures, policies, and techniques of the firms for which they have worked. Then there is

65 S.15.
66 Achiume, 2014.
67 See generally Burke et al, 2016.
68 See Susman, 2017.

also the nationalistic sentiment. For example, because majority of the employees of Hyundai are likely to be Koreans, this may naturally engender feelings of trust and confidence. Thus if Hyundai is awarded a job in Nigeria, it may be more comfortable working with Koreans than with Nigerians. The issue, however, is that some of the jobs that it may require Koreans to execute may be easily performed by locals in its host state of operation. Where this happens, it deprives locals of opportunities to develop their capacity, earn money, and pay taxes to their home governments.

Several PPCs would naturally desire to retain these jobs in-country, especially where their nationals have developed capacity and competence through training and industry exposure. Thus they may formulate policies which limit the use of expatriates in their petroleum industries, and allow expatriates to fill up gaps in local capacity and experience. Or they may stipulate expatriate quotas and work permits as a direct strategy of ensuring that petroleum firms keep the number of expatriates they employ to a minimum. For instance, section 8 of Nigeria's Immigration Act of 1963 provides that expatriates can only work in Nigeria after a permit is obtained from the Minister of Internal Affairs pursuant to an application in that regard.[69]

The challenge, however, is that in the absence of effective implementation and monitoring, expatriate quota provisions may be easily abused by petroleum firms. In Nigeria, for example, it has been severally alleged that petroleum firms abuse their expatriate quota, sometimes with the connivance of some government officials, and engage the services of expatriates for jobs which could be carried out by Nigerians.[70] Keen to address some of these concerns and to create more jobs for Nigerians, NOGICDA copiously regulates the degree to which foreigners can work in the NPI.

First, it mandates operators to give Nigerians first consideration in their employment.[71] Section 34 provides that all projects or contracts whose total budget exceeds $100 million must contain 'Labour Clauses'. These clauses obligate operators to utilise a minimum percentage of Nigerian labour in specific cadres as may be stipulated by the NCDMB.[72] And under section 35 of the Act, only Nigerians can be employed in the junior and intermediate cadres of any operator. Prior to applying to the Minister of Internal Affairs for an expatriate quota, prospective employers in the NPI are to apply first to the NCDMB for approval. The application must detail the proposed job titles, description of responsibilities, duration of the proposed employment, and any other information required by the NCDMB for the purpose of implementing the provision of the Act.[73]

69 For example under art.23(2) of the PSC of Equatorial Guinea, expatriates may only be employed after contractors and their subcontractors have exhausted all possibilities of recruiting adequately qualified local personnel in the required area of specialisation.

70 See Okpe, 2015; see also See Izeze, 2013.

71 S.28(1).

72 S.34.

73 S.33.

Foreign firms operating in the NPI are, nevertheless, entitled to retain a maximum of 5 percent of expatriate management staff in order to cater for investors' interests, subject to the approval of the NCDMB.[74] They may also employ expatriates in areas where skills are lacking. Firms which employ expatriates to fill in-country capacity gaps must, however, make every effort within a reasonable time to fill them by providing training locally or elsewhere, to the satisfaction of the NCDMB. Details of the effort made, and the procedure for its implementation are to be contained in the operator's E&T plan.[75] In order to secure employment for Nigerians in managerial and strategic positions, operators are obligated to submit succession plans which explain how Nigerians will eventually occupy positions which are currently occupied by expatriates. Under section 31, the E&T plan is required to outline a programme for Nigerians to understudy their foreign counterparts for a maximum period of four years, at the end of which, any such positions not currently occupied by Nigerians would be Nigerianised. Nigerianised positions are to attract salaries, wages, and benefits as provided for in the operator's conditions of service for Nigerian employees.[76]

NOGICDA appears very restrictive and nationalistic with respect to the use of expatriates. The Act ignores the fact that Nigeria struggles with skills shortages, not only because of Nigeria's weak tertiary institutions, but also because the country continues to suffer from brain drain. Thus even where Nigerians acquire skills and capacity either from practical experience or by overseas training, they often seek 'greener' pastures outside the shores of Nigeria. In this respect, the strict stance on expatriates also ignores the fact that Nigerians are engaged in the petroleum sectors of other countries. From Angola to the Middle East, Brunei, the UK, America, to Angola and Equatorial Guinea, Nigerians are engaged as expatriates in the global petroleum industry.

What this means is that if the same four-years-only rule contained in section 31 of NOGICDA is applicable to Nigerians in those countries on the basis of reciprocity, a large number of Nigerians who earn funds and repatriate home in the form of foreign exchange would be adversely affected. In essence, while there is need for protection of local industries and jobs in the NPI, Nigeria should exercise caution and not be overly protective or restrictive. It is also pertinent to highlight that unduly restricting an operator's quota may 'force' such firms into creative techniques geared towards their desire to actualise their business objectives. Be that as it may, it is equally unfair for foreign firms to abuse their privileges by utilising expatriates for simple jobs which do not require a high technical ability or competence.

In order to properly assess the performance of operators with respect to the implementation of the E&T plan, NOGICDA makes it obligatory for operators or project promoters to submit quarterly reports to the NCDMB. The report details the E&T activities of these firms for the reporting period, and compares same with

74 S.32.
75 S.30.
76 S.31.

the plan. The E&T plan is also required to include the number of new employees hired during the year, their place of residence at the time of hiring, their employment status, and any other information required by the NCDMB for the purpose of implementing the provisions of the Act.[77] The NCPR required under section 61 should also outline the operators' employment achievement in terms of hours or days worked by Nigerian and foreign workers, and their status.[78]

In addition to the detailed requirements analysed above, NOGICDA also addresses three other equally salient aspects of local content development: transfer of technology, investment in R&D, and the domiciliation of operations in-country. These aspects are now considered below.

4.4.3 Technology transfer and R&D

Technology transfer between established IOCs and international service firms to indigenous firms, is a critical component of local content development in that it enables PPCs to develop capacity, acquire technological expertise, and reduce their dependence on foreign firms over time. For that reason, several PPCs desire foreign firms operating in their terrains to execute agreements for the transfer of petroleum related technology to indigenous firms. These firms are however, sometimes reluctant to share their technology and expertise with local firms since this would understandably diminish their relevance over time. There are also intellectual property issues which may make technology transfer not as easy as it appears.

In order to 'compel' foreign-based petroleum firms to transfer technology to indigenous-based firms, some PPCs extract technology transfer commitments from them as a pre-condition for the award of oil blocks.[79] Others endeavour to provide enabling business environments in order to attract such firms to establish research centres in their terrains. For example in the 1970s, Norway encouraged its IOC partners to invest in R&D, first, by creating a suitable and attractive working environment, and, secondly, by giving preferences to firms which did so, in the allocation of petroleum concessions. Hence, the country '... offered preferential access to new concession blocks to oil companies that invested more heavily in R & D with Norwegian researchers in Norwegian institutions ...' the more '... critical the technology and the greater the investment, the more preferential was the access to new blocks'.[80] This strategy deepened the knowledge base of the Norwegian petroleum industry, and ultimately resulted in the increase of its local content.[81] Another strategy is to require petroleum firms to contribute a certain percentage of their profits to a fund created for the promotion of R&D.[82] For instance, Angola makes investment in R&D a precondition

77 S.29.
78 S.61(a).
79 See generally, Blair, 1983.
80 McCreery, 2012.
81 See Heum, 2008, at p 15.
82 For instance, Brazil requires concessionaires to reinvest a certain percentage of gross receipts from fields generating special participation fees in R&D. See ANP, 'P & D

for executing a PSC with IOCs. It requires its PSC partners to contribute a specified amount of money to a proposed Sonangol Research and Technology Centre.[83]

In keeping with the trend among several PPCs, Nigeria makes technology transfer a central component of its local content agenda.[84] Section 45 of NOGICDA provides that all operators in the NPI are to carry out technology transfer programmes which satisfy the NCDMB and are in accordance with Nigeria's plans and priorities. Operators are therefore required to submit annual technology transfer plans to the NCDMB, which set out their programmes of planned initiatives aimed at promoting the effective transfer of technology to Nigerian individuals and companies.[85] In order to ensure compliance, submission of annual reports to the NCDMB describing the outcome of their technology transfer initiatives is made compulsory.[86]

In recognition of the fact that active collaboration between foreign and locally based firms is an important medium for local content development as the Norwegian experience shows, NOGICDA requires operators to give full and effective support to technology transfer by encouraging and facilitating the formation of JVs. These firms are also required to support agreements geared towards partnerships and the development of licensing agreements between Nigerian and foreign contractors and service or supplier companies, for all such JVs or alliances, to the satisfaction of the NCDMB.[87]

Closely allied to technology transfer, R&D is another critical component of local content development, being a prerequisite for the development of new and innovative technologies. It entails sustained investment in training and retraining of staff, and in ground-breaking research aimed at combating local problems, among other things. The most vibrant NOCs, IOCs, and service firms all over the world invest billions of dollars annually in R&D in order to attain or maintain a competitive edge.[88] Some of these firms also establish development centres in

Investments in Exploration and Production' http://www.anp.gov.br/wwwanp/pesquisa-desenvolvimento-e-inovacao, accessed 21 November 2017.

83 See the model PSC which Sonangol executes with petroleum firms operating in Angola: http://www.sonangol.co.ao/English/AreasOfActivity/Concessionary/Documents/Licitacoes/modeloCPPonshore_en.pdf, accessed 22 November 2016. In 2014 it was reported that Sonangol obtained $350 million from BP for the proposed centre, but to date the centre appears not to have been established, raising concerns of fraudulent enrichment by some government officials. See 'Oil Companies Are Funding Mysterious Angolan Research Centre That May Not Exist' *Huffington Post* (5 August 2014) http://www.huffingtonpost.com/2014/08/05/oil-transparency-africa-bp_n_5649291.html, accessed 19 September 2017.

84 Ss 43, 45 and 46.

85 S.44.

86 S.46.

87 S.45.

88 The role of NOCs in the development of science and technology through R&D is treated more fully in Chapters 6 and 7.

their operation areas as a basis for the development of much-needed manpower and petroleum technology.[89]

Cognisant of the linkages which exist between R&D and local content, section 36 of NOGICDA authorises the Minister to set R&D targets for petroleum firms through regulations. In relation to their work programmes and activities, operators are required to carry out programmes and make expenditures to the satisfaction of the NCDMB for the promotion of R&D, education, and industrial attachments in Nigeria. These firms are also obligated to submit R&D plans to the NCDMB once every six months. These plans outline revolving three- to five-year strategies which these firms intend to undertake in Nigeria. The plan will also include a breakdown of expected expenditures which these firms intend to make in the process of implementation, as well as strategies through which members of the public may submit proposals for R&D initiatives associated with the activities such firms.[90] In order to ensure adequate monitoring, the Act directs operators to submit quarterly reports to the NCDMB with respect to their R&D activities, which will be compared with the plan for purposes of assessment and evaluation.[91]

4.4.4 Requirements for the domiciliation of operations of multinationals within Nigeria and utilization of Nigerian goods and services

It is widely believed that the domiciliation of the operations of petroleum firms in the countries in which they operate can benefit host PPCs immensely. This accounts for why some PPCs obligate petroleum firms operating in their terrains to domicile their operations in-country either directly or through subsidiaries, while others endeavour to create conducive operational environments in order to make their climes more attractive to foreign investors. Prior to NOGICDA, it was contended that IOCs and their service counterparts routinely outsourced the important aspects of their operations outside Nigeria, instead of establishing centres within Nigeria, from where some of those jobs could be carried out. This meant that fabrication and manufacturing jobs were executed in dock yards and centres in South Korea, America, and Europe, etc., and thereafter exported to Nigeria. The cost implication for Nigeria was huge, since such contracts bore a large chunk of the expenses of the operations of these IOCs by virtue of its JV/PSC arrangements.[92]

In order to address the trend, NOGICDA authorises the Minister to make regulations mandating operators to invest in, or set up, facilities, factories,

89 For instance, the Institute of Petroleum Studies of the University of Port Harcourt, Nigeria, was established in 2003 with the support of Total. Its objective was to enable Nigerians acquire relevant petroleum technology and expertise. IPS, 'Our History' http://www.ipsng.org/ips/index.php/about-ips/about-ips, accessed 14 June 2017.

90 S.38.

91 S.39.

92 Through NNPC, the Nigerian government has majority stake in the JVs executed with IOCs, and bears the expenses associated with it in proportion to its stake. Similar arrangements exist in the PSC, although they are slightly different.

production units, or other operations within Nigeria for the purpose of carrying out any production, manufacturing, or provision of services which would have otherwise been imported from other countries.[93] These regulations would also require petroleum firms to promote the full utilisation and steady growth of indigenous petroleum companies, seismic data processing, engineering designs, reservoir studies, manufacturing, and fabrication of equipment, and other facilities, as well as providing other support services for the NPI.[94] The Act also requires all fabrication and welding activities relating to the NPI to be carried out in Nigeria.[95] Foreign operators working in Nigeria through Nigerian subsidiaries are also obligated to demonstrate that a minimum of 50 percent of the equipment they deploy in their operations are owned by their Nigerian subsidiaries.[96] In furtherance of this objective, the NCDMB has voiced its desire to ensure that all projects executed in the NPI leave behind fabrication or integration yards as legacy assets which will continue to run even after the projects are completed.[97]

Although requiring companies to domicile their operations in Nigeria without more, is a good start, it is not enough. Granted that the idea may have been properly conceived, but it will require that the Nigerian government address security and infrastructure issues, as well as improve on the ease of doing business in the country. The onus is on the FGN to guarantee security of lives and property, and to provide infrastructure that would make the Nigerian terrain investor friendly, steps should also be taken to improve the ease of doing business in the country. Other factors include the country's judicial, legal, and fiscal regimes, which should be adequately designed to cater for the needs of the industry.

In other to incentivise firms which domicile their operations in Nigeria, the Minister is authorised to confer with other relevant arms of government on the appropriate fiscal framework and tax incentives to be conferred on firms which establish facilities, factories, and production units, and carry out other operations within Nigeria.[98] The degree to which these incentives, if put in place, will make the Nigerian terrain attractive, remains to be seen.[99]

93 S.48.

94 S.41(1). See also the 4.3 Equipment Component Manufacturing Initiative and Certification Process made in pursuance to s.41 of NOGICDA, the guideline on Crude Oil Lifting and Other Petroleum Products' Contracts, and the Free Trade and Export Processing Zones: Guidelines for Inter Organisational Implementation of NOGICDA: http://ncdmb.gov.ng/images/GUIDELINES/NCDMBHANDBOOKOFOPERATIONALGUIDELINES.pdf, accessed 26 April 2017.

95 S.53.

96 S.41(2).

97 Okonji, 2014.

98 In addition to NOGICDA, the Petroleum Profits Tax Act 1958 (PPTA), disallows petroleum firms from claiming capital allowances for the importation of certain goods which could have been purchased in Nigeria See s.13(i) of the PPTA.

99 For example, there is the guideline on Crude Oil Lifting and Other Petroleum Products' Contracts, and the Free Trade and Export Processing Zones: Guidelines for Inter Organisational Implementation of NOGICDA.

4.4.5 Patronage of the Nigerian services subsector

Nigeria requires a vibrant and competitive service sector in order to take full advantage of the provisions of NOGICDA. For that reason the Act also aims at improving the Nigerian services sector by making it mandatory for petroleum firms to patronise Nigerian insurers, banks, and lawyers, etc. NOGICDA prohibits operators from using foreign insurance firms without obtaining a prior written approval from the National Insurance Commission. This approval will be granted only if the Nigerian local capacity has been fully exhausted.[100] The Act requires all insurable risks related to the business operations of petroleum firms to be undertaken by Nigerian insurance firms.[101] Petroleum firms are thus required to submit to the NCDMB a list of all insurance companies and brokers through which they obtained insurance covers in the past six months. The list will also outline the class of insurance covers obtained, and the expenditures made in that regard.[102] Each operator is also mandated to have an insurance programme which would include a comprehensive list of insurance covers obtained in the past six months.[103] The programme will also provide details of insurance by expenditure, a forecast of covers required during the next six months, projected expenditure for insurance covers, a list of all insurance brokers through which covers were obtained in the past six months, the class of insurance covers obtained, and the expenditures made by the operator. Other items include an annual insurance premium budget for the past one year in naira and in foreign currencies.[104]

As with insurance, all operators, contractors, and other entities engaged in any operation, business, or transaction in the NPI are required to retain the services of only Nigerian legal practitioners whose offices are located in any part of Nigeria.[105] They are also mandated to submit a legal services plan to the NCDMB once every six months, which shall include a comprehensive report on the legal services utilized in the past six months, a forecast of legal services required during

100 S.50.

101 These are firms which under s.49(1) of the Act, have been registered in accordance with the provisions of the Nigerian Insurance Act. After the passage of NOGICDA, the National Insurance Commission also issued guidelines geared towards the promotion of the Nigerian insurance business, in pursuance to the provisions of the Insurance Act 2003 and the National Insurance Commission Act 1997 and s.50 of NOGICDA. Its aim is to facilitate compliance with NOGICDA as well as ensure value-added service(s) within the context of the Insurance Act 2003 and the National Insurance Commission Act 1997. See the Guidelines for Oil Insurance Business http://www.sicl.standardinsgroup.com/admin/kcfinder/upload/files/GUIDELINES%20FOR%20OIL%20AND%20GAS%20INSURANCE%20BUSINESS.pdf, accessed 3 April 2017.

102 S.49(2).

103 The use of the phrase 'in the past six months' in s.49(2) and (3)i and ii, appears untidy since there is no reference to the time frame from which to measure the six-month period. It would, however, appear that what the Act requires is for these details to be submitted once every six months to the NCDMB, explaining what transpired in the 'past six months'. This can be gleaned from other related sections such as ss 38, 51 and 52.

104 S.49(3).

105 S.51(1).

the next six months, and projected expenditure for legal services.[106] The plan shall also contain a list of external solicitors utilized for legal services in the past six months, the nature of work done, the expenditure made by operators, and the annual legal services budget for the past one year in naira and foreign currencies.[107]

In like manner, NOGICDA mandates all operators, contractors and any other entity engaged in any operation, business or transaction in the NPI to retain only the services of Nigerian financial institutions or organizations, except where they can satisfy the NCDMB that this is impracticable.[108] As with insurance and legal services, operators must submit a financial services plan to the NCDMB once in every six months.[109] The details of the plan are similar to those of the legal services plan, although in addition, operators, contractors, and subcontractors must maintain a bank account in Nigeria in which they shall retain a minimum of ten percent of their total revenues accruing from their Nigerian operations.[110]

4.4.6 Information technology and local content: the e-marketplace and the JQS

The NCDMB is mandated to establish an e-marketplace in other to provide a virtual platform for the facilitation of transactions required for efficient delivery of goods and services in the NPI. The e-marketplace would also facilitate the provision of a functional interface with the JQS and the provision of a universal and transparent governance structure drawn from relevant industry stakeholders. In addition, it would perform all other functions to be set out in regulations to be made by the Minister, and track and monitor the Nigerian content performance of operators, project promoters, as well as suppliers and service providers through the provision of relevant feedback.[111]

At the time of writing, the NCDMB has not established an e-marketplace. That gap is filled to some extent by the Nigerian Petroleum Exchange (NIPEX). NIPEX is operated by NAPIMS (a subsidiary of NNPC). NIPEX's e-marketplace covers most of the NPI since NNPC is directly or indirectly involved in about 80 percent of Nigeria's petroleum production through PSC/JV/RSC collaborations. The NIPEX e-marketplace is an:

> online platform designed to facilitate contract processing between Buyers (Operators), Suppliers and the Nigerian National Petroleum Corporation (NNPC [Approvers]). It enables communication and data exchange between Suppliers, Buyers and Approvers. The e Marketplace is deployed using mySAP Supplier Relationship Management (SRM) technology which provides a

106 S.51(2).
107 S.51(3).
108 S.52(1).
109 S.52(2).
110 S.52(3).
111 S.54.

comprehensive suite of capabilities including a platform for approving and monitoring contracting activities in the industry.[112]

Another development related to the e-marketplace is the JQS which was established to ensure that all relevant skills and capacities in the NPI are adequately captured and deployed efficiently. The JQS was established by the NCDMB in pursuance to NOGICDA in order to ensure a safe and verifiable pool of information about service providers, their products, capacities, capabilities, quality approach, HSE, and experience.[113] It is an important source of skilled and qualified personnel. Besides this, it is used for the Nigerian content registration and pre-qualification of contractors, and for the verification of contractors' capacities and capabilities. It is also used for the evaluation of the application of Nigerian content in the operations of petroleum firms and contractors, and serves as a database for national skills development and for the ranking and categorisation of service companies based on capabilities and Nigerian content.[114]

4.4.7 Community local content

One of the thorny issues confronting the NPI is the militarisation of the Niger Delta Region (NDR), which prior to 1999 was largely neglected by the FGN despite being the source of most of Nigeria's petroleum resources. The militarisation of the region is largely viewed as being an offshoot of what is loosely referred as the Niger Delta question, whose multifaceted dimensions and implications are discussed in detail later.[115] It is worthy of mention at this stage that perhaps with a view to giving the NDR some sense of belonging, NOGICDA requires all operators to establish project offices in the catchment areas where their projects are located, for the purpose of making decisions in relation to project management and procurements.[116] They are also required to locate personnel with decision making authority in those offices.[117] Similarly, the Act mandates the NCDMB to require operators to maintain offices in communities where they have significant operations,[118] and to maintain a reasonable number of personnel from those areas.[119] The Act also provides that the headquarters of the NCDMB must be located in one of the oil producing states of Nigeria.[120] The current difficulty in implementing some these provisions is that the spate of kidnappings, insecurity, and crime in some parts of the

112 NIPEX https://www.nipexng.com/irj/servlet/prt/portal/prtroot/com.sap.portal.navigation.portallauncher.anonymous, accessed 14 June 2016.
113 The JQS has been established by the NCDMB and has an operational website, see JQS, https://nogicjqs.gov.ng/, accessed 26 April 2017.
114 S.56.
115 See Chapter 9.
116 S.25.
117 S.26.
118 S.27.
119 S.28(2).
120 S.71(2).

NDR have increased to a worrying level. These challenges notwithstanding the above requirements are the right step in the right direction, and indicate a recognition of the need to accommodate producing communities in the scheme of things.

4.4.8 Other local content initiatives contained in NOGICDA

4.4.8.1 The NCCF

In addition to the JQS and the e-marketplace, NOGICDA requires the NCDMB to establish a consultative body to be known as the NCCF. The forum is a platform for information sharing and collaboration in the NPI with respect to upcoming projects, available local capabilities, and other policy proposals that may be relevant to the Nigerian content development.[121] The NCCF is constituted by key industry stakeholders, government, and regulatory agencies, and representatives from the following sectors: fabrication, engineering, finance, legal and insurance services, shipping and logistics, materials and manufacturing, information and communication technology, the Petroleum Technology Association of Nigeria, education and training, and any other professional services nominated by the NCDMB.[122]

4.4.8.2 The Nigerian Content Development Fund

Then there is the Nigerian Content Development Fund established by NOGICDA in order to address funding challenges faced by indigenous operators in the NPI. The difficulty in accessing financial facilities on the part of indigenous petroleum E&P companies, as well as indigenous oil and gas service firms, is currently one of the biggest impediments to the development of local content in Nigeria.[123] The petroleum industry is capital intensive and entails more than the average business risk. Banks therefore demand higher interest rates and sureties before granting loans to the industry.[45] Funding is not, however, only a Nigerian problem; in fact, Brazil liberalised its petroleum industry primarily to tackle funding challenges,[46] and a 1986 study conducted by the University of Aberdeen indicated that of the over 1,000 petroleum related firms in Aberdeen, many were subsidiaries, or affiliates of American firms. The study also noted that most of the British owned firms in Aberdeen were involved in insurance and catering, and not in core petroleum operations.[47] Commenting on the study, Locke notes that it demonstrated that '… the barriers to entry for local firms in such a capital-intensive (and more recently, technologically intensive) industry are significant, even with an aggressive local preference policy and a significant pool of producing facilities.'[124]

121 S.57.

122 S.58.

123 Amanze-Nwachukwu and Alike, 2010. See Chima, 2012. See also Humphries, 1995, Xavier, 2008, at p 399, and Hallwood, 1986.

124 See W Locke, 'Exploring Issues Related to Local Benefit Capture in Atlantic Canada's Oil and Gas Industry' (2004) http://publications.gc.ca/collections/collection_2010/apeca-acoa/AC5-10-2004-eng.pdf, accessed 14 July 2017.

Besides charging high interest rates, few Nigerian banks have the capacity to fund major projects in the NPI, when compared to their Western counterparts. In some instances, entrepreneurs have had to rely on syndicated loans to fund certain projects in the Nigerian economy.[125] In order to alleviate the funding challenge, NOGICDA provides that 1 percent of every contract awarded to any petroleum company or any other entity involved in any project, operation, activity, or transition in the upstream sector of the NPI, shall be deducted at source and paid into the Fund. The Fund is managed by the NCDMB and is to be employed for projects, programmes, and activities directed at increasing the Nigerian content.[126] In addition to the Fund, there are other related initiatives which have been introduced by the industry, with the support of some E&P firms under the aegis of the Oil Producers Trade Section (OPTS) of the Lagos Chamber of Commerce.[127] The OPTS reports that its individual members have contributed about $20 billion towards the promotion of the Nigerian content by making funds available to local entrepreneurs.[128] For instance, in 2012 Shell partnered with some Nigerian banks to establish a $5 billion fund to support local oil and gas firms.[129] In a similar vein, in 2013, NLNG also set up a $1 billion fund to support its local contractors in the industry.[130]

4.5 Conclusion

Nigeria's legislative approach to local content as embodied in NOGICDA has been the focus of this chapter. The chapter essentially attempted to review the salient portions of the Act as they relate to the advancement of the Nigerian content. First, it reiterated some of the points noted in the previous chapter, that NNPC's inability to further the Nigerian content through the contractual model saw Nigeria turn to an increasingly protectionist regime in the form of NOGICDA. The chapter then examined the extensive scope and powers of the NCDMB, as well as the obligations the Act imposes on operators and subcontractors in the NPI.

NOGICDA, which appears to be the first comprehensive legislation in the world on local content in the petroleum industry, is detailed and rigid in its approach to local content development.[131] Its provisions, as seen above, span the length and breadth of the NPI, covering not only the upstream, but also the downstream operations, and applying to all stakeholders and participants in

125 See Chima, 2014.
126 S.104.
127 The OPTS is an association grantees of OPLs and OMLs in Nigeria. Its members include Shell, Total, Eni, Moni Pulo, Chevron, ExxonMobil, Seplat, and Oando, etc.
128 OPTS, 'Local Content Strides in the Oil and Gas Industry' (2014) http://www.opts-ng.com/file/20140430092552Nigeria%20Stride%20High%20(web%20reduced).pdf, accessed 6 January 2017.
129 Chinwo, 2012.
130 Amanze-Nwachuku and Alike, 2013.
131 See also Msimang and Cull, 2014.

the industry. From authorisations and certifications to the award of contracts, E&T, technology transfer, information technology, as well as providing for the Nigerian Content Development Fund, NOGICDA codifies and embodies Nigeria's local content expectations. And its provisions have served as a model for several African PPCs such as Ghana, Kenya, and Tanzania, etc. Legislating on local content may, however, be the easiest part. There is also the issue of implementation, enforcement, and administration of its provisions. The question then is, how far has the Act been successfully implemented? Secondly, should Nigeria have adopted so stringent an approach as legislation when other alternative approaches may exist? The following chapter analyses the impact of the Act on Nigeria's local content, and its propriety, as well as implementation and enforcement challenges.

Bibliography

Achiume TA, 'Beyond Prejudice: Structural Xenophobic Discrimination against Refugees' (2014) 45 *Georgetown Journal of International Law*, 323.

Adepetun S, 'Production Sharing Contracts – The Nigerian Experience' (1995) 12 *Journal of Energy & Natural Resources Law*, 21.

Amanze-Nwachuku C and Alike E, 'Capacity Building Will Enhance 100% Local Content' *Thisday* (10 August 2010) http://www.thisdaylive.com/articles/-capacity-building-ll-enhance-100-local-content-/81350/, accessed 9 July 2013.

Amanze-Nwachuku C and Alike E, 'NLNG Floats $1bn Financing Scheme for Contractors' *Thisday* (5 December 2013) http://www.thisdaylive.com/articles/nlng-floats-1bn-financing-scheme-for-contractors/165960/, accessed 30 March 2017.

Atsegbua LA, 'The Nigerian Oil and Gas Industry Content Development Act 2010: an examination of its Regulatory Framework' (2012) 36(4) *OPEC Energy Review*, 479.

Blair HO, 'Overview of Licensing and Technology Transfer' (1983) 8(2) *North Carolina Journal of International Law and Commercial Regulation*, 167.

Burke B et al, 'Life on the Edge: EFTA and the EEA as a Future for the UK in Europe' (2016) 22(1) *European Public Law*, 69.

Chima O, 'Nigeria Leads Africa's Syndicated Loans Mkt with $10bn Deals' *Thisday* (30 April 2014) http://www.thisdaylive.com/articles/nigeria-leads-africa-s-syndicated-loans-mkt-with-10bndeals/146336/, accessed 10 March 2014.

Chima O, 'Multinationals Shun Nigerian Banks over High Interest Rates' *Thisday* (7 September 2012) http://www.thisdaylive.com/articles/-multinationals-shun-nigerian-banks-over-high-interest-rates/124326/?, accessed 17 March 2013.

Chinwo C, 'Local Content: Shell, Banks Create $5 billion for Contractors' *Thisday* (17 September 2012) http://www.thisdaylive.com/articles/local-content-shell-banks-create-5bn-fund-for-contractors/125153/, accessed 18 June 2017.

Hallwood P, *The Offshore Oil Supply Industry in Aberdeen: The Affiliates – Their Characteristics and Importance* (University of Aberdeen, Aberdeen, 1986).

Heum P, 'Local Content Development: Experiences from Oil and Gas Activities in Norway' (2008) *SNF Working Paper No. 02/08* https://brage.bibsys.no/xmlui/bitstream/handle/11250/166156/1/A02_08.pdf, accessed 22 November 2016.

Humphries ME, 'The Competitive Environment for Oil and Gas Financing' (1995) 23 *Energy Policy*, 991.

Izeze I, 'Nigeria: Oil Companies and Criminal Abuse of Expatriate Quota' *Sahara Reporters* (30 April 2013) http://saharareporters.com/2013/04/30/nigeria-oil-companies-and-criminal-abuse-expatriate-quota-ifeanyi-izeze, accessed 1 July 2017.

Lange S and Kinyondo A, 'Resource Nationalism and Local Content in Tanzania: Experiences from mining and consequences for the petroleum sector' (2016) 3(4) *The Extractive Industries and Society*, 26.

Machmud TN, 'Production Sharing Contracts in Indonesia: 25 Years' History' (1993) 11 *Journal of Energy and Natural Resources Law*, 179.

McCreery J, 'How National Oil Companies Can Fuel Economic Development' *Forbes* (1 May 2012) http://www.forbes.com/sites/baininsights/2012/05/01/how-national-oil-companies-can-fuel-economic-development, accessed 12 July 2017.

Msimang A and Cull J, 'Operators Must Carefully Navigate Nigerian Content Rules' (2014) http://www.velaw.com/uploadedFiles/VEsite/Resources/OffshoreOperators CullMsimang122314.pdf, accessed 4 January 2016.

Nwaokoro JE, 'Signed, Sealed but will it Deliver? Nigeria's local content Bill and Cross-Sectoral Growth' (2012) 4(1) *Journal of World Energy Law & Business*, 56.

Okonji E, 'Nigerian Local Content Development Attracts Foreign Interests' *Thisday* (24 February 2014) http://www.thisdaylive.com/articles/nigerian-local-content-development-attracts-foreign-interests/172252/, accessed 31 March 2014.

Okpe FO, 'Economic Development and the Utility of Local Content Legislation in the Oil and Gas Industry: Conflicts and Effects of Nigeria's Local Content Act in the Context of International Investment Law' (2015) 28 *Pacific McGeorge Global Business & Development Law Journal*, 255.

Olawuyi DS, 'Local Content Requirements in Oil and Gas Contracts: Regional Trends in the Middle East and North Africa' (2017) 36(1) *JERNL*, 30.

Oni A, 'Nigerian Local Content Act: A Status Report' *BusinessDay* (28 July 2012) http://www.businessdayonline.com/NG/index.php/law/legal-culture/41722-the-nigerian-local-content-act-a-status-report, accessed 7 August 2016.

Susman DD, 'Immigration, Trump and Agenda Settling in the 2016 Election' (2017) 41 *Fletcher F. World Affairs*, 75.

Xavier Y, 'Energy for the Future: Brazilian Law and Policy' in DN Zillman et al (eds), *Beyond the Carbon Economy: Energy Law in Transition* (Oxford University Press, Oxford, 2008), at p 399.

5 An analysis of the impact, necessity, and challenges of the Nigerian Oil and Gas Industry Content Development Act 2010

5.1 Assessing the impact of the Nigerian Oil and Gas Industry Content Development Act 2010

The passage of the Nigerian Oil and Gas Industry Content Development Act 2010 (NOGICDA) moved local content from the realm of contract and corporate social responsibility to a mandatory legislative obligation with which operators must comply, or be sanctioned. Undoubtedly, the Act is a bold attempt to address Nigeria's local content challenges in a comprehensive and in-depth manner by aiming at providing opportunities for growth and development of Nigerian firms involved in the Nigerian petroleum industry (NPI).[1] NOGICDA is a landmark legislation in that it addresses virtually every aspect of the NPI. Its requirements with respect to fabrication, engineering, manufacturing, the service sectors, as well as its requirement that indigenous Nigerian petroleum firms be given preference in the NPI are quite extensive and ambitious.[2] And by conferring extensive regulatory and monitoring powers on the Nigerian Content Development and Monitoring Board (NCDMB), the Act for the first time provides a vibrant regulatory mechanism whose operations are targeted directly at petroleum firms for the singular purpose of developing the Nigerian content. But are there actual facts and figures to prove whether or not the Act is achieving its objectives?

As far back as 2012, Mr Ernest Nwapa, the first chief executive of the NCDMB, had announced that $4 billion out of the $20 billion estimated for expenditure in the NPI in that year was retained in Nigeria by virtue of the impact of NOGICDA.[3] In terms of the ability of the Act to attract investments into the NPI, it was also reported that between 2010 and 2012, about $2.8 billion was invested in the NPI.[4] In terms of job creation, Diezani Madueke, Nigeria's past minister for petroleum resources

1 Atsegbua, 2012, at p 490.

2 On average, the schedule to the Act requires firms to utilize about an average of 67 percent Nigerian content in projects executed in the NPI. Besides NOGICDA, the Petroleum Profits Tax Act 1958 (PPTA), also contains some local content provisions. For instance, it disallows petroleum firms from claiming capital allowances for the importation of certain goods which could have been purchased in Nigeria. S.13(i) of the PPTA.

3 Olayinka, 2012, see also NCDMB, 2012. See also Okonji, 2012.

4 Okonji, 2012. See also Nwachukwu, 2012.

announced in February 2013 that NOGICDA resulted in the creation of 30,862 jobs in the NPI, besides increasing the man-hours performed by Nigerians by 350 percent.[5] In 2014, Mr Nwapa reported that about 90 percent of the engineering required in the NPI, and 50 percent of the tonnage required for the fabrication of all field development facilities, were carried out in Nigeria.[6] In terms of overall percentage, it has been reported that since the enactment of NOGICDA the Nigerian content has grown from less than 5 percent to 14 percent in 2014, and to over 20 percent in 2018.[7] It has also been claimed that there has been a remarkable growth from about 40 percent pre-2010, to 75 percent in 2015, with respect to contracts awarded to indigenous supply and service firms (ISSFs) in the NPI.[8]

Some industry observers, however, argue that NOGICDA's impact has been minimal. They cite frequent breaches of the Act's provisions by international oil companies (IOCs) in their contracting and employment to justify their claims.[9] There may also be valid reasons to doubt whether the figures published by the NCDMB are comprehensive and reflect what is on the ground in the NPI. For one, it appears that the NCDMB unduly relies on the submissions and reports of operators, but may not have sufficient independent evidence to verify its claims. Ovadia also observes that the NCDMB has been slow to 'move into the evaluation of Nigerian content in bidding for oil licences—an important priority both for ensuring Nigerian content and for ensuring full benefit from the awarding of oil licences'.[10] It is therefore important to ascertain the criteria used by the NCMDB in arriving at its conclusions. Does it for example base its claims on the number of contracts awarded to Nigerians in the NPI by IOCs and other petroleum firms, or does it actually ascertain whether a considerable amount of goods and services used by operators and service firms are actually produced in Nigeria?

Section 106 of the Act defines the Nigerian content as '… the quantum of composite value added to or created in the Nigerian economy by a systematic development of capacity and capabilities through the deliberate utilization of

5 Akpan, 2013.
6 Akpan, 2013.
7 NCDMB News Release 'NCDMB to Sue Offenders of Local Content Act' (6 March 2018) https://www.ncdmb.gov.ng/2018/03/ncdmb-sue-offenders-local-content-act/, accessed 6 August 2018.
8 NCDMB, 'Ugandan Officials Visit NCDMB to Seek to Model local content Policies After Nigeria' (13 June 2016) http://www.ncdmb.gov.ng/index.php/newsupdates/news-updates/6517-ugandan-officials-visit-ncdmb-seek-to-model-local-content-policies-after-nigeria, accessed 17 June 2016.
9 See Isineds, 2015. See also 'PENGASSAN calls for Appropriate Compliance with Nigerian Content Act' *Leadership* (Abuja, 29 October 2012) http://www.leadership.ng/nga/articles/38668/2012/10/29/pengassan_calls_appropriate_compliance_nigerian_content_act.html, accessed 20 November 2017. See also Onuegbu, 2012. See also 'PENGASSAN urges Total Enforcement of local content Act' (Sweet Crude, 30 October 2012) http://sweetcrudereports.com/2012/10/30/pengassan-urges-total-enforcement-of-local-content-act/, accessed 20 November 2016.
10 See Ovadia, 2013.

Nigerian human, material resources and services in the Nigerian oil and gas industry'. The key words as far as local content is concerned therefore are: Nigerian human or material resources, and Nigerian services. What the NCDMB requires is a holistic criteria for appropriately measuring Nigeria's local content, which will enable the proper identification of gaps which need to be filled, besides enabling the government to adequately reward compliant firms and sanction defaulters. In this respect, the example of Brazil may offer some insights which may be useful for Nigeria.

Brazil's petroleum industry regulator, the National Agency for Petroleum, Natural Gas, and Biofuels (ANP) developed the 'Cartilha' booklet in 2005 as its official methodology for measuring local content in its petroleum industry. The booklet defines methods for local content measurement and sets out the criteria for identifying actual manufacturers of components which make up each piece of equipment used in the Brazilian petroleum industry. It also sets out the criteria for calculating the level of local content in relation to goods, services, goods for temporary use, and local content in connection to systems and subsystems.[11] This method, which focuses on locally made goods, and excludes the value of imported parts, is used to calculate local content of services by taking into account salaries and additional taxes of Brazilian citizens and foreigners, who hold Brazilian permanent visas.[12] In the event of violations, the ANP is able to impose sanctions which are proportional to the missing value that would have been necessary to attain the minimum required local content in each particular case.[13] It is proposed that the NCDMB extracts lessons from the Cartilha booklet and perhaps the measurement criteria adopted by other petroleum producing countries (PPCs) in order to formulate a suitable approach to appropriately measuring the Nigerian content.

It is irrefutable, however, that domestic participation has increased in Nigeria since the passage of NOGICDA. In this regard, Ovadia noted that despite its enormous challenges, the:

> NCDMB has done a relatively good job. While there are also local content provisions in joint operating agreements and production sharing contracts between the national oil company and IOCs, these have never been well enforced. Although it is not difficult to find faults with NCDMB in its implementation of the NCA,[14] some important improvements have been made and the danger of Nigerian companies serving merely as fronts for foreign ones seems to have been largely avoided.[15]

11 Olsen, 2013.
12 See ANP, 'Local Content Booklet of Goods, Goods for Temporal USE, Sets, Materials MDO Services, Systems and Systems for Temporal Use Related to the Sector of Oil and Natural Gas' (2007).
13 Olsen, 2013.
14 Nigerian Content Act.
15 Ovadia, 2016.

Attesting to the success of the Nigerian story, it has been argued that the Act has clearly created backward linkages at least in fabrication and construction, well construction and completions and control systems, and information and communications technology,[16] as well as ensuring that petroleum firms operating in the NPI purchase majority of their goods from Nigerian firms.[17]

The Act's requirement that Nigerian firms be preferred by petroleum firms operating in the NPI in the supply of goods and services, has resulted in some growth in the Nigerian services sector. NOGICDA has thus served as a spring board for the development of in-country capacity in the NPI. It has also impelled Nigerians to innovate and develop capacity in order to qualify for jobs in the NPI. To a certain degree, NOGICDA represents a legislative guarantee to qualified Nigerian firms that they would be preferred for critically important jobs, provided they are able to meet the demands of the industry. The Act has also made IOCs and other exploration and production (E&P) firms operating in Nigeria to factor in local content in their policies and operations. These firms have thus been spurred to establish local content departments which are manned by professionals, and are saddled with ensuring compliance with the provisions of the Act in their projects.

Perhaps the most notable contribution of the Act is that it has created a general awareness of the obligations of petroleum firms in relation to local content in the industry. By imposing restraints on the outsourcing of jobs which can be performed locally, NOGICDA has also created opportunities in those areas where Nigerian firms already have adequate capacity. Some of these indigenous firms not only employ Nigerians, but they also retain most of their profits in-country. The Act has also spurred Nigerian entrepreneurs to take on new challenges and attain new heights in their bid to rise to meet the demands of the industry. Some of the local content strides of Nigerian firms in the NPI deserve further examination.

Prior to the enactment of the Act, virtually all the fabrication, engineering, and procurement in the NPI were outsourced to foreign firms.[18] But that is not the case today as Nigerian service firms have since invested massively in acquiring sophisticated vessels and rigs, once the exclusive preserve of foreign firms. Currently, ISSFs now enjoy patronage and even exclusivity in certain areas. In addition, several fabrication, manufacturing and engineering facilities have also been developed and upgraded, while indigenous and marginal field producers now account for about 15 percent of Nigeria's crude oil production, besides contributing about 53 percent of domestic gas supply requirements.[19] Currently, the total value of contracts awarded to Nigerian companies in the NPI is reported to have risen to 83 percent, while the average Nigerian content retention in-country is about 28 percent.[20]

16 Adewuyi and Oyejide, 2012.
17 Adewuyi and Oyejide, 2012, at p 452. See also, Ayoola, 2017, at p 53.
18 S Wabote, 'Eight Years of Local Content Act' *The Nation* (23 April 2018) http://thenationonlineng.net/eight-years-of-local-content-act/, accessed 8 August 2018.
19 Ibid.
20 Ibid.

In 2013, a local content feat was recorded in the NPI when Niger Dock and Dorman Long Engineering Limited[21] (both indigenous Nigerian firms), fabricated two major well heads for Mobil Producing Nigeria.[22] This project was, at the time, the largest fabrication job executed in-country for joint venture (JV) operations carried out between the Nigerian National Petroleum Corporation (NNPC) and Mobil Producing.[23] Another milestone recorded in the NPI was the upgrade of NNPC/Mobil's JV facilities, production system, and processes by SSC Pipe Mill.[24] In 2010, SSC Pipe Mill delivered the first ever set of made in Nigeria double submerged arc welded helical to the NNPC/Mobil JV.[25] And for first time in Nigeria's history, EIFFEL Construction Metallic of France, in collaboration with OOP Engineering Limited, another indigenous firm, were contracted to build offshore living quarters for Total's Ofon Phase 2 project.[26] But perhaps the greatest achievement since the passage of NOGICDA was the arrival in 2018 of Total E&P's Egina floating production storage and offloading vessel at the SHI-MCI Yard, LADOL Free Zone, Lagos for the integration of six modules which were fabricated in Nigeria. [27]

These feats have boosted the confidence of IOCs and E&P firms operating in the NPI, which are increasingly committing to utilizing locally made pipes for the transportion of crude oil in their operations. But while these feats are laudable, it is noteworthy that the actual 'local content' may have been minimal. This is because some of the jobs touted as local content milestones, were either outsourced to foreign firms by ISSFs, or utilised mainly imported materials. This, in effect, undermines the Nigerian content policy to a considerable degree since the essence of local content is to secure the use of locally produced goods and services, as well as the award of jobs to Nigerian firms.[28] Thus while the construction in 2011 of

21 Although this firm was originally a subsidiary of a British firm, it is now 100 percent Nigerian owned following Nigeria's indigenisation policy of 1977. See Dorman Long Engineering, 'History' (2014) http://www.dormanlongeng.com/Content/viewcontent.aspx?linkLvl1Id=7&linkId=37, accessed 7 April 2017.

22 See OPTS, 'Local Content Strides in the Oil and Gas Industry' (2014) http://www.opts-ng.com/20140430092552Nigeria%20Stride%20High%20(web%20reduced).pdf, accessed 8 November 2016.

23 'Nurturing Nigerian Content to Reality' *Thisday* (17 September 2014) http://www.thisdaylive.com/articles/nurturing-nigerian-content-to-reality/159163/, accessed 10 March 2017.

24 'Nigeria sees Local Content Prospects at SSC Pipe Mill' *Vanguard* (7 February 2012) http://www.vanguardngr.com/2012/02/nigeria-sees-local-content-prospects-at-scc-pipe-mill/, accessed 8 November 2016.

25 OPTS (n 22).

26 Ajoro, 2016.

27 Wabote (n 18).

28 For instance, although Fenog Nigeria Ltd was able to complete its seven Horizontal Directional Drilling fleet in 2011, the truth remains that the manufacturing was done in Germany by Prime Drilling HDD technology, according to Fenog's specifications. See Fenog Nigeria Ltd, 'HDD Rigs' (2016) http://www.fenog.com/index.php?option=com_content&view=article&id=52%3Ahdd-rig&catid=26&Itemid=144, accessed 4 February 2016.

seven horizontal directional drilling fleets by Fenog Nigeria Limited, an indigenous firm, was widely hailed as a local content milestone, the truth was that Fenog relied almost exclusively on German manufacturers to implement the job.[29]

The point being made is that the focus of Nigeria's local content agenda should be more about the development of local industries than the award of contracts/concessions to Nigerian firms. While the latter is somewhat beneficial, the former is by far more important. In fact, a foreign owned petroleum firm which utilises Nigerian employees and locally manufactured equipment to an appreciable degree, may have satisfied Nigeria's local content objectives more than a Nigerian firm which outsources most of its jobs to foreign owned firms. A proper appreciation of these dynamics should be kept in view by policy makers and regulators in their measurement and review of the progress being made in the development of the Nigerian content in order to properly appreciate whether the Act is actually producing desired results.

In spite of some of the achievements of the Act, Nigeria's adoption of a legislative approach to local content is still regarded by some as being unnecessary, unrealistic, and over-ambitious, besides the fact that it risks violating Nigeria's international trade and investment obligations. This chapter now evaluates whether the legislative approach to local content, which is widely accepted among African PPCs, is a necessary and better alternative to the contractual approach.

5.2 Is the legislative approach to local content necessary?

The dominant position of Nigeria, first, as a petroleum producer, and, secondly, because of its massive economy and huge population, means that the country, one way or another, remains a model for several African countries, particularly in the petroleum industry. This explains why Nigeria's adoption of the legislative template for the furtherance of its local content has been followed by several African PPCs. For example, Ghana's Petroleum (Local Content and Local Participation in Petroleum Activities) Regulation of 2013 appears largely to have been inspired by NOGICDA. In the same vein, there is the Petroleum (Local Content) Regulations, 2017 of Tanzania made in pursuance to its Petroleum Act of 2015, and the Local Content Regulations for its mining sector which was made in pursuance to the Tanzanian Mining Act of 2010. Other countries such as Uganda and Kenya are also at various stages of enacting local content legislations. There is also a Local Content Bill (2016) in Kenya. The question is whether it is necessary for African countries to rely on legislation to advance national participation in their petroleum industries, or whether other alternatives exist in that respect. This question is analysed with reference to responses to NOGICDA.

In three separate articles on the Nigerian content regime, Joseph Nwaokoro dismissed NOGICDA as being an unnecessary 'overkill', since a more viable contractual alternative for local content development already exists, in the form of NNPC's JVs/production sharing contracts (PSCs) interactions with its E&P

29 Ibid.

partners.[30] The author was of the view that 'new laws are hardly necessary to enhance the Nigerian local content' and that '... a collaborative framework between the IOCs and NNPC to implement existing contractual agreements is what is needed'.[31] He argued further that the collaborative contractual approach would avoid the arbitrariness of NOGICDA, as well as avoid potential legal issues which may be associated with it.[32] It was the author's position that Nigeria does not need another local content legislation since the Petroleum Act regime and NNPC's powers under the JVs/PSCs, sufficiently dealt with the Nigerian content. It was his view that legislation is not required to spur IOCs to patronise Nigeria's goods and services since it is actually cheaper and safer for them to do so.[33]

This writer's response to the learned author is that, at least for now, NOGICDA appears to be the best option available for the advancement of the Nigerian content. This is because far-reaching measures were necessary in order to overturn the unacceptably low Nigerian content pre-NOGICDA, it was therefore reasonable for Nigeria to turn to a more forceful approach. A top-down legislative approach to policy implementation is desirable, where 'milder' measures fail to yield expected results. And while it is conceded that some countries have developed their local content without necessarily relying on extensive legislation, the legislative approach is appropriate where there is the likelihood of deliberate non-compliance with the policy directives of a country.[34] Conceded again that legislation may result in rigidity, its merit lies in the fact that it represents a more permanent solution to a long standing issue. This means that in contrast to the contractual model, NOGICDA's requirements are 'standing and binding', and cannot be varied at the whims of NNPC, its IOC partners, or even by the NCDMB itself, without recourse to the legislature.

Conceded also that legislative local content requirements (LCRs) may become difficult to vary and may eventually become burdensome and overbearing. This weakness may, however, be easily overcome by empowering regulators to grant waivers where necessary, or by inserting LCRs in subsidiary legislations which may be easily varied without going through an expensive and time-consuming legislative amendment process. As shown in Chapter 2, although contractual LCRs have the advantage of flexibility and variability, they may result in adverse consequences if they are inadequately enforced. In Nigeria, for example, the closeness between NNPC/DPR/IOCs made effective monitoring of IOCs difficult. In fact, Nwaokoro conceded that violations of LCRs pre-NOGICDA occurred with the tacit consent of NNPC.[35] This fact all the more justifies Nigeria's shift from the

30 See Nwaokoro, 2011. See also Nwaokoro, 2012, and Nwaokoro, 2009.
31 Nwaokoro, 2011, at p 150.
32 Nwaokoro, 2011, at p 154, see also Nwaokoro, 2012, at p 62.
33 Nwaokoro, 2009, at p 53.
34 Commenting on the necessity of local content regulations with respect to mining firms, White notes that 'without policy or legal imperatives, mining companies would have little regard for local content'. White, 2017, at p 265.
35 Nwaokoro, 2011, at pp 148 and 152.

contractual and more collaborative approach, which did not yield desired results due to the absence of credible commitment to its implementation.

NOGICDA was also necessary to establish the NCDMB as a means of addressing the regulatory and monitoring weaknesses of NNPC/DPR with respect to the Nigerian content. Legislation is thus a more preferable vehicle for creating an institutional framework for policy implementation and for local content regulation.[36] For example, because Brazil established ANP in pursuance to legislation, the agency is manned by public officials who are accountable to the Brazilian legislature, and by extension to the Brazilian public.[37]

Again, in putting forward the argument that NNPC has sufficient powers to advance the Nigerian content, the learned author ignored the fact that the NPI extends beyond NNPC and its IOC partners, but also includes contractors and subcontractors, service sectors, and indigenous petroleum companies. It should also be noted that the majority of indigenous petroleum firms operate under sole risk arrangements without any recourse to NNPC.[38] The effect is that, pre-NOGICDA, firms operating under sole risk arrangements and their sub-contractors were not required to comply with the NCD guidelines in their purchasing, contracting, or employment.[39] And although they were required to comply with the local content requirements contained in the Petroleum Act, as well as other commitments they made when concessions or contracts were awarded, these requirements were very minor and not extensive enough. What is being alluded to here is that NNPC is only in a position to extract local content commitments from firms with which it has any direct relationship, but is powerless with respect to firms which operate under sole risk arrangements. The efficient monitoring of the various stakeholders therefore required a more comprehensive approach.

This institutional limitation has been addressed by NOGICDA, whose provisions apply to all operators in the NPI, and are enforced by the NCDMB across the whole industry.[40] Furthermore, NCDMB is able to function as a one-stop shop in its coordination and monitoring of the Nigerian content. This enables it to fast track the advancement of the Nigerian content policies of Nigeria while also reducing opportunities for inter-agency

36 ANP was established by Brazil's Petroleum Law of 1997, Law 9478. S.8 of the Law saddles it with responsibility for administering Brazil's petroleum resources and for regulating the industry.

37 See Rutter and Knigton, 2012.

38 They include Africoil and Marketing Ltd, Alfred James Nigeria Ltd, Amni, Dubri Oil, NPDC, Yinka Petroleum, and Moni Pulo, etc. See Department of Petroleum Resources, 'Oil and Gas Annual Report' (2016) https://dpr.gov.ng/index/wp-content/uploads/2016/01/2016-Oil-Gas-Industry-Annual-Report.pdf, accessed 6 March 2016, at p 31.

39 In contrast to Nigeria where concessions are vested in the FGN, Sonangol of Angola is able to exert a wider influence over Angola's petroleum industry because the Petroleum Activities Law of 2004 makes it sole concessionaire of Angola's petroleum assets. This unique and strategic position enables the firm to extract local content commitments from its partners, and monitor implementation unlike NNPC whose reach was limited to its partners. A similar approach to that of Angola, was adopted by Algeria pre-2005.

40 Ss 1 and 2.

conflicts.[41] For example, under the Act, the NCDMB is required to co-operate with the Nigerian Maritime Administration and Safety Agency (NIMASA), in the enforcement of compliance with relevant sections of the Coastal and Inland Shipping (Cabotage) Act 2003 (Cabotage Act), as they relate to local content in the NPI.[42] In addition to all these, another merit of NOGICDA is that its provisions are clear and accessible by all, and not shrouded in confidentiality. They are open to public scrutiny and evaluation. Civil societies, communities, and stakeholders are therefore in a better position to bring pressure to bear not only on the industry, but also on the regulator itself. The legislative approach also means that firms operating in the NPI are also clear on their responsibilities, sanctions, as well as the incentives available for furthering the Nigerian content.

In sum, it may therefore be necessary for African countries to rely on legislation as their primary legal template for the advancement of local content. They should, however, compliment their local content laws with other viable initiatives. This is because over-reliance on legislation without more, as shown below, may not yield desired results.[43] In this regard, it is crucial to ask whether African PPCs are ready to rise up to the challenge of protectionist top-down LCRs. The issue here is, first, whether they have the capacity to monitor and implement these laws, and, secondly, whether they have the wherewithal and political will to follow through. Legislative failure is bound to occur where the objectives behind the passage of laws are not achieved. This can lead to frustration on the part of the public, especially if the law in question is a public interest law. In the light of these realities, it is important to examine whether African countries which are 'rushing' on to protectionist local content measures can, in reality, rise up to the demands of these laws. The discussion that follows explores some of the challenges African PPCs may face in adopting protectionism in an industry that is highly capital intensive. Using Nigeria as a case study, it compares NOGICDA with other attempts by the Nigerian government to address weak local content in the Nigerian maritime industry via legislation.

5.3 NOGICDA and the challenge of weak capacity in Nigeria

NOGICDA is essentially a protectionist regime. Its extensive provisions which are couched in mandatory terms require operators to attain an average of 67 percent Nigerian content. Essentially, they severely limit the extent to which foreign firms and expatriates may operate freely in the NPI. The challenge with this approach is that most of Nigeria's capacity challenges which impacted its local content pre-NOGICDA, as shown in Chapter 3, have not been fully addressed. Some IOCs

41 For example, the NCDMB in its role as a local content regulator, was able to conclude the bid evaluations for Agip's Zabazaba Deepwater project within 14 months, as against the customary 36 months in the past. Wabote (n 18).

42 S.105.

43 Commenting on this issue, it has been advocated that the success of Nigeria's local content laws require nationwide support for local content policies as well as acceptance by petroleum firms. Gbegi and Adebisi, 2013.

have contended that Nigeria's weak capacity in relation to the requirements of NOGICDA displays of a lack of realism on the part of its policy makers.[44] Oguine has argued that rather than develop capacity to meet the needs of the NPI, Nigeria appears to over rely on regulation, and denial of approvals, etc., as a means of growing its local content.[45] In the light of Nigeria's capacity challenges, some have posited that literal compliance with NOGICDA will be difficult.[46] And according to Nwaokoro, NOGICDA's requirements ignore the systemic problems faced by Nigerian banks.[47]

That NOGICDA is quite ambitious is not in doubt. Its effective implementation will depend on the political will of the Nigerian government in creating the enabling environment under which local firms would rise to meet the demands of the NPI. Nigeria has a history of enacting far reaching legislations, which are often poorly implemented either because they were unrealistic to begin with, or because of the lack of political will. This has given rise to genuine concerns whether or not NOGICDA would go the same way. A review of two of such laws, which have largely failed to actualise the objectives of the government in passing them, drives home the point that is being made.

In response to a very weak domestic participation in its maritime industry, Nigeria turned to legislation. It enacted the Cabotage Act. As with the NCDMB, this Act established NIMASA to monitor and regulate the sector. The Act also contains extensive provisions aimed at growing a considerable Nigerian content in the maritime industry.[48] For example, section 3 prohibits vessels which are not wholly owned and manned by Nigerians, and built and registered in Nigeria, from engaging in the domestic coastal carriage of cargo and passengers within the coastal, territorial, inland waters, islands, or any point within the waters of the exclusive economic zone of Nigeria; while section 4(1) prohibits tugs or vessels which are not wholly owned by Nigerians from towing vessels from or to any port or point in Nigerian waters. Similar prohibitions are provided with respect to the carriage of materials or provision of supply services to and from oil rigs, platforms, and installations or the carriage of petroleum products between oil rigs, platforms, and installations whether offshore or onshore, or within any ports or points in Nigerian waters.[49]

44 See Oguine, 2011, at p 406.
45 Oguine, 2011, at p 419. Similar sentiments have been made elsewhere. See White, 2017.
46 The Schedule to NOGICDA itemises the required Nigerian content for about 280 separate aspects of the NPI. They include the required local man hours, finance/tonnage/usage of services, etc. While NOGICDA requires a 100 percent Nigerian content in some aspects of the industry, in other aspects it requires less, depending on the extent of local capacity and expertise. See also Atsegbua, 2012, at p 491.
47 Nwaokoro, 2012, at p 56.
48 See Anele, 2018, Ukpere and Ukpere, 2011. See also Damachi and Zhaosheng, 2005.
49 S.5. Similarly s.6 prohibits a vessel or whatever type or size from engaging in domestic trading in the inland waters of Nigeria except it is wholly owned by Nigerian citizens. And under s.7, in the rebuilding of vessels, a vessel shall only be eligible for cabotage

Many Nigerians were hopeful that the Act would usher in a new era of shipbuilding, create employment, and improve Nigeria's economy. The difficulty, however, was at the implementation and enforcement stage. It was found that due to the weak capacity of Nigerian ship builders, the Act could not be fully implemented. For instance, section 3 which requires all cabotage vessels to be built in Nigeria has been almost impossible to comply with because the country is not a shipbuilding nation, besides lacking trained personnel to operate all internally used vessels.[50]

Fifteen years after the Cabotage Act was enacted, it is now widely acknowledged that its impact has been negligible.[51] Nigeria still relies largely on foreign ships and vessels even though this violates the requirements of the Act. That the Cabotage Act has largely failed to meet its objectives was acknowledged by Ibrahim Zailani, a former executive director of Maritime Labour and Cabotage Services in NIMASA. Zailani, who was also a member of the National Assembly when Cabotage Act was enacted into law, noted during his tenure at NIMASA that now 'that I am in charge of implementing Cabotage, I have seen the practical difficulties of implementing the Act. The Cabotage Act, I will say, was virtually built on almost nothing; and, to me, you cannot build on nothing'.[52] In a similar vein, Louis Mbanefo, a senior advocate of Nigeria and maritime expert posited that Cabotage Act has failed not being well thought out and for being fundamentally flawed. He noted that:

> Whilst the object may be laudable, the foundation of the Act was faulty … as a policy statement of future aspiration it is fine but to make it applicable with almost immediate effect was most ill-advised. The Act then provides that waivers may be granted by the Minister to foreigners to operate cabotage vessels and foreigners continue to operate as before by virtue of waivers. It seems to me that the reasoning is flawed. You set targets that Nigerians cannot reach and then you grant foreigners the waivers to continue to operate! I think a radical restructuring is called for, not cosmetic amendments.

In order to remove obstacles to progress which the Cabotage Act has come to represent, a draft Bill for its amendment was tabled before the National Assembly in 2014, in order to bring it in line with current realities.[53] Like the Cabotage Act, the ambitious nature of NOGICDA demonstrates that either its framers ignored

services if the entire rebuilding including the construction of any major component of the hull or superstructure of the vessels is effected in Nigeria.

50 S.23 of the Cabotage Act 2003.

51 Echenim, 2012.

52 Echenim, 2012.

53 The effect of the amendment Bill which passed the second reading at the National Assembly, was to amend certain provision of the Cabotage Act and 'expand its scope to cover all offshore operations in the Nigerian coastal and inland shipping waters'. The amendment was also expected to address some gaps in the Cabotage Act which make violation of Nigeria's cabotage regime possible. It was not, however, passed into law in the 7th National Assembly, which ended in May 2015. See Etim and Afun, 2014. A Coastal and Inland Shipping (Cabotage Act) (Amendment) Bill 2016 Bill (HB529), has been tabled before Nigeria's 8th National Assembly.

Nigeria's capacity challenges or were very optimistic that they could be addressed within a very short period. But this has not been the case, and Nigeria's infrastructural reforms are still ongoing. Although there are prospects that some reforms may translate into a higher Nigerian content over time, an unrealistic and rigid local content regime may make Nigeria unattractive as an investment destination.[54] Where a protectionist local content regime becomes restrictive and unduly prohibitive, the PPC which enacts it may be compelled by market forces to tone it down through waivers, reforms, or revisions. This was the case of the Cabotage Act. It was also the case with Brazil, which struggled to implement its protectionist regimes, and took the only step available to it by revising it downwards in its 14th proposed bidding rounds, which was held in 2017, when it was removed as a bidding criterion.[55] Brazil also relaxed some LCRs for blocks awarded as far back as 2005, in a broad effort at increasing its appeal to foreign investors.[56]

Nigeria may in time be required to adopt a similar strategy at least with regard to some aspects of NOGICDA. This is more so as Brazil's capacity and NOC viability exceed those of Nigeria. It may be reasonable if Nigeria targets a 50 percent average, since the development of its considerable petroleum reserves makes dependence on foreign capital, technology, and goods, imperative. That said, exceptions and waivers, properly inserted into statutes, may be used to mitigate the consequences of stringent legislations. It is thus normal for regulators and administrators to grant waivers in the event of weak in-country capacity. It is in recognition of this fact that section 11(4) of NOGICDA provides that:

> Notwithstanding the provisions of subsection (1) of this section, where there is inadequate capacity to any of the targets in the schedule to this Act, the Minister may authorize the continued importation of the relevant items and such approval by the Minister shall not exceed 3 years from the commencement of this Act.[57]

One crucial drawback with the above section, however, is that the power to grant waivers by the Minister ended three years after the coming into effect of NOGICDA, which in effect was 2013. The challenge is that even as at 2018, eight years after the passage of NOGICDA, Nigeria continues to struggle with capacity and infrastructural challenges, which makes it imperative for the

54 Already the cost of producing oil in Nigeria is said to be among the highest in the world. C Okafor, 'WSJ: Cost of Oil Production: Nigeria now World's 3rd Most Expensive' *Thisday* (18 June 2016) http://www.thisdaylive.com/index.php/2016/06/18/wsj-nigerias-cost-of-oil-production-now-worlds-3rd-most-expensive/, accessed 20 June 2017.

55 See Almeida and Arruda, 2017.

56 See Parkin and Kiernan, 2016. And in 2013, Petrobras was 'forced' to write to the ANP to reduce Brazil's local content requirements in the face of daunting challenges it faced in Brazil's pre-salt region. Bryne, 2013.

57 Emphasis supplied.

subsection in question to be amended. Such amendment would make the power to grant waivers an open ended one in the event that there is inadequate capacity on the part of Nigerian firms.

Such power to grant waivers should, however, be judiciously applied for the best interest of the country. Care should also be taken in order to prevent waivers being the norm rather than the exception. This has been Nigeria's experience with respect to gas flaring. Nigeria enacted the Associated Gas Reinjection Act (AGRA) in 1979. Through the Act, it established a legal framework for the eradication of gas flaring by 1984. The conducive environment necessary for the successful implementation of the Act was not put in place, however. For the most part, Nigeria has not had a vibrant domestic gas market nor did it have the infrastructure it needed to re-inject natural gas to the ground. The fallout of these challenges, coupled with weak enforcement and pitiable fines has been that petroleum firms have continued to flare associated gas in Nigeria, despite its detrimental effect on the environment, by relying on waivers, or by paying the paltry fines where necessary.[58]

Thus while these waivers prevented AGRA from constituting a stumbling block on the development of the NPI,[59] they may also have engendered a lackadaisical attitude on the part of IOCs/NNPC towards the abolition of gas flaring. Care should be taken in relation to NOGICDA. Blanket waivers should not be conferred on the NCDMB or the Minister. Waivers should only be granted in limited instances. Again, AGRA and the Cabotage Act have demonstrated that legislation alone cannot produce desired results where there is a lack of political will to implement laws, or where the factors necessary for their successful implementation are absent.

Despite the capacity challenges it seemingly has, Nigeria's adoption of protectionism is not without its merits. First, in connection with the issue of capacity, the truth remains that while Nigeria is not a developed nation, it has immense potential which, if properly harnessed, will go a long way in meeting the demands of the NPI. The country can boast of a considerable number of engineers, geologists, and scientists, many of whom are engaged in the best petroleum firms all over the world. Besides that, NNPC has nearly 50 years' experience in the NPI, which can be harnessed for the advancement of the Nigerian content. Despite its reputational issues and numerous challenges, NNPC had demonstrated upstream promise in the past.[60] Furthermore, some Nigerian indigenous petroleum firms

58 As of 2017, Nigeria is the seventh largest gas flaring country in the world, behind Russia, Iraq, Iran, the USA, Venezuela, and Algeria. See, NNPC, 'Gas Flaring, Nigeria Achieves 26 Percent Reduction' (3 April 2017) http://nnpcgroup.com/PublicRelations/NNPCinthenews/tabid/92/articleType/ArticleView/articleId/755/Gas-Flaring-Nigeria-Achieves-26-Per-Cent-Reduction.aspx, accessed 3 July 2017; see also Ejiogu, 2013; Edino, 2010.

59 S.2 of the Act.

60 Nwokeji points out that the upstream unit of NNOC drilled its first well (OPL 96) offshore in 1976, at a time when Mobil was the only other firm operating offshore. An effort which was, arguably, the first successful deep water drilling by any operating firm

and service firms are performing relatively well in the NPI, as shown below. These all establish that while protectionism has its drawbacks, it may also throw a challenge to local industries to tap into their potentials and to devise localised strategies to address the needs of the NPI.

In the end, perhaps what Nigeria requires is a hybrid approach to local content regulation: one which straddles between the protectionist and the liberalised and more flexible approach. In those areas where it lacks in-country capacity, it may rely on a more collaborative approach similar to that of Norway in the North Sea. NOGICDA should therefore serve as a guide, and at the same time as a catalyst for local content development, while Nigeria aggressively addresses its capacity and infrastructural challenges in the background. It is suggested that the Act should retain its 'top-down' stance in order to protect budding industries that need protecting, but at the same time it should contain some 'bottom-up' aspects. This will create room for flexibility and compromise in those areas which require foreign participation and partnership.

It is also noteworthy that the top-down stance of NOGICDA notwithstanding, the NCDMB strives to combine elements of protectionism, while also collaborating with operators in the NPI in developing local content. Thus, beyond granting authorisations and granting or withholding approvals, it also conducts workshops, provides funding and training for local firms, and facilitates information sharing among stakeholders in the industry, etc.[61] This approach is more inclusive, and if pursued transparently and professionally, may generate win-win results, for operators and the Nigerian government.

5.3 Conclusion

This chapter ascertained the impact of NOGICDA in the NPI. It noted the Act's broad acceptance and its outcomes since 2010. It also noted that the Act has placed local content on the front burner of the NPI, rather than making it a corporate social responsibility affair. It found that since Nigeria took the bold step of enacting NOGICDA into law, indigenous firms have been spurred on by the Act to develop their capacities in order to be eligible to take on greater challenges in the NPI. It also noted that the Act serves as a model for several African PPCs, which have adopted the legislative approach, although to a slightly or less stringent manner than NOGICDA. The chapter also examined arguments against Nigeria's adoption of a legislative approach as an alternative to the milder and more flexible contractual approach.

It was also demonstrated that several countries which adopt protectionism often struggle with in-country capacity and, in addition, they risk violating their international trade obligations.[62] In this respect, it should be mentioned that local content measures not only place a burden on foreign firms which operate in

in Nigeria at a water depth of 122 meters. And that by 1979, NNPC had discovered more than one billion barrels of crude oil in different locations, based entirely on the work of Nigerians: see Nwokeji, 2007, at p 37.

61 See s.57, which mandates the Board to constitute the Nigerian Content Consultative Forum in order to promote collaboration in the industry in various aspects.

62 See Chapter 1, 1.4.

Africa, but they also place significant burdens on African PPCs in terms of regulatory commitment, and capacity building. And as was shown from the Nigerian experience, the successful enforcement of extensive local content provisions may not be easy for African PPCs, many of which struggle with weak in-country capacity, poor regulatory mechanisms, and corruption.

Going further, Chapter 6 analyses the available mechanisms for the enforcement and implementation of NOGICDA by the NCDMB, and in that light seeks to determine whether they are adequate enough to enable the agency fulfil its mandate. The chapter also seeks to determine the extent to which private citizens will be able to enforce the provisions of NOGICDA.

Bibliography

Adewuyi A and Oyejide A, 'Determinants of Backward Linkages of Petroleum industry in the Nigerian Economy' (2012) 37(4) *Resources Policy*, 452.

Ajoro CJS, 'National Participation in Nigerian Oil and Gas Industry: Prospects and Challenges' (2016) 6(1) *Petroleum Technology Development Journal*, 91 http://www.ptdjournal.com/?page_id=8, accessed 8 November 2016.

Akpan U, 'Local Content Initiative Creates 30,862 Jobs for Nigerians' *National Mirror* (27 February 2013) http://nationalmirroronline.net/new/local-content-initiative-creates-30862-jobs-for-nigerians/, accessed 10 March 2016.

Almeida B and Arruda E 'Evaluating Brazilian Bid Rounds: The Impact of a Plan to Grant Licences to Optimize Demand in the Upstream Sector' (2017) 10(3) *Journal of World Energy Law & Business*, 235.

Anele K, 'A Study of the Cabotage Policy in Nigeria from the Prisms of Ship Acquisition and Shipbuilding' (2018) 17(1) *WMU Journal of Maritime Affairs*, 91.

Atsegbua LA, 'The Nigerian Oil and Gas Industry Content Development Act 2010: an examination of its Regulatory Framework' (2012) 36(4) *OPEC Energy Review*, 479.

Ayoola OT, 'Nigerian Oil and Gas Industry Content Development Act's Perceived Performance Impact' (PhD Thesis, Walden University 2017).

Bryne L, 'Petrobras Wants local content Changes' *Rio Times* (5 March 2013) http://riotimesonline.com/brazil-news/rio-business/petrobras-requests-local-content-changes/, accessed 9 November 2016.

Damachi BB and Zhaosheng Y, 'The Nigerian Shipping Industry and Indigenous Shipping Companies' (2005) 32 *Maritime Policy & Management*, 31.

Echenim S, 'Success of the Cabotage Act, Still a Major Concern to NIMASA – Zailani' *Leadership* (18 May 2012).

Edino M, 'Perceptions and attitudes towards gas flaring in the Niger Delta, Nigeria' (2010) 30(1) *The Environmentalist*, 67.

Ejiogu A, 'Gas Flaring in Nigeria: Costs and Policy' (2013) 24(6) *Energy & Environment*, 983.

Etim K and Afun A, 'Nigerian Cabotage Tides Are Turning – Good or Bad?' *Nigeria Shipping Bulletin* (7 February 2014) http://www.mondaq.com/x/292776/Marine+Shipping/SHIPPING+BULLETIN+Nigerian+Cabotage+Tides+Are+Turning+Good+Or+Bad, accessed 23 April 2014.

Gbegi D and Adebisi JF, 'Managing Local Content Policies in the Extractive Industry' (2013) 4(7) *Res J. Financ. Account*, 97.

Isineds I, 'Civil Society, Media call for Stiffer Punishment for Violation of Local Content Act' *Premium Times* (7 September 2015), http://www.premiumtimesng.com/business/business-interviews/189609-civil-society-media-call-for-stiffer-punishment-for-violation-of-local-content-act.html, accessed 8 November 2016.

NCDMB, 'Nigeria Content Support Fund Hits $100' (9 October 2012) http://www.ncdmb.gov.ng/index.php/public-relations/news-updates/127-nigeria-content-support-fund-hits-100-million, accessed 19 November 2016.

Nwachukwu C, 'Nigerian Content: Appreciable Success, Greater Challenges still Ahead' *Vanguard* (28 February 2012) http://www.vanguardngr.com/2012/02/nigerian-content-appreciable-success-greater-challenges-still-ahead/, accessed 20 November 2017.

Nwaokoro J, 'Beyond Legislation: a Contractual Alternative to Legislation local content in Nigeria' (2009) 18 *Currents: Int'l Trade L.J.*, 42.

Nwaokoro JE, 'Nigeria's National Content Bill: The Hype, the Hope and the Reality' (2011) 55(1) *Journal of African Law*, 128.

Nwaokoro JE, 'Signed, Sealed but will it Deliver? Nigeria's local content Bill and Cross-Sectoral Growth' (2012) 4(1) *Journal of World Energy Law & Business*, 56.

Nwokeji U, 'The NNPC and the Development of the Nigerian Oil and Gas Industry: History, Strategies and Current Directions' (2007) James A Baker III Institute for Public Policy of Rice University and Japan Petroleum Energy Center, https://www.bakerinstitute.org/media/files/page/9b067dc6/noc_nnpc_ugo.pdf, accessed 4 November 2017.

Oguine I, 'Nigerian Content in the Nigerian Petroleum Industry: Legal and Policy Issues' (2011) 29(4) *Journal of Energy & Natural Resources Law*, 405.

Okonji C, 'Local Content: Nigeria Records $2.8b Investment Inflow' *Nigerian Compass* (3 September 2012) http://www.compassnewspaper.org/index.php/special-desk/maritime/7218-local-content-nigeria-records-28b-investment-inflow, accessed 2 September 2017.

Olayinka C, 'Local Content Implementation Retains $4b, says Nwapa' *Guardian* (14 November 2012).

Olsen WH, 'Brazil's Local Content Policy, Strategy and Ambitions' (2013) http://10.64.0.51:2111/usg/NdxICC.htm?IP=10.64.0.51&MA=20107A247174&OS=http://www.intsok.com%2Fcontent%2Fdownload%2F249%2F1809%2Fversion%2F4%2Ffile%2FBrazil_Local_Content_Strategy.pdf, accessed 7 January 2017.

Onuegbu H, ' Nigerian Content Act: Issues and Workers Concerns' Port Harcourt International Oil and Gas Conference and Exhibition (26 September 2012) Rivers State House of Assembly, Port Harcourt, Nigeria http://www.tucrivers.org/The%20Nigerian%20Content%20Act%20 %20Issues%20and%20Workers%20Concerns.pdf, accessed 23 November 2012.

Ovadia J, 'Measurement and Implementation of Local Content – A Framework for Working With Stakeholders to Increase the Effectiveness of Local Content Monitoring and Development' (2013) *FOSTER Project MFP030703* http://cpparesearch.org/wp-content/uploads/2014/12/FOSTER-Measurement-and-Implementation-of-Local-Content.pdf, accessed 8 July 2018.

Ovadia JS, 'Local Content Policies and Petro-Development in Sub-Saharan Africa: A Comparative Analysis' (2016) 49 *Resources Policy*, 27.

Parkin B and Kiernan P, 'Brazil to Ease Local-Content Rules Ahead of Next Oil Bid Round' *Wall Street Journal* (17 October 2016) http://www.wsj.com/articles/brazil-to-ease-local-content-rules-ahead-of-next-oil-bid-round-1476731328, accessed 9 November 2016.

Rutter J and Knigton W, 'Legislated Policy Targets' (2012) *Institute for Government Briefing* https://www.instituteforgovernment.org.uk/sites/default/files/publications/Legislated%20policy%20targets%20final.pdf, accessed 20 November 2017.

Ukpere LO and Ukpere WI, 'A Strategic Reposition of the Maritime Industry for Economic Recovery and Sustainability: "The Cabotage Act"' (2011) 5(14) *African Journal of Business Management*, 5658.

White S, 'Regulating for Local Content: Limitations of Legal and Regulatory Instruments in Promoting Small Scale Suppliers in Extractive Industries in Developing Economies' (2017) *The Extractive Industries and Society*, 262.

6 An assessment of the frameworks for the enforcement of the Nigerian Oil and Gas Industry Content Development Act 2010

6.1 Introduction

The enforcement of local content laws is not very easy. Efficient enforcement of local content laws will require that regulators be able to adequately monitor the contracting and purchasing of petroleum firms and to be able to use sufficient criteria to measure the local content in the operations of petroleum firms. Because of the vast nature of the petroleum industry (upstream and downstream), local content regulation is a demanding and daunting task. Nonetheless, it is imperative that countries which enact local content requirements (LCRs) also take steps to position and empower their regulators to efficiently discharge their mandates. This is primarily due to the fact that because of the magnitude and volume of petroleum related contracts awarded annually in the petroleum industry, the impact of non-compliance with LCRs can be significant, not only economically, but also in terms of loss of exposure, experience, and capacity for local firms. For example, in 2018 the Nigerian Senate commenced a probe of the local content elements and cost variations of the $16 billion Egina deep water project which is being executed by Total. It embarked on the probe in response to allegations that Total, an upstream operator in the Nigerian petroleum industry (NPI), and its contractors, flagrantly infringed the provisions the Nigerian Oil and Gas Industry Content Development Act 2010 (NOGICDA), which resulted in the loss of billions of dollars in expatriated hard currency. The Senate committee which conducted the investigation claimed that Nigerian firms were used as conduits by their foreign counterparts as a direct means of circumventing the provisions of NOGICDA. It therefore proposed an amendment of NOGICDA in order to enable the National Assembly to grant final approvals for petroleum related projects.[1] It remains to be seen whether this proposed amendment will see the light of day, and it is also doubtful whether it will actually be good for the NPI. Breaches of employment regulations as well as other requirements can also have considerable economic implications on petroleum producing countries (PPCs), hence the need, in some instances, to take a firm stance against firms which deliberately default and violate LCRs. In this respect, it will be recalled that the National Agency for Petroleum, Natural Gas, and

1 Umoru, 2018.

Biofuels (ANP) of Brazil, takes a strong stance against violators of its LCRs. A 2015 record $71 million fine imposed on BG, an exploration and production (E&P) partner of Petrobras, for local content violations in an offshore project, is examined in Chapter 2. [2]

The establishment of the NCDMB has been hailed as a strategic move which positions Nigeria to advance its local content through a focused and legislatively empowered regulator. Commenting on the establishment of the NCDMB, Olawuyi notes that from the perspective of international oil companies (IOCs), Nigeria's establishment of a local content regulator '… reduces ambiguities and surprises with respect to LCR enforcement and implementation, while from a government and policy standpoint, it ensures that LCRs are indeed actually monitored and enforced such that they can result in real and quantifiable benefits in the long run'.[3] It is important, nevertheless, to ascertain whether the agency is actually able to rise up to meet the demands of its mandate. Secondly, if it lacks capacity or commitment, it is important to ascertain whether there are alternatives that can help further the Nigerian content. For example, what roles can private Nigerian citizens play in advancing the Act? In this respect, are there complimentary roles that the Department of Petroleum Resources (DPR) or even the Nigerian National Petroleum Corporation (NNPC) can play in advancing the Nigerian content in order to strengthen the enforcement of the Act? This chapter analyses the powers and strategies employed by the NCDMB in the advancement of the Nigerian content. It also seeks to determine the extent to which Nigerian citizens can enforce the provisions of the Act, drawing lessons from case law and recent happenings in the NPI.

6.1.1 A review of the strategies employed by the NCDMB in the implementation of NOGICDA

The NCDMB, as regulator/developer of the Nigerian content in the NPI is conferred with powers to administer the provisions of the Act.[4] As a developer it promotes local content initiatives, and also collaborates with petroleum firms in order to ensure that the Nigerian content is well represented in projects executed in the NPI.[5] Its involvement at every phase of the contracting cycle also positions it to insist on compliance with the Nigerian content. Furthermore, it relies on its powers to pre-authorise and issue certificates, as well as on its powers of inspection, to ensure that the Nigerian content is taken into cognisance by petroleum firms. In practice it may also ban the importation of certain items and require firms to source for them locally.[6]

2 See Chapter 2, 2.2.1.1.
3 See Olawuyi, 2017.
4 Ss 4, 5 and 105.
5 S.104(3).
6 'NCDMB to Ban Imported Cables for Oil Projects' *Punch* (23 February 2017) https://punchng.com/ncdmb-ban-imported-cables-oil-projects/, accessed 8 August 2018.

In spite of the strong protectionist language of NOGICDA, it is interesting to note that the NCDMB has largely adopted a collaborative and conciliatory approach to local content regulation. In its dealings with the industry, it would rather issue notices of non-compliance to defaulting firms than rely on strict law enforcement. As a local content developer, it constantly organises annual local content conferences, workshops, and sponsors skills development initiatives, mainly in collaboration with E&P firms. To a large extent the NCDMB functions like a 'big brother' in the NPI, settling or mediating local content disputes among contractors and operators, and it is for the most part, slow to issue sanctions, relying rather on administrative procedures to resolve local content issues. Thus in the implementation of the Act, the NCDMB focuses largely on promoting indigenous ownership of equipment used for operations in the NPI, while also advancing indigenous manufacturing of components used in the NPI. The Board has also sought to ensure that Nigerian content targets are met for projects and operations, while also utilising training and employment opportunities for Nigerian indigenes. Furthermore, it deploys the Nigerian content development fund for target capacity building, while also ensuing that local capacity investors amortize investments involving oil producing communities.

Adopting a collaborative approach by a top-down regulator is decidedly a welcome strategy which should be encouraged by the Nigerian state, and emulated by other African PPCs. The approach may also account for why there are fewer complaints about the NOGICDA than might have been expected the 'tough stance' of NOGICDA. That said, there is still the need for operators and firms in the NPI to be made to appreciate that the NCDMB is not only a local content partner, but also a regulator which may, where necessary, be able to hand down sanctions in the event of deliberate breaches. Nevertheless, since 2018, the NCDMB has evinced an intention to prosecute defaulters in a court of law as a means of propping up its enforcement mechanisms.[7]

Local content development is also promoted in Nigeria through the reward system. Accordingly, section 3(4), makes compliance with the provisions of the Act, and the promotion of Nigerian content development, a major criterion for award of licences, permits, and any other interest in bidding for oil exploration, production, transportation and development, or any other operations in the NPI. What this means is that firms which make local content a major aspect of their operations are likely to be 'rewarded' in the future, while firms which fail to comply are less likely to be considered by the Nigerian government. This explains why firms in Nigeria are quick to tout their local content achievements as a means of assuring the Nigerian government that domestic firms are taken in to consideration in all their operations.

In the enforcement of NOGICDA, the NCDMB is guided by its Guideline on Implementation and Enforcement of Nigerian Content Requirements ('the Guideline'), which was made in pursuance to sections 4, 5, 59 and 70 of the Act.[8]

7 NCDMB, 'NCDMB to Sue Offenders of Local Content Act' (6 March 2018) https://www.ncdmb.gov.ng/2018/03/ncdmb-sue-offenders-local-content-act/, accessed 6 August 2018.

8 These provisions authorise the NCDMB to make procedures to guide the implementation of NOGICDA, and to do anything legally necessary to facilitate the carrying out of its overall duties.

Under the Guideline, firms which breach their local content obligations are to be notified by the NCDMB, and given a specified time frame to address them, failing which they would be sanctioned appropriately.[9] The Guideline also classifies infractions into: minor, serious, and chronic. A minor infraction includes first time defaults, inadvertence, or deficits in meeting deadlines for periodic reports, and similar defaults.[10] Penalties for minor infractions include the issuance of warning letters, invitation of the management team of the operator/stakeholders, for corrective dialogues with the NCDMB.[11] Serious infractions include repeated or persistent defaults, as well as deliberate refusal to comply with directives issued by the NCDMB. Firms which persist in defaulting may also be reported to ministries, departments and other agencies of the Federal Government of Nigeria (FGN), and may suffer the withdrawal of tax privileges. They may also be prevented from getting 'cost recovery', while certificates of authorisation and approvals issued for the project in respect of which the infraction occurred, may be cancelled or withdrawn.

A serious infraction may, in some cases, also be classified as an economic sabotage. Where that happens, the 'saboteurs' in question may be arrested, while privileges/support, and/or approvals may also be withdrawn. Lastly, the NCDMB may disqualify firms which commit serious infractions from participating in future projects in the NPI for specified periods.[12] For example, in 2014, the NCDMB banned Saipem, an Italian-based petroleum service firm from operating in Nigeria because it violated its obligations under NOGICDA in the Egina deepwater oil field project currently being operated by Total. Saipem was alleged to have abused its expatriate quota as well as its procurement processes.[13] In the same year, the NCDMB banned Hyundai Heavy Industries (HHI) of Korea from bidding for contracts in the NPI for violating sections 28, 33 and 41(2) of NOGICDA in Ofon II, an offshore oilfield located in oil mining lease (OML)102. HHI was alleged to have used non-compliant assets and expatriates on the project. For instance, it was alleged that of its 184 HHI staff on the project, only two were Nigerians.[14]

Under the Guideline, chronic local content infractions refer to flagrant attempts to undermine or circumvent the implementation of the functions of the NCDMB, and the deliberate refusal to comply with specific directives. Sanctions applicable to chronic infractions include entry into the premises of the defaulter with the intention of closing down operations, impounding and quarantining products or goods which constitute the infraction or which are subject-matter of a default. The NCDMB may also issue cease/desist notices, or cause chronic defaulters to be prosecuted under section 68 of the Act.[15] These sanctions are, however, subject to review by the office of the Executive Secretary of the NCDMB.[16]

9 3.
10 4.2.1.
11 4.2.2.
12 4.3.
13 Alike, 2014.
14 See Alike, 2016.
15 4.4.
16 5, see also the Review Procedure of the NCDMB.

Sanctions are sometimes necessary to enforce local content directives because not all firms will comply willingly. In effect, the higher costs associated with local procurement, and the time and effort required to invest in the training of local personnel, may not naturally endear petroleum firms operating in the NPI to 'willingly' develop and promote the Nigerian content. This means that – notwithstanding that local content may have long-term benefits not only for PPCs, but also for petroleum firms – the latter may be unlikely to willingly promote it, if they can find cheaper and quicker alternatives in procuring foreign goods or utilising 'ready-made' expatriates.[17] Sanctions are thus necessary to deter future infractions. With respect to the sanctions regime in NOGICDA, three issues may require further elucidation. The first is whether the sanctions regime in the Act is adequate to compel compliance and enable the NCDMB to further the Nigerian content. The second is whether the Act confers on the NCDMB the power to impose and enforce sanctions. The third is whether or not the NCDMB requires a court order before it can impose sanctions on defaulting firms.

NOGICDA contains a two pronged sanction provision in section 68. Under the section, it is an offence for operators, contractors, or subcontractors to carry out projects contrary to the provisions of NOGICDA. The first leg of the sanction is that firms which default will be liable to pay a fine of 5 percent of the total sum for each project in which they infringe the Act's provisions. The second leg is that the project itself in respect of which the offence is committed is liable to be cancelled.[18] Apart from this section, no other sanctions are provided for in the Act. It appears that the sanctions regime as currently contained in the NOGICDA itself is not exhaustive enough.

This has caused the NCDMB to rely more on the sanctions contained in the Guideline in its enforcement of the provisions of the Act itself. But those sanctions are primarily administrative, and may not necessarily have the force of law. This is more so as the Act does not expressly authorise the NCDMB to impose sanctions. It is therefore submitted that in order to clothe the infractions, and the procedures contained in the Guideline, with the force of law, they should be transferred to the main body of the Act, given that they are sufficiently elaborate. In the alternative, NOGICDA should be amended in order to authorise the NCDMB to define sanctions through regulations, and enforce them accordingly. The circumstances under which the 'threat' of cancelling projects for infractions of the Act should also be made more detailed and specific in the body of the Act. The blanket threat to 'cancel' is too wide and arbitrary. It may be too harsh to cancel billions of dollars' worth of projects for minor or even serious infractions, without first exploring other viable and more reasonable alternatives. Perhaps in recognition of the need to put things in clearer perspective, the Guideline provides that only chronic infractions are liable to be cancelled.

17 See White, 2017, at p 263.
18 S.68.

6.1.1.1 How sufficient are the NCDMB's powers of enforcement?

Another issue which requires some scrutiny is whether the NCDMB has adequate and clear powers to enforce NOGICDA. Adequacy of regulatory powers is a pre-requisite for efficient regulation and monitoring. Thus while the NCDMB has reserved for itself the right to impose sanctions on firms which commit infractions of NOGICDA, it is uncertain whether this power clearly derives from the Act. This is especially so when it comes to enforcing the sanction provided for in section 68 of the Act. This uncertainty is borne out from the fact that NOGICDA did not specify the institution which has responsibility to cancel projects for local content violation, nor does it stipulate the procedure for the recovery of the 5 percent fine.

Does the NCDMB, for example, have the right to cancel an upstream E&P licence granted by the FGN to Mobil on the ground that there are violations of NOGICDA, or would it rather make recommendations to the FGN in that regard? It is difficult to see how the NCDMB would be able to cancel an oil mining lease which it did not award in the first place. Secondly, does it have the right to cancel a subcontract awarded by Shell to Halliburton on the basis that the latter imports, rather than utilises local equipment and goods, or would it make a recommendation to the Minister of Petroleum to carry out the 'cancellation'? While the NCDMB may 'muscle' its way in regard to subcontracts between an E&P firm and its contractors, it may not find it easy in interfering with agreements between the FGN and E&P firms. It is interesting that in other climes such as Norway or Brazil sole regulators are responsible for local content as well as conducting bid rounds and awarding petroleum licenses. It would thus be much easier for the regulator to 'cancel' an upstream licence for local content breaches than it would in Nigeria, where local content is divorced from other regulatory aspects of the NPI. For now, this would require co-operation between DPR and the NCDMB, since only DPR, acting on behalf of the Minister may be able to 'cancel' an upstream licence awarded to a petroleum firm.

It is also remarkable that because the violation referred to in section 68 is referred to as an 'offence', it would require an agency with prosecutorial powers to enforce it in court. The issue is that NOGICDA does not vest direct prosecutorial powers on the NCDMB. Whether such powers are inferable from its general powers to implement and administer NOGICDA, however, remains to be seen.[19] There is thus need for clarification in that respect, since any presumption to prosecute the offence stipulated in section 68 may be challenged in a court of law. Should a court find that the NCDMB lacks prosecutorial powers, it would have to rely on the Federal Ministry of Justice, (which ordinarily has the power to prosecute offences against the laws of the Federation of Nigeria) to enforce any breaches of the Act. But this inter-agency reliance may limit the NCDMB's efficiency, and expose it to political interplays and government bureaucracy. It is therefore suggested that NOGICDA be amended in order to confer positive and clear

19 Ss 5, 59, 70(1) and 100.

powers on the NCDMB to prosecute 'offenders' and impose sanctions, where necessary.

Assuming, further, that the NCDMB is expressly authorised to 'cancel' projects or impose sanctions on firms which violate NOGICDA, it will still be unclear whether recourse to the courts would first be required before such sanctions can be imposed. Recently, the right of administrative authorities to impose fines in Nigeria has been increasingly subjected to challenge. Some firms operating in the NPI have challenged administrative fines on the basis that they amount to a usurpation of the powers of the judiciary, besides infringing on their right to fair hearing.[20] This has led to conflicting decisions by various High Courts in Nigeria.

In 2017, for instance, in *Mobil Producing Nigeria Unlimited v NOSDRA*, the Federal High Court sitting at Uyo held that the imposition of fines by NOSDDRA was unlawful.[21] In that case, NOSDRA had imposed a fine of 10 million naira on Mobil for breaching portions of the NOSDRA Act 2006. The same reasoning of the court may be applied to an agency such as the NCDMB, whose ability to impose sanctions against erring firms in the implementation of its mandate may be challenged on grounds that it is acting as a judge and jury over its own matter. In 2018, however, a Federal High Court sitting in Lagos in a suit between *NOSDRA v Shell Nigeria Exploration Company*, held that the imposition of a $3.6 billion fine on Shell did not amount to a violation of Nigeria's constitution nor to Shell's right to fair hearing.[22]

These conflicting decisions call into question whether an administrative regulator such as the NCDMB can actually impose fines without first going through the long route of litigation. This is not only costly, but may also detract it from its core monitoring focus. It is perhaps in a bid to avoid any potential challenge to it sanctions' jurisdiction that the NCDMB announced in 2018 that it would adopt the litigation route.[23]

6.1.1.2 Does the NCDMB have the requisite regulatory independence where NNPC is concerned?

Another pertinent issue that may have a bearing on the efficiency of the NCDMB is whether it possesses sufficient independence to regulate NNPC, and by extension, its IOC partners. First, NNPC is a member of the NCDMB council,[24] and its chairman who is the Minister of Petroleum also has oversight over the NCDMB.[25] Conceded that some ministerial oversight of the NCDMB is in order,

20 There have been conflicting decisions on whether or not the imposition of administrative fines by regulators amounts to a derogation of the courts' powers and whether it also violates the constitutionally guaranteed right to fair hearing. Ojameruaye, 2012; Omojuyigbe, 2018.

21 Suit NO FHC/UY/CS/1623/2016, Unreported.

22 See Omojuyigbe, 2018.

23 NCDMB (n 7).

24 S.72b.

25 S.72a. See also. Ss 36, 40, 41, 42, 44, 47, 48, 54, 101 and 102.

and some measure of closeness between the NCDMB and NNPC/IOCs may also create opportunities for better collaboration and dialogue in local content development. The issue is that such closeness may frustrate arm's length regulation.[26] It may also expose the NCDMB to 'capture' by NNPC/IOCs, which will weaken its ability to enforce the provisions of the Act. And because IOCs control over 75 percent of upstream operations in the NPI, for the most part, the NCDMB will have to contend with conflict of interest issues in carrying out its operations in the NPI.[27]

In order to address these issues, it is suggested that the FGN should either remove the Minister of Petroleum and NNPC from the NCDMB council, or take steps to partially privatise NNPC as a direct means of creating some distance between it and the NCDMB. The experience of Brazil with respect to local content regulation was mentioned in Chapters 1 and 2. Those chapters show that because Brazil's petroleum industry regulator, ANP, operates as a separate and independent regulator from Petrobras, it is able to assert its authority over the firm and its partners.[28] The ANP is thus positioned to publish local content regulations for the Brazilian Petroleum Industry, besides imposing fines in the event of infringements. All of these are made possible largely because Petrobras is partially privatised, and enjoys some arm's length distance from the Brazilian government.[29]

6.2 Private Nigerian citizens and the enforcement of the provisions of NOGICDA

By nature, NOGICDA is a public interest legislation whose impact cuts across the spectrum of the Nigerian economy, although its administration and enforcement is left solely with the NCDMB. The question is whether private citizens have the locus standi to enforce the Act's provisions through the courts. And if that were possible, would such actions strengthen the enforcement of the Act? Concerned private citizens may resort to litigation if they are convinced that there are infringements of NOGICDA and little is being done by the NCDMB to address them. Such actions may be instituted by indigenous petroleum firms involved in the NPI,[30] professionals involved in petroleum

26 S.72(b)i. See also Nwaokoro, 2011, at p 155.

27 See Nwapi, 2015, for a detailed analysis of the risks of capture of the NCDMB.

28 See Pereira, Gergio and Amorium, 2017, where the authors note cost and time implications of Brazil's local content laws in its pre-salt regions.

29 Chapter 8 delves deeper into the prospects of privatisation for improving NNPC's performance.

30 In another suit instituted by Hydrodive, an indigenous Nigerian firm, it was alleged that Addax Petroleum awarded an oil well contract to a foreign firm, in violation of NOGICDA. The awardees Ranger Offshore and Rangers Subsea were named as third and fourth defendants to the suit, while Addax Petroleum, Kaztec Engineering Limited and the Nigerian Content Development and Monitoring Board were named as first, second and fifth defendants. See 'Addax Petroleum Sued over Award of Oil Well Contract to Foreigners' (2014) http://dailyindependentnig.com/2014/08/addax-p

related disciplines,[31] artisans, and in some cases, host communities. Such persons may seek to enforce portions of NOGICDA if they perceive that contracts from which they expect to benefit are awarded to foreign firms in express violation of the Act. These actions may complement the efforts of the NCDMB. They may also serve as alternative enforcement mechanisms which may prove useful if regulatory complacency or negligence sets in.

It is not out of place for private citizens while acting in their personal capacities, through civil societies, impacted communities, or affected groups, to institute public interest litigation to protect the environment or to advance human rights. Such actions where successful, often have some regulatory component, and may be justified especially if there is evidence of government complicity or negligence in enforcing laws strictly. Public interest litigations which seek to enforce statutory provisions can have consequential implications, should they be prosecuted successfully. Besides, they will bring pressure to bear on regulators to work efficiently. Two notable public interest litigations that were instituted in the NPI against Shell/NNPC in the light of enforcement laxity on the part of the FGN deserve mention at this stage. They are: *Gbemre v Shell*, and *Douglas v Shell.*

Through the Associated Gas Reinjection Act 1979 (AGRA), Nigeria prohibits gas flaring in Nigeria. This is because of the fact that gas flaring is inimical to the human environment, besides amounting to a waste of vast sums of money. Despite the ban, however, gas flaring has continued in Nigeria, with the tacit consent of the FGN. Political and economic considerations on the part of the FGN, coupled with the fact that NNPC is directly involved in the operations of IOCs, has hindered the strict enforcement of the provisions of AGRA by government agencies. The perceived 'reluctance' on the part of the FGN to strictly enforce AGRA against IOCs and to abolish and stop gas flaring, eventually gave rise to a private citizens' litigation in the case of *Gbemre v Shell Petroleum Development Company Nigeria Limited and 2 others.*[32] In that case the applicant, suing for himself and on behalf of the Iwherekan community of Delta State, sought and obtained a perpetual injunction from the court, restraining Shell and its associates

etroleum-sued-award-oil-well-contract-foreigners/, accessed 9 June 2016. Again, in 2014, Ofserv Nigeria Ltd sued Weatherford International and its Nigerian affiliate, Weatherford Nigeria Limited for breach of NOGICDA. Udoh, 2016.

31 In 2014, for instance, an action was instituted at the Federal High Court against NNPC, Nigeria's Finance Minister, and accounting giant PricewaterhouseCoopers, by SIAO partners, a conglomerate of three indigenous accounting firms. The claimants, Messrs Robert Ade-Odiachi, Ladi Smith, and Ituah Ighodalo, alleged that the appointment of PricewaterhouseCoopers to audit NNPC was in gross violation of ss 10, 11 and 15 of the Act. They also claimed that the contract was awarded without any bidding by the local industry or from any Nigerian accounting firm. See 'Missing $20bn: Okonjo-Iweala Disowns Pricewaterhousecoopers, says she didn't hire firm' *Premium Times* (30 April 2015), https://www.premiumtimesng.com/news/headlines/182286-missing-20-billion-okonjo-iweala-denies-appointing-pricewaterhousecoopers.html, accessed 6 March 2018. See also Opeisetain, 2014.

32 Heard in the Federal High Court of Nigeria, Benin Judicial Division, Suit No. FHC/B/C/153/05 delivered on 14 November 2005. See also Ebeku, 2007.

from flaring associated gas within the community. The applicants had argued that continued gas flaring contravened their human rights as guaranteed under Nigeria's Constitution of 1999, and under the African Charter on Human and People's Rights (Ratification and Enforcement) Act of 1983. Whether the judgment was complied with is beyond the scope of this book. Suffice to note, though, that the action and the ruling which followed are demonstrable of the enforcement potential which private citizens' litigation can bring to bear on the NPI.

In *Oronto Douglas v Shell Petroleum Development Company Limited and 3 others*, [33] the applicant challenged the commissioning of a plant belonging to the Nigerian Liquefied Natural Gas Company Ltd (NLNG) in Bonny, Rivers State, Nigeria. The ground for the action was the refusal on the part of the respondents to comply with the 1992 Environmental Impact Assessment Act, which required the conduct of an environmental impact assessment before such projects could commence.[34] The case was dismissed by the trial court on procedural grounds. On appeal, the judgment of the trial court was overturned and a retrial was ordered. The trial could not proceed, however, because the NLNG plant had already been commissioned – in essence, the matter was already overtaken by events.

As with the *Gbemre* and *Oronto* cases, some Nigerian citizens have instituted some local content actions, as shown below. These actions are, or may be, founded on the assertion that a petroleum firm operating in the NPI has awarded or seeks to award a contract to a foreign firm in contravention of the clear provisions of NOGICDA. They may also arise where foreigners are employed to carry out responsibilities which may be carried out by Nigerians, or where a firm imports goods or utilises the services of foreigners which are available in Nigeria. In such actions, it would also be usual for the complainant to claim that he/it is entitled to be awarded the contract complained about. These actions require closer scrutiny.

6.2.1 Disputes between Nigerian service firms and their service partners

Most of the local content disputes which have given rise to litigation in the NPI have, so far, arisen out of partnership relationships between indigenous supply and service firms, with their foreign service partners.[35] These partnerships are common and beneficial to both sides. For the foreign firm, aligning with a local content partner increases its chances of securing jobs in Nigeria. The foreign firm will also benefit from the information, market intelligence, contacts, experience, and local presence of the Nigerian firm. For the Nigerian firm, and the Nigerian government, such partnerships will facilitate technology transfer and guarantee technical assistance. They will also expose Nigerian firms to more challenging projects, and

33 Suit No. FHC/2CS/ 573.

34 Ss 2 and 13 of the Environmental Impact Assessment Act.

35 Some of these disputes include actions filed by Ofserv Nigeria Ltd (indigenous) against Weatherford Nigeria Limited (foreign), Hydrohive Ltd (Nigerian) against Addax Petroleum (foreign), and Arco (Nigerian), and LADOL (Nigerian) against Samsung (foreign).

provide access to funding. For these reasons, NOGICDA requires operators to give full and effective support to the formation of joint ventures, partnerships, and the development of licensing agreements between Nigerian and foreign contractors and service or supplier companies. Such partnerships must however, satisfy the requirements of Nigerian content development to the satisfaction of the NCDMB.[36] It is therefore not out of place for service contracts to be awarded jointly to indigenous firms and foreign firms. But disputes may arise in the course of executing such joint ventures/partnerships, and if not resolved they may give rise to litigation which may contain some local content element. A hypothetical scenario may perhaps explain this point further.

TTB Ltd, an IOC operating an oil block in Nigeria, may decide to award a well drilling contract to ADZ Ltd (French), and to BBC Ltd (Nigerian). The facilitation of the job will require the execution of at least two contracts. First, there will be a tripartite contract between TTB as concessionaire, and ADZ/BBC, as contractors. The two partners will also execute a typical partnership agreement among themselves. Problems may arise if ADZ terminates its arrangement with BBC, and elects instead to partner with YBY (another Nigerian firm), or with DDD (German). Should this happen, an aggrieved BBC may lodge complaints with the NCDMB, and with TTB as well. In the event that the dispute is not amicably resolved, it may resort to litigation.

It would be left for the court to determine whether or not the termination by ADZ was legal. To do that it would have to scrutinise the terms of the partnership contract between ADZ/BBC, and the basis upon which both firms were awarded the contract by TTB. Beyond that, it may also rule on whether ADZ's actions were in breach of NOGICDA. Should the court find that the contract was awarded jointly to ADZ/BBC as equal partners, it may hold that ADZ lacks the capacity to unilaterally and arbitrarily terminate or 'sack' BBC in violation of the partnership contract, without recourse to TTB and the NCDMB. ADZ may justify its actions by arguing that it was the main party to which the contract was awarded, and that BBC was nothing other than an 'addendum'. It may also argue that BBC is bankrupt, lacks capacity, or is sabotaging the performance of the contract.

Should the court hold that ADZ is, indeed, the main awardee of the contract, and that BBC is its subcontractor, it may hold that the termination is lawful and not in violation of NOGICDA, provided ADZ replaces BBC with YBY. But if ADZ, in terminating the contract, choses to partner instead with DDD, the German firm, the court may hold that its actions are in violation of NOGICDA. A similar scenario arose in an action filed before the Federal High Court between *LADOL v Samsung Heavy Industries Nigeria Ltd. (SHI).* [37]

In 2014, LADOL, an indigenous logistics firm sued SHI, Total Nigeria, as well as the NCDMB at the Federal High Court. It alleged violations of NOGICDA with respect to the construction and installation of a floating, production, storage, and offloading facility (FPSO) at Total's Egina oilfield, a project that was valued at

36 S.45.
37 Unreported in Suit No: FHC/L/CS/1768/2014.

about $3.5 billion. LADOL alleged that SHI 'used' it as its local content partner to secure the contract, and thereafter, sought to 'dump' it for another firm, on flimsy excuses. It sought a declaration that the Egina FPSO project contract was awarded by Total to Samsung, with the approval of the Nigerian regulatory authorities including NNPC, National Petroleum Investment Management Services (NAPIMS), NCDMB and the Ministry of Petroleum. And it was on the basis that inter alia, a considerable proportion of the steel fabrication and the integration of the FPSO topsides would be carried out at LADOL's yard in the LADOL Free Zone, Tarkwa Bay, Lagos, and, as such, it argued that the said termination was unlawful. The suit was, however, settled out of court before a definitive decision was handed down. This meant that the court was unable to reach any conclusion on the germane issues it raised.[38]

6.2.2 Disputes between E&P service firms and Nigerian service providers

Local content disputes may also arise out of direct relationships between E&P firms and Nigerian service providers. For example, if an E&P firm terminates a contract it had awarded to a Nigerian firm, and re-awards it to another firm, the Nigerian firm may challenge the termination, and in so doing, may assert that the provisions of NOGICDA have been violated by the former. Such action is unlikely to succeed if the E&P firm re-awards the contract to another Nigerian firm, although damages may be awarded to the claimant if the termination was in breach of the contract. In effect, Nigerian courts may be reluctant to direct an unwilling E&P firm to retain a Nigerian firm against its will. For although NOGICDA seeks to secure the participation of Nigerians in the NPI, it gives firms operating in the NPI the freedom to decide with whom they would contract. Section 3(2) of NOGICDA requires *exclusive* consideration to be given to Nigerian indigenous service companies which demonstrate ownership of equipment, Nigerian personnel, and have capacity, to bid for jobs on land and swamp areas. This means that petroleum firms may award contracts in the NPI to any capable indigenous firms of their choice which demonstrate capabilities and personnel. The issue is, what if only one Nigerian firm has the capability to execute a contract which is to be awarded in the swamp or land areas of an E&P firm? Must such contracts be awarded to it, since *exclusive consideration* is reserved only for Nigerian firms in this area? A similar question arose in the case of *Arco v NAOC*, [39] except in that case the claimant was unable to establish that it was the only Nigerian firm that had capacity to execute the job in issue.

In 2014, Arco an indigenous petrochemical firm instituted a suit against the Nigerian Agip Oil Company (NAOC), NNPC, Conocophillips Petroleum Nigeria Limited, and NAPIMS. Relying on section 3(2) and (3) of NOGICDA, it claimed exclusive right to be granted an extension of a contract for the maintenance and servicing of a rotating equipment at NAOC's gas plants at OB/OB, Ebocha and

38 Aderigbibe, 2014.
39 Unreported in Suit No: FH/PH/CS/02/2015.

Kwale. It founded its claim on the basis that it had demonstrated ownership of equipment, personnel, and capacity to execute the job. Arco also argued that it had scored the highest in the bidding process for the contract, but that NAOC refused to award the job to it.

After hearing arguments from lawyers on both sides, Justice Abdullah Liman of the Federal High Court sitting in Port Harcourt dismissed Arco's case on the ground that it failed to establish that it was the *only capable* Nigerian indigenous firm that bid for the contract. In effect, the court held that Arco was not exclusively entitled to be considered and awarded the contract in question. Certain conclusions can be extracted from the judgment, which appears to be the first local content action bordering on NOGICDA to be decided with finality. First, the case appears to sanction the right of interested Nigerian firms to enforce the provisions of NOGICDA through the courts, especially where there was a prior contractual relationship between the claimant and the respondent. Secondly, it also established the fact that no Nigerian firm can claim to be exclusively entitled to be awarded contracts by operators provided other Nigerian firms also qualify for the same job, with respect to capacity and personnel. Thus it is irrelevant whether the claimant in question scored the highest in the bidding process, as long as it has not been awarded a contract by an operator, it cannot claim to be exclusively entitled to that contract. This is more so as an invitation to pre-qualify and bid for a job is only an invitation to treat, while the bid is the offer itself.[40]

Lastly, it may appear that where a Nigerian firm is the only firm that has capacity to execute a job in the NPI, it may be entitled to be awarded a contract in the NPI, and should the operator award same to a foreign firm in violation of NOGICDA, an aggrieved private citizen would be allowed to institute a local content challenging it. In essence, were Arco the only capable firm in Nigeria that could execute the job which formed the subject matter of the dispute, it would have been able to claim to be entitled to it. It remains to be seen, however, how this will work in practice, since the law generally will not compel a person or company to contract against his/its will. It is submitted that even if Arco alone had the personnel and capacity to execute the job, NAOC would have still had the choice to decide whether or not to award the contract to it, provided it does so in good faith, and does not contract with a foreign firm to execute the job in question.

6.2.3 Do private citizens have locus standi to challenge infractions of NOGICDA?

This segment now investigates whether private Nigerian citizens actually have the locus standi to enforce the provisions of NOGICDA in court, and if so, under what circumstances can such actions be instituted? Put another way, is the power to enforce NOGICDA the exclusive privilege of the NCDMB? Can Nigerian citizens seek, by way of either injunction or declaration, remedies from the court

40 See the English case of *Spencer v Harding* (1870) LR, 5 CP, 561.

where NOGICDA is infringed, especially if there is evidence that complaints made to the NCDMB have not been adequately responded to?

While some content actions have been instituted in Nigeria by private citizens, it appears that only *Arco* was decided with finality on its merits. Whether or not a court countenances a private citizen's litigation which claims that NOGICDA has been infringed may depend on the way the claim is couched in the first place, and whether or not a prior contractual relationship existed between the parties. Actions instituted by firms which already have a direct contractual relationship with the respondent are more likely to be countenanced in court, as was the case with *Ladol* and *Arco*. In other words, a local content complaint is likely to be countenanced by the court if it supports another claim which is founded on a breach of contract. In *Arco*, for example, the Federal High Court did not object to the reliance of the claimant on the provisions of NOGICDA in support of its claim against the respondent. This, perhaps, was borne out of the fact that there already existed a prior contractual relationship between both parties, the breach of which was being challenged by the complainant. Similarly, in the *LADOL* case, the claimant's action bordered not only on breach of NOGICDA, but also that the respondent was awarded the said contract jointly with it.

Local content actions instituted by claimants which did not have direct contractual relationships with the respondent may, however, be discountenanced on the basis of lack of locus. For instance, a claim by a Nigerian lawyer that Chevron's engagement of a Ghanaian lawyer is in violation of NOGICDA may be discountenanced by the court on the basis that only the NCDMB can make such complaints. However, if the claimant is challenging the termination of his engagement by Chevron, and in addition to that claim, alleges that his replacement with a Ghanaian is in breach of the Act, his second claim may be 'saved' by the first. As such, the court may, accordingly, be 'forced' to make a pronouncement on the legality of the engagement of the Ghanaian. But if the action is not 'supported' by a main claim which is founded on a pre-existent contract between the parties, it is likely to be dismissed on the ground that the parties lack the locus to institute it. In *Prince Alfred Omamuminogho and four others v SPDC*, [41] the applicants, suing for themselves and as representatives of Aja-Omamuminogho Uba Ikata community in Warri South Local Government Area of Delta State, had sought to compel the respondent to recognise their right as host communities, and to accord them the privileges accruable to them in that regard. Their action was challenged by the respondent on the basis that the Federal High Court lacked jurisdiction to determine the matter, which bordered on the recognition of host communities' rights and privileges attachable to same. Responding to the objection, the claimants, without citing any particular section, claimed to be entitled to their 'rights' as contained in NOGICDA. Upholding the objection and dismissing the action, the Federal High Court, per Justice Shitu Abubakar, held that:

41 Unreported Suit No FHN/WR/CS/8/2013.

> … nowhere did the Act vest any legal right in communities to enforce any of its sections against companies. This is because the Act did not give the community any justiciable right to enforce. In fact it appears to me that it is only the Federal Government of Nigeria that has the legal right to enforce the provision of the Act.

A similar conclusion was reached by the Edo State High Court per Esohe Ikponwen in the case of *CMES Flanges and Fittings Ltd v Chevron, Shell, and Mobil Oil Producing Companies.* [42] The claimant had alleged that the respondents breached NOGICDA with respect to contracts for the provision of flanges. The respondents, however, challenged the jurisdiction of the court to hear the matter. In upholding the objection of the counsel to Chevron, the court held that indigenous firms in Nigeria lack the locus standi to institute local content actions against IOCs for violation of NOGICDA, since the Act already gave that role to the NCDMB.

Although the rulings in *Omamuminogho* and *CMES Flanges and Fittings Ltd* are quite instructive, a more definitive ruling from a higher court (Court of Appeal or the Supreme Court) is required to create some certainty on whether or not private citizens have the locus to complain when the provisions of NOGICDA are being violated. As it stands, it is unclear whether aggrieved Nigerian stakeholders who rely entirely on NOGICDA, but had no prior relationship with an E&P firm, can either seek a declaration of the court that a contract in violation of NOGICDA is illegal, or obtain an injunction to stop the performance of such contract.

It is contended that, in light of the need to promote the Nigerian economy, courts should take a more liberal stance as far as private enforcement of NOGICDA is concerned. Of particular interest is the fact that in both the *Gbemre* and *Douglas* cases, the Nigerian government was a direct 'culprit' in the infractions complained against by its direct participation in the operations of Shell in the *Gbemre* case through a joint venture, and its ownership of 49 percent of the NLNG. Direct government participation means that the state may be sometimes reluctant to take action against firms which infringe the provisions of laws that are enacted for the benefit of the people. Where this is so, the doorway to the courts should be opened as in the *Gbemre* and *Douglas* cases, in order for private citizens to institute actions which would compel compliance especially where there are clear violations of the law.

The regulatory impact of public interest litigation in Nigeria has been relatively minimal when compared to countries such as the USA[43] and Brazil.[44] This is due in part to the absence of a comprehensive class action procedural framework, and a rigid application by Nigerian courts of the locus standi rule due to a strict adherence to conservative principles of statutory interpretation.[45] It is important that private citizens be allowed to act as watchdogs in protecting the interests of Nigerians as far as NOGICDA is concerned. The courts should therefore allow

42 Unachukwu, 2017.
43 See Hadfield, 2007, Issacharoff, 2007.
44 See Gidi, 2003; and McAllister, 2008.
45 See Obinna, 1987.

relevant stakeholders to be able to challenge flagrant breaches of the provisions of NOGICDA if there is proof of complacency and complicity on the part of NCDMB after receiving complaints from the respondents of ongoing violations. Such actions will keep operators on their toes in ensuring that the provisions of the Act are complied with in their contracting and procurements. Successfully prosecuted local content litigations will have some regulatory impact, and to that extent would strengthen the enforcement of NOGICDA. But while the possibility of private enforcement of NOGICDA through litigation has its merits, such actions should be limited through carefully developed principles, in order to prevent unrestrained litigation which may disrupt the smooth running of the operations of petroleum firms.[46]

6.4 Conclusion

This chapter examined the framework for the enforcement of NOGICDA. In that respect, it analysed the roles and powers of the NCDMB as a local content developer and regulator. It was shown that the NCDMB relies first on collaborative approaches to local content development, but in some instances, may impose sanctions on defaulters. The sanctions regime contained in NOGICDA and in the NCDMB Guideline was also analysed. The chapter questioned the adequacy of the singular sanction contained in section 68 of the Act, and pointed out that the sanctions contained in the Guideline appear more elaborate than the scanty provision contained in section 68 of NOGICDA. It noted however that they may not have the direct backing of the Act itself. The chapter also inquired into whether the NCDMB has the requisite independence to proceed against NNPC and its IOC partners, noting that the closeness which exists between the NCDMB and the NNPC may expose the former to capture and conflict of interest issues. Lastly, the possibility of private enforcement of the Act was analysed, drawing lessons from some recent cases.

In conclusion, it is suggested that the FGN should give the NCDMB more support in the area of funding, and capacity development in order to enable execute its mandate more effectively. The NCDMB should also be conferred with a greater level of independence in order to be able to exercise its monitoring roles over IOCs, NNPC, indigenous firms, and the whole of the NPI. There is also need for continuous human capacity development in view of the fact that the NCDMB needs capable employees who are well trained and prepared to tackle the challenges of the industry. But beyond that, there is the need for a more integrated approach to local content enforcement. Due to its overall importance to the NPI and the Nigerian economy, it is suggested that there should be some level of partnership between the NCDMB, DPR, and NNPC. DPR, as industry regulator, cannot be totally alienated from local content regulation. In awarding petroleum contracts and concessions, it should be able to insist on local content commitments which may sometimes exceed the provisions in the Act. In its

46 See Glover, 2012.

monitoring, it should also be able to determine whether or not the Nigerian content is being complied with. NNPC, as the fully owned NOC of the Nigerian state, can also continue to play vital roles in the advancement of the Nigerian content through its partnership with IOCs. Its direct involvement in contracting continues to provide it with viable opportunities which can be tapped by the Nigerian government to further the Nigerian content. At the head of all of these institutions should, however, be the NCDMB, coordinating, enforcing, and giving support, where necessary.

Protectionist LCRs, especially where embodied in legislation, risk contravening international trade law. The following chapter analyses protectionist local content laws in the light of international trade law, using NOGICDA as a case study. In that light, it enquires into whether waivers or policy spaces exist which may be used to justify the continued application of LCRs by African PPCs.

Bibliography

Aderigbibe N, 'Samsung-LADOL Truce: Nigeria's Local Content Act has Passed First Efficacy Test' *Ventures* (22 September 2014) http://venturesafrica.com/samsung-ladol-truce-nigerias-local-content-act-has-passed-first-efficacy-test/, accessed 16 November 2016.

Alike E, 'Challenges of Enforcing the Nigerian Content Act' *Thisday* (29 April 2014).

Alike E, 'House Committee Accuses Hyundai, Samsung of Breach of Local Content Law' *Thisday* (6 December 2016) http://www.thisdaylive.com/index.php/2016/12/05/house-committee-accuses-hyundai-samsung-of-breach-of-local-content-law/, accessed 3 July 2017.

Ebeku K, 'Human Rights Approaches to Environmental Protection in Nigeria: Gbemre v. Shell Revisited' (2007) 16 *REICEL* 312.

Gidi A, 'Class actions in Brazil: a Model for Civil Law Countries' (2003) 51 *American Journal of Comparative Law*, 311.

Glover JM, 'The Structural Role of Private Enforcement Mechanisms in Public Law' (2012) 53 *Wm. & Mary L. Rev.*, 1137.

Hadfield GJ, 'Don't Forget the Lawyers: The Role of Lawyers in Promoting the Rule of Law in Emerging Market Democracies' (2007) 56 *Depaull. Rev.*, 401.

Issacharoff S, 'Regulating After the Fact' (2007) 56 *Depaul L. Rev.*, 375.

McAllister LK, *Making Law Matter, Environmental Protection and Legal Institutions in Brazil* (Stanford University Press, Palo Alto, 2008).

Nwaokoro JE, 'Nigeria's National Content Bill: The Hype, the Hope and the Reality' (2011) 55(1) *Journal of African Law*, 128.

Nwapi C, 'Corruption Vulnerabilities in Local Content Policies in the Extractive Sector: An examination of the Nigerian Oil and Gas Industry Content Development Act, 2010' (2015) 46(2) *Resources Policy*, 92.

Obinna OB, 'Judicial Activism or Passivity in Interpreting the Nigerian Constitution' (1987) 36(4) *International and Comparative Law Quarterly*, 788.

Ojameruaye E, 'A Commentary on the $5 Billion Fine Imposed on SNEPCO by NOSDRA' *Vanguard* (21 August 2012) http://community.vanguardngr.com/m/discussion?id=4565467%3ATopic%3A619545, accessed 26 July 2017.

Olawuyi DS, 'Local Content Requirements in Oil and Gas Contracts: Regional Trends in the Middle East and North Africa' (2017) 36(1) *JERNL*, 30.

Omojuyigbe O, 'Court Orders Shell to Pay $3.6 Billion to NOSDRA' *Punch* (21 July 2018) https://punchng.com/court-orders-shell-to-pay-3-6bn-fine-to-nosdra/, accessed 6 August 2018.

Opeisetain T, 'Examining Local Content Legal Framework' *Daily Independent* (27 August 2014) http://uncova.com/examining-local-content-legal-framework, accessed 8 August 2017.

Pereira EG, Gergio F and Amorium L, 'The Brazilian pre-salt case: Governmental Interference and Challenges for Potential Joint Ventures' (2017) 35(4) *Journal of Energy & Natural Resources Law*, 456.

Udoh B, 'Nigerian Oil Firm Battles IOC Alleged Breach of Local Content Law' *Premium Times* (2 June 2016) http://www.premiumtimesng.com/business/business-news/204587-nigerian-oil-firm-battles-ioc-alleged-breach-local-content-law.html, accessed 9 June 2016.

Umoru H, '$16 Egina Probe: NASS to Amend Local Content Act' *Vanguard* (29 January 2018) https://www.vanguardngr.com/2018/01/16bn-egina-probe-nass-amend-local-content-act/H, accessed 22 February 2018.

Unachukwu JA, 'Companies Lack Power to Enforce Local Content Act, says Court' *The Nation* (3 October 2017) http://thenationonlineng.net/companies-lack-power-enforce-content-act-says-court/, accessed 24 March 2018.

White S, 'Regulating for Local Content: Limitations of Legal and Regulatory Instruments in Promoting Small Scale Suppliers in Extractive Industries in Developing Economies' (2017) *The Extractive Industries and Society*, 262.

7 Protectionist local content measures in Africa and international trade law

7.1 Introduction

Globalisation, market liberalisation, and free trade often present a challenge to countries that adopt protectionist measures.[1] This is because most countries in the world are signatories to some form of bilateral or multilateral trade or investment related treaties or agreements, which promote free trade on a reciprocal and non-discriminatory basis.[2] In essence, these agreements constrain the imposition of measures such as tariffs, import and export quotas, and performance requirements which are discriminatory in nature and have the tendency to restrict free trade. A number of free trade frameworks also provide amicable dispute settlement mechanisms, and establish avenues for the imposition of retaliatory measures against countries which breach their trade or investment obligations.[3] The most popular free trade frameworks are contained in the World Trade Organization (WTO) system. The WTO system is global in scope and reach, and comprises several multilateral trade liberalisation agreements designed to boost free trade among contracting parties. In addition to being signatories to several bilateral investment treaties (BITs) or multilateral investment treaties (MITs), most countries are members of continental or regional blocs such as the African Union, European Union, East African Community, and the Economic Community for West African States, etc.[4]

When applied to the petroleum industry in Africa, multilateral and bilateral free trade agreements tend to discipline the ability of African petroleum producing countries (PPCs) to restrict market access or to discriminate against foreign

1 See generally Ravenhall, 1999.
2 It is estimated that about 170 countries are involved in around 2,500 investment treaties. See Salacuse, 2007.
3 For further reading, see Hudgins, 1996.
4 They include the North American Free Trade Agreement (NAFTA) of 1994, and the European Economic Area (EEA) Agreement of 1992, and the Economic Community of West African States' Trade Liberalisation Scheme of 1979, the East African Community which was originally founded in 1967, then there is the recently African Continental Free Trade Area agreement which has been signed by 44 out of 55 members of the African Union, and will come into effect after it is ratified by 22 of its member states.

products through local content, and other measures.[5] The issue is that weak in-country capacity in countries such as Nigeria, Ghana, Tanzania, Sudan, Gabon, and Equatorial Guinea, would make it next to impossible for local sectors to compete on an equal basis with American, European, and Asian firms, which are decidedly more advanced in technology, capacity, and funding. Internal weakness of developing countries explains why international free trade regimes are often perceived as being disadvantageous to developing countries, but heavily biased in favour of developed capital exporting countries.[6]

Signatories to free trade agreements from the developing world are often caught in a dilemma. They desire to access global and regional markets for trade purposes, but by so doing they risk stifling local industries. This is because the opportunity cost for gaining access to foreign markets is that they expose their budding industries to unrestrained competition with firms which have greater capacity. Some form of protectionism therefore appears reasonable and sensible to these countries in the form of tariffs, export quotas, and performance requirements. Recently, these countries have increasingly resorted to local content requirements (LCRs) as a protective measure, not minding that, in so doing, they risk violating their trade obligations, and may be exposed to trade disputes as well as retaliation from countries which are adversely affected by their measures, besides making countries that adopt them unattractive to foreign investors.[7] Despite these risks, protectionism has continued to increase,[8] surprisingly, not only in developing countries, but also in emerging economies such as India, and Brazil, in even more advanced economies such as Canada and the United States of America (USA).

This chapter evaluates the free trade rules contained in the WTO system as they relate to LCRs, in order to determine why they have continued to flourish. It argues that there is a moral justification for protectionism which is borne out by the fact that developing countries cannot compete on equal footing with their developed counterparts. It also identifies certain gaps in the WTO system which may justify protectionist local content measures.

7.2 International free trade law and LCRs

7.2.1 The international free trade regime

The WTO system regulates trade relationships among contracting parties. It provides a framework for negotiating trade agreements among countries on a

5 See Crosby, 2012.

6 See Langhammer, 1980; see also Schriver, 1995, at p 223.

7 In that regard, see criticisms of NOGICDA 2010: Nwaokoro, 2012, see also Atsegbua, 2012.

8 An OECD Trade Policy Notes that since 2008 about 140 LCRs have been introduced by states in an effort to improve domestic employment and industrial performance. See 'Economic Impact of Local Content Requirements' (February 2016) https://www.oecd.org/tad/policynotes/economic-impact-local-content-requirements.pdf, accessed 6 July 2018.

multilateral basis. It also establishes a dispute resolution mechanism.[9] The most prominent WTO rules are contained in the General Agreement on Tariffs and Trade (GATT) of 1947 which was superseded by the GATT of 1994, the Agreement on Trade Related Investment Measures (the 'TRIMs Agreement'), the Agreement on Subsidies and Countervailing Measures (ASCM), the General Agreement in Trade in Services (GATS), and the plurilateral Agreement on Government Procurement (GPA). With the exception of the GPA, the rest of these agreements were the product of the 8th round of multilateral trade negotiations, conducted within the framework of the GATT 1947 at Uruguay.

The GATT regime is the most comprehensive of the WTO system as far as free trade is concerned. It prohibits discriminatory trade practices among contracting states based on national origins. Article 1, for example enjoins contracting states to confer most favoured nations status on all other contracting party states to the agreement.[10] Article 3.1 of the GATT also provides that:

> Internal taxes and other internal charges, and laws, regulations and requirements affecting the internal sale, offering for sale, purchase, transportation, distribution or use of products, and internal quantitative regulations requiring the mixture, processing or use of products in specified amounts or proportions, should not be applied to imported or domestic products so as to afford protection to domestic production.

What this means is that the products of contracting party states imported into the territories of other contracting parties are to be accorded treatment no less favourable than what is accorded to like products of importing countries with respect to all laws, regulations, and requirements.[11] This principle, which is referred to as the 'national treatment obligation', prohibits contracting parties from conferring preferential advantages on locally produced goods over and above what they confer on imported goods from contracting parties. Article 2 of the GATT also prohibits measures which limit quantities of imports or exports among parties, while Article 3.5 prohibits the application of internal quantitative measures pertaining to the mixture, processing, or use of products in specified amounts or proportions, which require directly or indirectly that any specified amount or proportion of any product which is the subject of the rule in question be supplied from domestic sources.

Like the GATT, the TRIMs agreement serves to constrain contracting parties from carrying out measures which restrict free trade. It is, however, limited to trade in goods, and does not apply to trade in services. The agreement prohibits trade related measures which infringe on the national treatment obligation of

9 See generally, 'Understanding the WTO' (2015) https://www.wto.org/english/thewto_e/whatis_e/tif_e/understanding_e.pdf, accessed 3 March 2017.

10 This requirement is also reiterated in Art.2 of the GATs, and Art.4 of the TRIMs.

11 See also, Art.27 of the GATS, and Art.3 of the Agreement on Trade-Related Intellectual Property Rights. See also Hestermeyer and Nielsen, 2014, at p 566.

states, as well as measures which infringe on the prohibition of quantitative restrictions.[12] In order to successfully challenge a TRIM as being in violation of the agreement, an aggrieved party would have to establish that the measure is mandatory, or enforceable under domestic law, or an administrative ruling, or that compliance with the measure is tied to an advantage. Furthermore, for a TRIM to be in violation of the national treatment obligation, it must also require the purchase or use of products of domestic origin, in terms of volume or value of products, or it may make mandatory the use of imported products in a limited sense.[13]

A TRIM may violate the prohibition on quantitative restrictions if it restricts importation by an enterprise of products used in or related to its local production, or restricts it to an amount related to the volume or value of local production which it exports. Alternatively, the measure may restrict the importation of products used in or related to the enterprise's local production, by restricting its access to foreign exchange to an amount related to the foreign exchange inflows attributable to it. Furthermore, it may restrict the exportation or sale for export by an enterprise, of products, whether specified in terms of particular products, in terms of volume or value of products, or in terms of a proportion of volume or value of its local production.[14]

Then there is the GATS, which in contrast to the TRIMs, focuses entirely on trade in services. Article 17 of the GATs reiterates the national treatment obligation by requiring members to accord to services and service suppliers of other members in respect of all measures affecting the supply of services, treatment no less favourable than what they accord their own like services and service suppliers. The agreement recognises the right of countries to regulate the supply of services, but requires reasonableness, objectivity, and impartiality in their application.[15] Under the GATS, contracting parties may nevertheless, be bound by their expressly scheduled commitments. Put in another way, countries which have not made scheduled commitments may legitimately introduce LCRs such as technology related requirements, financial contribution for the support of research, requirements that firms train indigenes, award scholarships, employ locals or introduce expatriate quotas.

Lastly, there are the ASCM and the GPA. The ASCM prohibits government subsidies which are contingent in law or fact, whether solely or as one of several other conditions, upon export performance. It also prohibits subsidies contingent, whether solely or as one of several other conditions, upon the use of domestic, over imported goods.[16] In order to establish that a country has contravened the ASCM, an aggrieved party must establish that the subsidy in question relates to a specific enterprise or industry, or group of enterprises, and that it has had an

12 See Art.2 of the TRIMs, which specifically refers to Arts 3 and 11 of the GATT.
13 See illustrative list attached to the TRIMs, para.1.
14 See illustrative list attached to the TRIMs, para.2
15 Art.6.
16 Art.3.

adverse effect on its related domestic industries.[17] The agreement allows WTO members to impose countervailing duties on subsidised imports, if there is proof that they cause injury to domestic markets.[18] The GPA on the other hand imposes the national treatment obligation in connection with government procurements.[19] It aims at ensuring a level playing ground for local and foreign suppliers through the national treatment obligation. The GPA, however, is a plurilateral agreement, which means that its obligations are only binding on members of the WTO which accede to it. Currently, no Africa country is signatory to the GPA.

In addition to belonging to the WTO, most countries in the world, as shown previously in this chapter, are signatories to some BITs, MITs, as well as some regional free trade agreements. These agreements typically contain non-discrimination clauses which embody the spirit of the WTO system of promoting free trade to some extent.[20] A typical BIT would require country A to observe the national treatment obligation and to confer most favoured nation status on country B as regards investments and income made in either country by the other. It will also restrict country A from providing incentives or subsidies and from granting privileges on its indigenous investors, over investors from country B. Moreover, parties to a BIT will be required to treat investors from both countries fairly and equitably. For that reason, the BIT would prohibit the introduction of harsh, unfair, and discriminatory practices that would harm foreign investments. Other matters dealt with by a typical BIT would include a blanket prohibition of expropriation and nationalisation of foreign investments, and guarantees for unrestricted transferability of earnings and profits by investors from each state. Some BITs may also restrict the introduction of performance requirements. For example, country A may be prohibited from requiring investors to utilise local services and goods, transfer technology to local industries or locate their headquarters in a particular location. Lastly, they would also address measures which relate to nationality of management staff and expatriate employees, while providing dispute settlement mechanisms.

The issue is, what happens where a country contravenes its WTO or BIT obligations? Since 1994, a dispute settlement mechanism was established under the WTO system to address some perceived weaknesses in the preceding GATT years.[21] Under the mechanism, trade disputes among contracting parties are submitted first to a panel or court of first instance, consisting of between three to five members. The Panel hears complaints from contracting parties, and issues reports with findings and recommendations on such disputes. Aggrieved parties may appeal to a standing appellate body. The recommendations of the panel attain

17 Arts 1 and 2 of the ASCM.
18 Art.10 of the ASCM.
19 See GATT 3.8, which provides that 'The provisions of this Article shall not apply to laws, regulations or requirements governing the procurement by governmental agencies of products purchased for governmental purposes and not with a view to commercial resale or with a view to use in the production of goods for commercial sale'.
20 There are over 3,000 BITs in force in the world today.
21 Ali, 2003.

legal status if they are adopted by the WTO's Dispute Settlement Body FD (DSB), which is a political organ comprising of all WTO members. The DSB operates on the basis of one member, one vote.[22] Where a contracting party is found to have breached its WTO obligations, the DSB will recommend that it brings the measure into conformity with the violated WTO agreement in question.[23] Where its recommendations are not implemented within a reasonable period, the other party may request for authorisation to apply counter measures which may result in the imposition of trade sanctions.[24] Like the WTO system, BITs also contain dispute settlement mechanisms. Under these, country A would agree to submit disputes that may arise between it and nationals of country B, concerning investments made by those nationals in the territory of country A, to an international dispute settlement authority for settlement by conciliation or arbitration.[25]

Despite the fact that the provisions in the WTO system and BITs potentially constrain protectionist measures, protectionist LCRs have continued to rise across the spectrum of developing and emerging resource rich countries.[26] At least three reasons can be adduced for this rise. To start with, there are certain gaps in the WTO system which leave room for some leverage for countries to adopt protectionist LCRs. Then there is the issue of weak enforcement of the WTO rules by affected countries, particularly within the extractive industry. Lastly, LCRs have flourished because multinational firms operating in the extractive sectors of developing countries choose largely to quietly comply with them. The reasons why LCRs have flourished require further interrogation and analysis.

First, LCRs have flourished perhaps because states have exploited certain gaps or policy spaces within the WTO in advancing their local content. For example, because the GATT system does not prohibit tariffs but rather requires states to 'bind' them, some countries have resorted to the imposition of tariffs as a means of restricting imports and support domestic industries. And with respect to the GATS, the scheduled commitments of developing countries, which determine the extent to which they are bound by its provisions, are quite shallow. This has left them with a latitude of discretion to regulate their services industry as they deem fit.[27] Contracting parties are thus left with a wide latitude of policy space to make

22 Ali, 2003.
23 Art.19.1 of the DSB Rules.
24 See Hudec, 1999.
25 See Art.9 of the Nigeria/Netherlands BIT and Art.8 of the Nigeria/Italy BIT. See also See Joffe et al, 2009.
26 For example, over 90 percent of resource rich countries have some form of LCR in place. Ramdoo, 2015. Again, A recent study claims that in the wake of the 2008/2009 recession more than 100 new LCRs have been adopted, amongst others by Australia, Canada, the USA, Argentina, Brazil, China, India, Indonesia, and Kazakhstan. See Hufbauer et al, 2013.
27 Ramdoo, 2015, at p 22. For example, Nigeria which has made commitments only in its communications and financial services sectors. Even at that, a number of these commitments are unbound. This, in essence, allows Nigeria to introduce or maintain measures inconsistent with market access or national treatment.

LCRs relating to service suppliers and employment in sectors, without necessarily contravening the GATs. Furthermore, the GATs do not constrain state owned enterprises, which though fully owned, may be used to further local content in their contracting systems surreptitiously. The TRIMs agreement and the GATT also allow some temporary deviation from the obligations they impose on developing economies.[28]

Similarly, the ASCM contains some allowances for developing and least developed countries.[29] Thus states have continued to provide subsidies in spite of the obligations contained in the ASCM, primarily because subsidies are not prohibited outrightly by its provisions. The subsidies conferred by a state on its local industries, may nevertheless be subjected to countervailing measures if an aggrieved state is able to establish that they relate to a specific enterprise or industry or group of enterprises, and that they have had adverse effect on its domestic industry.[30] Another gap in the ASCM is the fact that subsidies on innovation and research are not actionable under Article 8.2. This leaves states with the right to advance local content through provisions bordering on investment, research, and innovation.

The second reason LCRs have continued to flourish is because WTO rules are not comprehensively or effectively enforced. This is partly because it is expensive and time consuming to bring cases through dispute settlement procedures, and partly because some countries refrain from highlighting abuses by other states which are similar to policies they implement at home. Nowhere is this truer than in the extractive sector, where most countries of the world have some form of protectionist measure or another. It is instructive that, to the knowledge of this writer, no dispute has ever been initiated under the WTO system against local content measures in the extractive sector.[31] Enforcement of WTO rules are also restrained by poor surveillance and lack of transparency on the part of contracting parties, which make it difficult for aggrieved parties to gather relevant evidence. This is more so in those countries whose local content measures are not necessarily contained in express statutes, but are rather 'covertly' applied to operators and to select industries.[32]

Furthermore, enforcement under the WTO system is hampered by technical hurdles which complainants have to overcome. For example, in order to establish that a country has violated its national treatment obligation under the GATT, an aggrieved country would have to, among other things, establish that there is some 'likeness' between goods or produce from both countries. Establishing this element is not easy, however, because the panel of the DSB has not always been consistent in its interpretation of what comprises 'likeness'.[33]

Lastly, LCRs have continued to flourish in extractive sectors of developing and emerging countries because a number of multinational firms prefer to quietly

28 See Art.18 of the GATT and Art.2 of the TRIMs.
29 Art.27.3.
30 See Art.5 of the ASCM.
31 Ramdoo, 2015, at p 25.
32 See Cossy, 2006.
33 See Hestermeyer and Nielsen, 2014, at p 569.

comply with them, rather than challenge them openly. In some cases, these firms even go as far as establishing local content departments which advise them and direct their local content integration plans.[34] In Nigeria, for example, IOCs have been known to provide funding and logistics support for local suppliers in the states in which they operate.[35] Quiet compliance has a number of advantages. First, it endears foreign firms to the indigenous populations among which they operate. Secondly, it may also prove less expensive in the long run, as these firms may find it less expensive to use locals than expatriates to carry out less technically demanding jobs. A company such as Mobil, for example, may prefer to contract a pipeline surveillance contract to locals rather than to foreigners, for obvious reasons. Lastly, compliant firms tend to be rewarded subsequently in the award of contracts, and are viewed more favourably by current and subsequent governments.

7.3 NOGICDA in the light of Nigeria's international free trade obligations

Nigeria, like most African PPCs, is a member of the WTO, and has been since 1995.[36] As an active member of the international community, it has also signed BITs with a number of countries as well as being a member of the Economic Community of West African States' Trade Liberalisation Scheme.[37] The question is, do these LCRs actually inhibit free trade? Specifically, does NOGICDA actually violate Nigeria's free trade obligations under international trade and investment laws/agreements? If indeed it does, what options are available for Nigeria? A blanket assumption is not adequate. There is need for an in-depth analysis of the Nigerian approach vis à vis the international trade and investment regime. To that extent the following analysis compares some of the provisions of NOGICDA in the light of the WTO system. It also evaluates Nigeria's BIT obligations, using the Nigeria/Netherlands and the Nigeria/Italy BITs as case studies.

34 On the contributions of IOCs to local content development, see Ayoola, 2017, at p 53, see also Ngoasong, 2014.

35 In Nigeria for instance, IOCs such as Shell, Mobil, and Agip have been known to provide funding and grants to local suppliers, as well as investing in capacity building. See Shell, 'Nigerian Content Development' https://www.shell.com.ng/media/nigeria-reports-and-publications-briefing-notes/nigerian-content-development.html, accessed 11 July 2018, ExxonMobil, 'Capacity Development Initiatives' http://corporate.exxonmobil.com/en/company/worldwide-operations/locations/nigeria/community/development-initiatives, accessed 11 July 2018, Eni, 'Local Content', https://www.eni.com/en_NG/sustainability/community/local-content/local-content.shtml, accessed 11 July 2018.

36 It actually became a member of the GATT as far back as 1960.

37 Nigeria has signed BITs with Algeria, Austria, Bulgaria, Canada, China, Egypt, Ethiopia, France, Finland, Germany, Italy, Jamaica, Montenegro, The Netherlands, Republic of Korea, Kuwait, Romania, Russia, Serbia, South Africa, and Spain, etc., some of which are in force.

7.3.1 NOGICDA and the WTO system

Prima facie, several stipulations in NOGICDA appear to violate some of Nigeria's obligations under the WTO system. Of particular note is the national treatment obligation. This is because the Act seeks to confer benefits on the condition that goods produced within Nigeria are used in the NPI, and to that degree, it tends to discriminate against foreign goods on the basis of their territorial origins. For example, section 3 of the Act, which requires Nigerian independent operators to be given first consideration in the award of oil blocks, oil field licences, oil lifting licences, and in all projects for which contracts are to be awarded in the NPI, appears to discriminate against foreign petroleum firms operating in the NPI. While section 48, which authorises the Minister of Petroleum Resources to confer tax incentives on firms which establish facilities, factories and production units, or other operations in Nigeria for the purpose of carrying out production, manufacturing, or for providing services and goods otherwise imported into Nigeria, may also contravene the national treatment obligation as contained in the GATT.[38]

The requirement for yearly certification and submission of plans may also violate Article 3.5 of the GATT as same may be interpreted as being an internal quantitative regulation,[39] while the penalties provided for under section 68 of NOGICDA for noncompliance, may violate Article 11.1 of the GATT, especially if they are deemed as being prohibitive.[40] The creation of the Nigerian Content Development Fund in section 104 may also violate the provisions of the ASCM if they are interpreted as subsidies which confer an unfair advantage on local industries vis à vis their foreign counterparts.

The directive in NOGICDA that all operators and subcontractors comply with a minimum local content,[41] the prohibition of the importation of welded or fabricated products,[42] as well as its stipulation that operators utilise locally produced goods,[43] all risk violating the national treatment obligation. The same obligation may be infringed by the prohibition on quantitative restrictions which is contained in Article 2 of the TRIMs. Some provisions of NOGICDA may also violate the GATs, although Nigeria may have a valid defence if any of the measures in the Act do not infringe any of its scheduled commitments. For example, the requirement

38 See s.13 (i) of the PPTA. The PPTA in essence disallows petroleum firms from claiming capital allowances for the importation of certain goods which could have been purchased in Nigeria.

39 See United States – Measures Affecting the Importation, Internal Sale and Use of Tobacco, (1994) Report of the Panel adopted by the Council on 4 October 1994 (DS44/R) https://www.wto.org/english/tratop_e/dispu_e/gatt_e/94tobaco.pdf, accessed 11 July 2018.

40 See also the panel decision in Brazil – Retreated Tyres, WT/DS332/19/Add.6, 15 September 2009. It was held in that case that fines which imposed limiting conditions in the relation to the imports, restricted imports within the meaning of Art.11.1.

41 See s.11(3) as well as and the first Schedule to the Act.

42 S.53.

43 Furthermore, ss 10, 11, 12 and 13.

in section 10, that operators and contractors give first consideration to Nigerians in training, employment, and to goods manufactured in Nigeria, may violate the national treatment obligation contained in the GATs. Similarly, the directive that operators apply for expatriate quotas, and insert a 'labour clause' in projects exceeding $100 million may violate Article 26 of the GATs, which deals with market access.[44]

The directive in section 52 of NOGICDA that all financial services in the NPI be provided by Nigerians, may infringe the express inclusion of financial services in Nigeria's scheduled commitments which it made under the GATs system.[45] Nevertheless, because insurance was expressly excluded in the Schedule, and no mention was made of legal services in the commitments, sections 49 and 51 of the Act, which require insurance and legal services in the NPI to be provided by Nigerians, would certainly not violate the GATs. As no African country has signed the GPA to date, NOGICDA does not stand any chance of infringing that agreement. Moreover, assuming Nigeria were a signatory to the GPA, it is doubtful whether the Act would have had any bearing on its requirements. This is because the Act deals directly with petroleum firms and operators, while the GPA deals with government procurement.

As noted earlier, Nigeria, has also signed BITs with a number of countries, which among other things, constrain the extent to which it may introduce protectionist measures which impair free trade in its relations with its BIT partners.[46] The Nigeria/Netherlands BIT (signed in 1992, came into force in 1994) is used here as a case study. The Netherlands is used as an example, primarily because it is home to Shell, which plays considerable roles in the NPI. The Nigeria/Netherlands BIT typically contains non-discrimination clauses which embody the spirit of the WTO system of promoting free trade. For example, it requires both countries to observe the national treatment obligation and to confer most favoured nation status on investments made by nationals of either country.[47] The BIT also restricts both countries from providing incentives or subsidies and from granting privileges on their indigenous investors over and above what is conferred on investors from the other country, and to treat investors from both countries fairly and

44 See, for instance, ss 32 and 33 of NOGICDA which limit the number of expatriates that may work in the NPI, in addition to requiring companies to obtain the permission of the NCDMB before apply for expatriate quotas.

45 See GATs, 'Nigeria: Schedule of Specific Commitments' GATS/SC/65 15 April 1994 https://docs.wto.org/dol2fe/Pages/FE_Search/FE_S_S006.aspx?Query=(@Symbol=%20gats/sc/*)%20and%20((%20@Title=%20nigeria%20)%20or%20(@CountryConcerned=%20nigeria))&Language=ENGLISH&Context=FomerScriptedSearch&languageUIChanged=true#, accessed 25 June 2018.

46 See the Comprehensive and Progressive Agreement for Trans-Pacific Partnership which signed in 2016 among Australia, Brunei, Canada, Chile, Japan, Malaysia, Mexico, New Zealand, Peru, Singapore, and Peru –countries which together represent over 13 percent of the world economy. There is also the unsigned Regional Comprehensive Economic Partnership between the ten members of the Southeast Asian Nationals, Japan, Sought Korea, Australia, China, India, and New Zealand.

47 See Art.3.2. See also Art.3(1) and (3) of the Nigeria/Italy BIT of 2000.

equitably.[48] Thus it prohibits the introduction of harsh, unfair, and discriminatory practices that would harm foreign investments.[49] The Nigeria/Netherlands BIT also prohibits expropriation and nationalisation of foreign investments except for a public purpose which is not discriminatory, and provided there is provision for adequate compensation.[50] It also guarantees that investors from both countries have unrestricted transferability of earnings and profits.[51]

As with the WTO rules, a cursory comparison of NOGICDA with Nigeria's BIT obligations may indicate that the Act risks infringing some of Nigeria's obligations to the Netherlands. This is because several of its provisions as contained in sections 3, 10, 11, 12 and 13 which give preference to Nigerian services, goods, and entitlements in the award of exploration and production licenses, appear discriminatory against investors from the Netherlands. To that extent, the Act may violate the prohibition on discrimination against investors/goods from the Netherlands, as the most favoured nation obligations, contained in Articles 3 and 4 respectively of the Nigeria/Netherlands BIT.

7.4 Discussion and analysis

Countries whose LCRs infringe their international trade/investment obligations may be exposed to liability under the international trade system, and may be required to remove/alter/amend the measures in question, failing which they may face sanctions or be exposed to reciprocal treatments from affected countries. Lastly, such measures have the tendency of making such countries unattractive to foreign investors. The pertinent question then is what should African PPCs which have enacted protectionist LRCs, such as Nigeria, Ghana, and Tanzania, do? Should they jettison their protectionist local content drive in favour of a liberalised approach?

Three options present themselves. To start with, in view of the fact that the legality of the LCR measures of these countries is not necessarily dependent on whether or not they violate their international trade obligations, coupled with the fact that these measures may help shore up local participation, it is suggested that African PPCs should continue to apply them, notwithstanding the consequences.[52] The other option is for them to repeal/alter/amend the infringing aspects of their local content laws, in order to ensure conformity with their international trade obligations. Thirdly, they may take the extreme measure of opting out of the WTO system and reviewing some of their BITs. This last option is, however, hardly practicable.

Of the above measures, it is suggested that African PPCs should adopt the first measure, at least for now. First, because LCRs are not unique to African countries.

48 Art.3.1. See also Art.2.3 of the Nigeria/Italy BIT.
49 See Art.3.1. See also Art.2.3 of the Nigeria/Italy BIT.
50 Art.6. See also Art.5 of the Nigeria/Italy BIT.
51 Art.5. See also Art.6 of the Nigeria/Italy BIT.
52 This may entail reprisal actions by contracting parties or payment of compensation.

Secondly, as discriminatory as a number of these measures may appear, the truth remains that not all LCRs violate international trade and free trade obligations. Furthermore, because of enforcement and monitoring challenges under the WTO system, it is very unlikely that LCR measures of African PPCs would be challenged under the WTO system. That several foreign firms operating in African PPCs prefer to quietly comply rather than challenge LCR provisions is another reason why these countries should retain their LCRs, although they should be ready to revise them downwards or upwards as occasion demands.

It is conceded that several provisions in protectionist LCRs adopted by countries such as Ghana, Nigeria, and Tanzania, can potentially violate their BIT obligations. But these measures, while discriminatory in nature, are not perhaps radical and extreme to such an extent as to warrant a response from the international community. Rather, they evince an intention among third world countries, which have still not benefited from the industrial revolution, to shore up capacity, and emerge from the shadows of poverty and backwardness. In fact, it is perhaps because LCRs of African countries are not extensive and outright expropriatory that other developed countries often choose to look the other way.

NOGICDA for example, would have provoked the ire of the Netherlands if its provisions had operated retrospectively, or had nationalised the assets of foreign firms from that country. The Act does neither of these. It does not affect previously signed oil and gas agreements, but rather, requires all subsequent agreements and contracts entered into in the NPI to comply with its provisions.[53] It is also not expropriatory in nature. Unlike recent reforms in Venezuela and Bolivia,[54] which nationalised foreign assets, the Act does not attempt to seize the assets of foreign nationals, cancel their contracts, or revise fiscal agreements. Again, even if its provisions tend to favour locals against foreign firms, they are noticeably applicable to all operators in the NPI. What is being said is that if the Act is a burden at all, it is a burden to all: Nigerians and foreigners alike. Thus its provisions are as binding on Shell (Netherlands) as they are on Dubri Oil (Nigeria).

Again, NOGICDA does not impose discriminatory taxes on one foreign investor over another, instead, it mandates all firms and operators in the NPI (foreign or local) to comply with the Nigerian content in their purchasing, contracting, and employment. Again, while the Act is heavily tilted in favour of local investors, it gives all foreign firms a level playing ground. Hence, the China National Offshore Oil Corporation is not discriminated against, in favour of Statoil of Norway.

53 S.6.

54 For example, through the 2001 Organic Hydrocarbons Law of Venezuela, and the 2005 Hydrocarbons Law No 3,058 of Bolivia, the way was set for the nationalization of hydrocarbons in both states. For example, in pursuance to the Bolivian law, President Evo Morales, issued the 'Nationalization' Supreme Decree No 28,701 (SD), which in effect gave the State control of the entire commercial and production chain of the oil and gas sector and required IOCs to renegotiate their contracts with Bolivia so that YPFB could hold the majority control. For the Venezuelan experience, see Fry and Ibrahim, 2013. For the case of Bolivia, see Ribeiro, 2009.

Furthermore, it is instructive that while NOGICDA enjoins Nigerian firms to be considered in contracting, it does not exclusively confer benefits on them, perhaps except with regards to service firms operating in swamp areas and on land.[55] But even here, they must demonstrate ownership of equipment and personnel in order to be exclusively considered. What is being alluded to here is that while the Act appears to have 'shut' the gate on foreign IOCs and their service partners, an incisive scrutiny will reveal that they still have considerable roles to play in the NPI. The dominance of foreign firms in offshore operations which ordinarily requires more funds, as well as advanced technology for example, will remain for a considerable time to come. Furthermore, foreign firms still have a chance to compete in the NPI, and their chances are even brighter if they collaborate with local firms. Then there is the fact that IOCs and foreign elements operating in the NPI have been known to take advantage of certain leakages in the Nigerian system, which is made possible by weak enforcement of laws and regulations.[56] In the final analysis, perhaps all that countries such as Nigeria, Ghana, Angola, and Tanzania have sought to do in enacting protectionist LCRs is to create a chance for the 'consideration' of local suppliers who demonstrate capacity and own relevant equipment. And it is contended that they have a moral justification to do so.

The question is, would LCRs not give rise to reciprocal treatments from the developed countries of America and Europe? This possibility is low due primarily to the fact that several developing countries trade mainly in natural resources rather than in finished goods. Hence they stand to lose little from reciprocal protectionist measures which may be taken against them by their developed counterparts. The risk of retaliation would have been stronger if Nigeria or Ghana were major trading nations such as Britain, Japan, Germany, or the USA, etc. Then there would be a high possibility that their LCRs would have been visited with a backlash. For example, the ongoing American-Europe trade disagreement, and the American-China trade disputes have resulted in reciprocal treatments mainly because these countries trade in finished goods among themselves.[57] Again, it should be pointed out that several countries which are staunch proponents of free trade have also resorted to some form of protectionism either directly via tariffs, or via local content measures.[58] The revival of American protectionism as manifested in imposed, or threatened tariffs on imports from Mexico, Canada, China, and the

55 S.3(2).

56 Okafor and Aniche, 2014, at p 87. See also Umoru, 2018.

57 John, 2018, see also Banks, 2018.

58 The USA, for instance, enacted the American Recovery and Reinvestment Act of 2009 (ARRA), which required all iron and steel procured using ARRA stimulus funds be produced domestically. India's National Solar Mission is another local content initiative, under which feed-in tariffs and power purchase agreements are extended by the Indian government to solar developers under conditions that solar photovoltaic projects utilize cells and modules manufactured in India, with some exceptions. See Cimino, Hufbauer and Schott, 2014. Canada had also recently applied Ontario's Feed-in Tariffs programme, although it was challenged as being in violation of the country's obligations under Art.2.1 of the TRIMs Agreement, and Art.3.4 of the GATT in the case of *Canada – Renewable Energy. See Canada – Certain Measures Affecting the*

European Union, all indicate the country's desire to become 'Great Again'. The argument that free trade can be unfair to domestic businesses was cited by Donald Trump in his objections against the North American Free Trade Agreement (NAFTA) and the America-EU free trade agreements. The American example demonstrates that even the most viable economies in the world are now placing local industries[59] first in their interactions with the outside world.

The question is, if America, with its size, manpower, and capacity can resort to protectionism on the basis that free trade is unfair, is it not understandable that developing African PPCs would resort to protectionist LCRs in their desire to create some space for local firms to secure jobs in their petroleum industries? The truth remains that free trade has not always benefitted many developing countries. Some Latin American countries which experimented with it in the 1980 and 1990s were no better off at the end. In fact, the liberal economic policies they adopted were later perceived as not doing enough to address the wide gap between the rich and the poor, resulting in the region having one of the widest unequal income distributions in the world at that time.[60] In the end, it created a perception in Latin America that trade liberalisation agreements are exploitative and imperialistic.[61] It also justified the resurgence of protectionism in the region in the form of nationalisation of foreign assets, and renegotiation of previously concluded contracts entered with multinational firms.[62] While not advocating the extreme measures of Bolivia and Venezuela, it is still important that some level of protectionism be inserted for developing countries which require participation as a means of developing capacity and expertise, over time.

Still relying on the developing countries argument, it is instructive to note that one of the guiding principles of the WTO system is the desire to protect developing countries, in view of their economic limitations.[63] This explains why special and differential treatments are allowed for them in certain cases.[64] Thus developing countries were thus given longer time periods to implement agreements and commitments. The WTO system also requires its members to safeguard the trade

Renewable Energy Generation Sector Appellate Body Report, WT/DS412/AB/R, DS426/AB/R (6 May 2013).

59 Wingrove and Olorunnipa, 2018.

60 Levitsky and Roberts, 2011, at p 7.

61 See Veltmeyer, 2008, at p 140.

62 See n 54.

63 See the preamble to the Marrakesh Agreement, which established the WTO. See also the DOHA WTO Ministerial Declaration (2001) WT/MIN(01)/DEC/1 which, in recognition of the fact that majority of WTO members are developing countries, sought to place their needs and interests at the heart of the Work Programme adopted in the Declaration. Making Reference to the Preamble to the Marrakesh Agreement, there was an express commitment to continue to make positive efforts designed to ensure that developing countries, and especially the least-developed among them, secure a share in the growth of world trade commensurate with the needs of their economic development, see https://www.wto.org/english/thewto_e/minist_e/min01_e/mindecl_e.htm, accessed 11 July 2018.

64 For example, under Part 4 of the GATT, developed countries are not to expect developing countries to reciprocate with match making offers.

interests of developing countries, as well as support to help developing countries develop capacity to carry out WTO work.[65] Furthermore, some other initiatives which have been put in place at the WTO system tend to support the need to protect developing countries. For example, there was a 1996 Plan of Action for Least Developed Countries, which included technical assistance to enable them participate better in the multilateral system as well as a pledge from developed countries to improved market access for least-developed countries' products.[66] And in 2002, there was a work programme for least-developed countries which deals with matters such as: improved market access, technical assistance, and provision of support for agencies working on the diversification of least-developed countries' economies, etc.[67]

Perhaps in the end what is needed is mutual respect of the aspirations of developing PPCs, on the one hand, and the entrepreneurial drive of capital and technology exporting countries, on the other. A partnership based on trust and mutuality is what is needed. Interestingly, it appears that IOCs and their service counterparts have accepted the inevitable and are adapting to same, while academics of the liberal bent are still dealing with semantics and idealism. In the end, things come down to their level. Market forces, reality, and competition, are able to better discipline LCRs than the international trade system. The Brazilian example is a case in hand, as seen earlier. The country was not 'forced' by any threat of sanctions or retaliation, but when faced with market realities, it toned down on its protectionism. In the end, that is perhaps what would happen in Africa.

7.5 Conclusion

The extent to which protectionist LCRs infringe on international trade law has been the focus of this chapter. The chapter assessed the international free trade obligations of African PPCs in the light of the WTO system (GATT, GATS, ASCM, TRIMS, etc.) and BITs. Using NOGICDA as a case study, it concluded that certain provisions of the Act may infringe Nigeria's trade obligations and may expose the country to retaliatory actions. It also noted that the Act may make Nigeria unattractive as an investment destination in an industry where the competition for capital is intense. Even at that, it was shown that LCRs have continued to rise due to a number of factors which include lapses in the WTO system, the fact that a number of countries also have protectionist measures in place, and the fact that companies often comply quietly rather than complain. Lastly, the chapter made a case for the continued retention of NOGICDA as it is, particularly because of Nigeria's weak position as a developing country.

65 WTO, 'Special and Differential Treatment Provisions' https://www.wto.org/english/tratop_e/devel_e/dev_special_differential_provisions_e.htm, accessed 11 July 2018.

66 https://www.wto.org/english/tratop_e/devel_e/action_plan.htm, accessed 11 July 2018.

67 WT/COMT/LDC/11.

A work of this nature would be incomplete if it does not address the importance of national oil companies (NOCs) in the advancement of local content. NOCs all over the world, from Nigeria, Pertamina, Petrobras, Aramco, Petronas, NIOC of Iran, Sonangol, to Statoil, are involved in one way or another in the advancement of local content in their home states. As such, it is important to understand, first, why these mammoth firms were established in the first place, the strategies they have employed in the advancement of local content, and the challenges and limitations that they have faced. The following chapter therefore concentrates on local NOCs and local content development.

Bibliography

Ali A, 'Non-Compliance and Ultimate Remedies Under the WTO Dispute Settlement System' (2003) 14 *Journal of Public and International Affairs*, 1 https://jpia.princeton.edu/sites/jpia/files/2003-1.pdf, accessed 10 December 2016.

Atsegbua LA, 'The Nigerian Oil and Gas Industry Content Development Act 2010: an examination of its Regulatory Framework' (2012) 36(4) *OPEC Energy Review*, 479.

Ayoola OT, 'Nigerian Oil and Gas Industry Content Development Act's Perceived Performance Impact' (PhD Thesis, Walden University 2017).

Banks M, 'EU Braces for Trade War as US Announces Steel Tarrifs' *The Parliament Magazine* (9 March 2018).

Cimino C, Hufbauer GC and Schott JJ, 'A Proposed Code to Discipline Local Content Requirements' (2014) *Policy Brief No. PB14-6*, Petersen Institute for International Economics, https://piie.com/publications/pb/pb14-6.pdf, accessed 18 June 2018.

Cossy M, 'Determining "likeness" under the GATS: Squaring the circle?' (2006) *Working Paper of the Economic Research and Statistics Division of the WTO* https://ideas.repec.org/p/zbw/wtowps/ersd200608.html, accessed 11 July 2018.

Crosby DC, 'Energy Discrimination and International Rules in Hard Times: What's New This Time Around, and what can be done?' (2012) 5(4) *Journal of World Energy Law & Business*, 327.

Fry JD and Ibrahim E, 'Reassessing Venezuela's Organic Hydrocarbon Law: a Balance between Sovereignty and Efficiency?' (2013) 6(3) *Journal of World Energy Law & Business*, 234.

Hestermeyer HP and Nielsen L, 'The Legality of Local Content Measures under WTO' (2014) *Journal of World Trade*, 553.

Hudec R, 'The New WTO Dispute Settlement Procedure: An Overview of the First Three Years' (1999) 8 *M.J.I.L.*, 1.

Hudgins EL, 'Regional and Multilateral Trade Agreements: Complementary Means to Open Markets' (1996) 15 *Cato Journal*, 231.

Hufbauer G et al, *Local Content Requirements: Report on a Global Problem* (Peterson Inst. Intl. Econ, Washington DC, 2013).

Joffe G et al, 'Expropriation of Oil and Gas Investments: Historical, legal and economic perspectives in a New Age of Resource Nationalism' (2009) 2(1) *Journal of World Energy Law & Business*, 4.

John B, 'White House Hits China with New Tariffs, Ramping up Trade War' *Roll Call* (15 June 2018).

Langhammer RL, 'Multilateral Trade Liberalization among Developing Countries' (1980) 14 *Journal of World Trade Law*, 508.

Levitsky S and Roberts K, *The Resurgence of the Latin American Left* (Johns Hopkins University Press, Baltimore, 2011).

Ngoasong MZ, 'How International Oil and Gas Companies Respond to Local Content Policies in Petroleum-Producing Developing Countries: A Narrative Enquiry' (2014) 73 *Energy Policy*, 471.

Nwaokoro J, 'Beyond Legislation: a Contractual Alternative to Legislation local content in Nigeria' (2009) 18 *Currents: Int'l Trade L.J.*, 42.

Nwaokoro JE, 'Signed, Sealed but will it Deliver? Nigeria's local content Bill and Cross-Sectoral Growth' (2012) 4(1) *Journal of World Energy Law & Business*, 56.

Okafor J and Aniche E, 'A Critical Appraisal of Enforcement of Nigerian Oil and Gas Industry Content Development (NOGICD) Act, 2010' (2014) 31 *Journal of Law, Policy and Globalisation*, 82.

Ramdoo I, 'Unpacking Local Content Requirements in the Extractive Sector: What Implications for the Global Trade and Investment Frameworks?' (2015) *E15 Expert Group on Trade and Investment in Extractive Industries, Think Piece*, http://e15initiative.org/wp-content/uploads/2015/07/Extractive-Ramdoo-FINAL.pdf, accessed 9 January 2017.

Ravenhall J, 'APEC and the WTO: Which Way Forward for Trade Liberalization?' (1999) *Working Paper No. 11.*

Ribeiro MR, 'Sovereignty over Natural Resources Investment Law and Expropriation: The case of Bolivia and Brazil' (2009) 2 *Journal of World Energy Law & Business*, 139.

Salacuse S, 'The Treatification of International Investment Law' (2007) 13 *L. and Bus. Review Am.*, 155.

Schriver S, 'Sovereignty over Natural Resources: Balancing Rights and Duties in an Interdependent World' (PhD Thesis, University of Groningen, 1995), http://www.rug.nl/research/portal/files/3265518/dissertatie.pdf, accessed 11 July 2017.

Umoru H, '$16 Egina Probe: NASS to Amend Local Content Act' *Vanguard* (29 January 2018) https://www.vanguardngr.com/2018/01/16bn-egina-probe-nass-amend-local-content-act/H, accessed 22 February 2018.

Veltmeyer H, *New Perspectives on Globalization and Anti-Globalization: Prospects for a New World Order?* (Ashgate Publishing, Ashford, 2008).

Wingrove J and Olorunnipa T, 'Trump Repeats He'd Quit NAFTA and May Seek Separate Talks' *Bloomberg* (8 June 2018) https://www.bloomberg.com/news/articles/2018-06-08/trump-says-he-ll-quit-nafta-if-countries-can-t-reach-new-deal, accessed 15 August 2018.

8 National oil companies and local content development

8.1 The rise and relevance of national oil companies in the petroleum industry

A treatise of this nature would be incomplete without a discourse on the roles national oil companies (NOCs) play in advancing local content in petroleum producing countries (PPCs). This is because if African PPCs are going to succeed in implementing their local content policies, it would be important for them, first, to appreciate the relevance of NOCs in this respect, and, secondly, to understand what it would entail for them to channel the resources of these firms in the advancement of local content. But first it is pertinent to understand why most PPCs in the developing world adopt the NOC model.

It was shown in Chapter 1 that from the inception of the petroleum industry in the late 19th century up to the global oil crisis of in the early 1970s, most of the world's petroleum deposits were dominated by international oil companies (IOCs).[1] The larger part of the operations of these firms were carried out in the Middle East, South America, and Africa, through concessionary arrangements, most of which were awarded to them pre-1945. The terms of these arrangements were later deemed to be extremely unfavourable and unacceptable to their host states because they were couched in such a way as to give the IOCs virtual ownership and total control over the petroleum resources of their host states.[2] For example, the life span of an average concession awarded to IOCs in the Middle East during this period was considered to be quite extensive, coupled with the fact that their scope in terms of land mass was also disproportionately vast.[3] Furthermore, royalties which were paid by these IOCs to their hosts were predetermined, and

1 The most prominent of these IOCs, which had their principal places of business in Europe and North America, were termed the Seven Sisters by Enrico Mattei of Italian firm Eni. They include Anglo-Persian Oil Company (now BP), Gulf Oil, Standard Oil of California (now Chevron), Texaco, Royal Dutch Shell, Standard Oil of New Jersey (now Esso/Exxon), and Standard Oil Company of New York (now ExxonMobil). These firms together controlled around 85 percent of the world's petroleum reserves.

2 See Stevens, 2008, at p 10.

3 The average age of concessions signed in Iran, Iraq, Kuwait, and Saudi Arabia for instance, was 82 years and there were no relinquishment clauses. Again, about 88 percent of the combined national areas of the aforementioned four countries were covered

totally unrelated to the profits they made. This meant that little could be done by host countries to increase government take in the event of an upward swing in the prices of petroleum products. Another disquieting thing was that most of these IOCs did not operate under scheduled timelines and could thus sit on their acreages and do nothing by way of development for a long period of time.

After the Second World War, increasingly dissatisfied PPCs in the developing world, felt the need to renegotiate the terms under which they interacted with IOCs.[4] They were spurred on by the concept of permanent sovereignty over natural resources,[5] rising oil demand, and the clamour for a new economic world order. And as most of these countries, which perhaps with the exception of PPCs from South America, were colonies or mandate territories of European powers, became independent, they began to clamour for the right to control their natural resources. These agitations led to the formation of the Organisation of Petroleum Exporting Countries (OPEC) in 1960. OPEC was, and has remained, an oil cartel which protects and furthers the interests of its members in the global petroleum industry.[6] Keen to counter the dominance of IOCs, which were perceived as tools of neo-colonialism and imperialism, OPEC mandated its members to participate directly in their petroleum industries, largely through NOCs.[7] This gave rise to the establishment of NOCs among all OPEC members.

The rapid rise of NOCs among countries which control most of the world's petroleum resources (Saudi Arabia, Iran, Iraq, Venezuela, and Kuwait, etc.), signalled an irreversible shift in the control of global petroleum resources from IOCs to NOCs.[8] Currently, NOCs control over 80 percent of the world's hydrocarbon reserves, and 70 percent of daily crude oil

by concessions which were controlled by IOCs: this included the whole land mass of Iraq and Kuwait.

4 Stevens, 2008, at p 10.

5 The concept was embodied in UN Resolution 1803 of 1962, which recognised the permanent sovereignty of states over their natural resources. There was also UN Resolution 2158, which advised host countries to secure maximum exploitation of natural resources by the accelerated acquisition of full control over production operations, management and marketing, see http://www.refworld.org/docid/3b00f1c64.html, accessed 16 May 2018.

6 The founding members of OPEC included Iran, Iraq, Kuwait, Saudi Arabia, and Venezuela.

7 It is noteworthy, however, that the first NOC was established in 1908 by Austria. And in 1922 Argentina established YPF, while Mexico established Pemex in 1938 following its expropriation of the assets of some American and European firms operating in its terrain during this period.

8 Prior to 1971, IOCs controlled over 70 percent of the world's petroleum resources. This figure changed when OPEC was created, as NOCs began to dominate the industry and dominated over 79 percent of the world's petroleum. See W Rasheed, 'The Oil Curtain and the Evolution of National Oil Companies', *Journal of Petroleum Technology* (2009) http://www.spe.org/jpt/print/archives/2009/02/JPT2009_02_11Management.pdf, accessed 26 March 2016. It is not in question that the size and influence of NOCs have vastly increased over the last several decades. From controlling less than 10 percent of global petroleum reserves, as at 2012, that number had increased to more than 90 percent. See Leis et al, 2012.

production.[9] Today, virtually every PPC in the developing world participates directly in its petroleum industry through an NOC.[10] It is also interesting that even when developing PPCs turn to privatisation of moribund state owned enterprises as a means of shoring up revenues and turning around their performances, they have been reluctant to completely privatise their NOCs.[11] Some of the reasons why PPCs have continued to in their petroleum industries through NOCs are now considered.[12]

First is the desire to generate profits. Most NOCs are vertically integrated into the value chain of the petroleum industries of their home states. Their activities in exploration and production (E&P), to pipelines management, gas development, production, refining and marketing, shipping, and petrochemicals, etc., mean that NOCs are able to rake in billions of dollars annually which fund the budgets of several PPCs.[13] It is a fact that NOCs are the highest revenue earners for the governments of many PPCs. For example, Mexico's NOC, Pemex, besides having immense symbolic national importance, provides about one-third of the revenues of the government.[14] Similarly, Petronas remains the single-largest contributor to Malaysia's government revenues.[15] Other notable examples in which NOCs are the highest revenue earners for the governments of their home states include Saudi Arabia, Nigeria, Iran, Nigeria, Brazil, and Angola, etc.

PPCs also use NOCs to implement socioeconomic and welfarist objectives as a means of distributing petroleum wealth to their citizenry and furthering government policies.[16] This accounts for why these firms are routinely required to maximize 'the net present value of economic rents from production of petroleum, inter-temporal equity, and the promotion of backward and forward linkages …'.[17] Several NOCs subsidize petroleum at home, award scholarships, and invest in research. Embarking on socially inclined programmes also means that several NOCs are required to prioritise their socio-economic mandates over profitability, in contrast to private oil companies (POCs), which prioritize profits and shareholder maximisation. For example, Venezuela uses its NOC, PDVSA, to fund healthcare, housing, education, and other socially inclined programmes at great cost, in addition to subsidizing fuel.[18] Not surprisingly, these projects affect its

9 See Tordo, Tracy and Arfaa, 2011; Eller et al, 2007.

10 Even some developed countries have had NOCs at one time or another. They include the British National Oil Company which was later privatised in 1982, Statoil of Norway, and Italy's Eni (still part state owned).

11 The nearest some PPCs have come to privatising their NOCs is partial privatisation. From Brazil, Norway, Saudi Arabia, to Russia, and Nigeria, direct state participation remains the norm and practice.

12 See Eller et al, 2007.

13 See Noreng, 1997.

14 See Samples and Vittor, 2011, at p 216.

15 Tordo and Anouti, 2013, at p 139.

16 Tordo, Tracy and Arfaa, 2011, at p 6. Angola, for instance, uses Sonangol not only as a revenue earner, but as a political tool. For example, the firm financed most of Angola's long civil war against separatists and rebels. See Stevens, 2016.

17 Tordo, Tracy and Arfaa, 2011, at p 8.

18 See Fry and Ibrahim, 2013, at p 247.

profits outlook, with the firm losing one-quarter of its revenues to fuel subsidies and oil imports.[19] Like Venezuela, NNPC, Sonangol, Petrobras, and a host of other NOCs have, at one time or another, been used to sell petroleum to the public at subsidized rates, causing significant economic losses to their home states.[20]

Thirdly, PPCs retain ownership of NOCs in their desire to secure the supply of petroleum products for domestic use, and to ensure 'oil sovereignty'. For many PPCs, it was thought that leaving such a strategic asset as petroleum in the 'hands' of IOCs would make PPCs vulnerable in the event of war, and sanctions, etc. For example, were Russia and Iran not directly involved in their petroleum industries through Gazprom/Rosneft or NIOC, respectively, both countries would have fared worse in the wake of sanctions which were recently imposed on both countries by the USA and its allies in Western Europe.[21]

Then there is the regulation and monitoring factor.[22] The complexities surrounding petroleum E&P often make it difficult for formal administrative regulators to have access to adequate and relevant information concerning the operations of petroleum firms.[23] These regulators invariably rely on petroleum firms for information, and sometimes for the logistics which they require to be effective in the discharge of their duties.[24] And while this reliance on petroleum

19 Hernández, 2018.

20 For example, Sonangol takes on other responsibilities geared towards public benefits such as the provision of low cost housing. See E Cropley, 'Exclusive: Isabel dos Santos Pledges Transparency, Efficiency at Angolan state Oil Giant' *Reuters* (9 June 2016) http://uk.reuters.com/article/us-angola-sonangol-exclusive/exclusive-isabel-dos-santos-pledges-transparency-efficiency-at-angolan-state-oil-giant-idUKKCN0YV26V, accessed 11 October 2017. Similarly, NNPC has recently diversified into Nigeria's health sector. NNPC, 'NNPC Commences Diversification into Health Sector' (21 April 2017) http://nnpcgroup.com/PublicRelations/NNPCinthenews/tabid/92/articleType/ArticleView/articleId/763/NNPC-Commences-Diversification-into-Health-Sector.aspx, accessed 11 October 2017.

21 Russia is currently facing sanctions because of its invasion of Ukraine in 2014. See Wang, 2015. Like Russia, Iran was subjected to a series of sanctions which, among other things, targeted its petroleum industry and, in essence, barred European and American firms from doing business with Iran. Despite these sanctions, the firm was able to maintain Iran's petroleum industry, albeit under some strain. See generally Brumberg and Ahram, 2007.

22 Some NOCs in the Middle East include the Kuwait Petroleum Company, Saudi Aramco, the National Iranian Oil Company (NIOC), and the Iraq National Oil Company.

23 Even in the USA, which has an extensive regulatory framework manned by competent regulatory personnel, regulating IOCs has proved difficult in some instances. In the wake of the BP Gulf of Mexico oil spill in 2010, it was reported that the now disbanded Minerals Management Service which regulated offshore exploration, 'captured' by BP. The regulator relied extensively on the regulated for information and logistics. See '"Shared Failure" in BP Spill Cited in Panel Report: Reforms Needed Since "Oversight Utterly Failed", Says Co-chair of Obama Commission', nbcnews.com (1 November 2011), http://www.nbcnews.com/id/41020738/ns/us_news-environment/t/shared-failure-bp-spill-cited-panel-report/, accessed 12 October 2016 ('Shared Failure').

24 Ibid.

firms occurs in developed[25] and developing countries alike, it is more pronounced in the latter, where regulators routinely struggle with weak capacity and funding challenges. Regulatory reliance on petroleum firms for crucial information was even more pronounced prior to the establishment of NOCs in many developing countries. In the Middle East, for example, the extensive domination of IOCs in the decades leading up to the formation of OPEC made it extremely difficult for countries such as Saudi Arabia, Iran, and Kuwait, to access relevant information about the operations of IOCs.[26] This hindered their capacity to monitor the operations of IOCs, and it invariably weakened regulation.[27]

The direct participation of PPCs in the operations of IOCs through collaborations with NOCs was designed to address this limitation. Unlike formal arm's length regulators, NOCs were better positioned to monitor their partners by virtue of their closeness with the industry. Their creation thus bridged information gaps and created room for more sustainable and efficient monitoring arrangements.[28] NOCs are thus able to insist that their IOC partners comply with safety and environmental regulations. That said, not all NOCs were successful in harnessing their capabilities to the benefit of their home states. In this light, the weaknesses of NNPC were considered earlier in Chapter 3.[29]

Finally, PPCs participate directly via NOCs in order to use them as institutional vehicles for the promotion of local content. These firms are thus used to spearhead the backward and frontward linkages between the industry and the rest of the economy of their home states. The rest of this chapter explores the role of NOCs in local content development, and the challenges they face in so doing.

The importance and types of institutional frameworks adopted by PPCs in relation to the advancement of local content are discussed in Chapter 2. [30] The chapter shows that the NOC model is the most widely adopted strategy among developing countries, and that among countries which establish NOCs, there are two primary submodels. First, there is the fused model, where NOCs act as operators, regulators, and in some cases, policy makers. Malaysia, Angola,[31] Saudi Arabia, Algeria, and Nigeria have all at one time or another adopted the fused model approach in their petroleum industries.[32] The merit of adopting the fused model is that it reduces inter-agency strife/in-fighting, saves cost, and perhaps time as well. Its danger lies in the fact that exclusive reliance on NOCs may increase the risk of such firms becoming too powerful to control. Such firms may thus end up acting as a state within a state. Where

25 Ibid.
26 Stevens, 2008, at p 14.
27 See Stevens, 2008, at p 15.
28 See Grayson, 1981, at p 199.
29 Chapter 3, 3.2.
30 See Chapter 2 in general.
31 See Chapter 2, 2.2.
32 Despite having formal regulators over the petroleum industries, the vast majority of these countries rely almost entirely on their NOCs to drive local content. Nigeria adopted this model between 1977 and 1988 following the merger of NNOC and DPR into NNPC. NNPC was thus responsible for policy formulation, regulation, partnering with IOCs, and sometimes functioned as an operator in its own right.

that is the case, rather than facilitate local content and other government policies, they may focus on furthering narrow and corrupt interests. For instance Venezuela's NOC, PDVSA, which spearheads the petroleum industry policies of that country, was once perceived as being too powerful. Constantly at loggerheads with the late President Hugo Chavez, it became subjected to reforms which led to the sacking of about 20 percent of its employees and most of its management staff.[33] In the same vein, Nigeria's NNPC, which was largely responsible for local content development prior to NOGICDA, has been difficult to control by the government, and is largely unaccountable.[34]

In contrast to the fused model approach, countries such as Brazil and Norway attempt to combine the efforts of their NOCs with those of formal regulators.[35] In essence, these countries confer responsibilities for policy, operatorship, and regulation on three separate institutions. What this means is that although some form of collaboration may exist between these NOCs and regulators, the roles carried out by each entity are discernible and separate. This enables some form of regulatory independence, and also strengthens NOC focus. It may, however, be more costly for governments to run combined NOCs and regulatory agencies, besides, this approach may engender delays for petroleum firms, as well as inter-agency competition. There is also the risk of the regulator being captured by the NOC, while the NOC's closeness to the regulator and, by extension, to the government, may weaken its autonomy.

Irrespective of the NOC model adopted by a PPC, its criticality to fostering local content at home is indisputable. NOCs can be used to facilitate the growth of local content in three primary ways. First, they may take advantage of their collaborations with E&P firms to insist on the patronage of domestic industries. Secondly, they may directly patronise domestic suppliers and service firms, and create employment for their citizens. Thirdly, NOCs may further local content through indirect initiatives (investing in technology, scholarships, and providing funds for local firms, etc.) geared towards the development of human capacity and the acquisition of relevant technology. The strategies employed by NOCs in the advancement of local content are now considered in detail.

8.2 Strategies employed by NOCs in furthering local content at home

First, NOCs advance local content by harnessing their collaborations with E&P firms. It is usual for PPCs to vest joint upstream rights on NOCs and E&P firms. In other instances, they may vest the title of the concession on the NOC, which will in turn collaborate with E&P firms through production sharing contracts

33 See Hults, 2012, at p 418; see also Fry and Ibrahim, 2013.

34 House of Representatives, 'Report of the Ad-Hoc Committee to verify and determine the actual Subsidy Requirements and Monitor the Implementation of the Subsidy Regime in Nigeria' (Rstn No. HR.1/2012) http://premiumtimesng.com/news/4747-premium_times_presents_the_full_oil_subsidy_probe_report.html, accessed 4 January 2017.

35 See n 32.

(PSCs). Irrespective of the approach adopted, these collaborations are implemented under frameworks which vest NOCs with powers to approve or veto the budgets and operating expenses of their partners (who often double as operators of these concessions). This power to veto or approve budgets and operating expenses places NOCs in a position to insist on compliance with local content requirements (LCRs) geared towards ensuring the patronage of locally produced goods and services.

Collaborative relationships abound in Nigeria, Angola, Algeria, Brazil, and Equatorial Guinea, etc. For example, NNPC collaborates with IOCs primarily via joint ventures (JVs) and PSCs in pursuance to joint operating agreements (JOA) which regulate their working relationships. A typical JOA would contain LCRs which NNPC's IOC partners would be required to comply with in their contracting and purchasing. For instance, clause 8(l) of the Model PSC which guides NNPC's interactions with IOCs, requires the latter to give preference to goods which are available in Nigeria, or services rendered by Nigerian nationals, provided the goods meet industry standards, and the services rendered, are of good quality, are offered at competitive prices, and are timely available. In a similar vein, clause 5.1 of the same Model PSC provides that:

> within two (2) months after the Effective Date and thereafter at least three (3) months prior to the beginning of each Year, the CONTRACTOR [IOC] shall prepare and submit for review and approval by the Management Committee, pursuant to Clause 6, a Work Programme and Budget for the Contract Area setting forth the Petroleum Operations which CONTRACTOR proposes to carry out during the ensuring Year, or in the case of first Work Programme and Budget, during the remainder of the current Year. The Management Committee shall review and approve such Work Programme and budget in accordance with Clause 6.3(e) prior to submission of the Work Programme and Budget to the Ministry.

In order to ensure equitable representation of the interest of all the collaborating parties, JOAs usually establish joint operating committees (JOCs), comprising of NOCs and their partners. Customarily, the position of chairman of the JOC would be reserved for the NOC, or a representative of the government who would also have veto powers in certain cases. JOCs are crucial to growing local content because they monitor and approve the work programmes and budgets of E&P firms with respect to JV/PSC operations. What this means is that membership of JOCs thus uniquely positions NOCs to support local content, first, by insisting on the patronage of local supplies and services, and, secondly, by vetoing contracts which do not comply with the minimum LCRs contained either in the law (NOGICDA, for example), or in the JOA.

The strategic positioning of NOCS notwithstanding, their functionality, commitment, and efficiency are a prerequisite to their effectiveness in driving local content. As such, an NOC may not further local content despite its strategic powers, either because it lacks the capacity to do so, or because it is corrupt. Other factors that may weaken its success include conflict of interest issues, or capture by its partners. This perhaps explains why despite its enormous powers, NNPC was unable to drive the Nigerian content pre-NOGICDA.[36] In contrast to NNPC, some other NOCs have made strides in growing local content by harnessing their strengths and unique positions in order to ensure that their E&P partners comply with LCRs. Angola's Sonangol and Malaysia's Petronas are two such examples.

After Libya and Nigeria, Angola has the third highest crude oil reserves in Africa.[37] The country relies extensively on Sonangol, a firm which is vertically integrated in every aspect of Angola's petroleum industry, while also functioning as industry regulator and asset manager. Although it is surrounded by an environment rife with corruption and inefficiency, Sonangol has, surprisingly, striven to protect Angola's interests in its petroleum industry in an efficient manner.[38] Unlike the larger number of African NOCs which do not operate abroad, the firm has been able to expand its operations into Brazil and Iraq.[39] Thurber et al note that '… flying in the face of the canonical Norwegian Model, Angola has managed to build a highly productive petroleum sector by means of Sonangol acting as a single multipurpose agent, achieving steady growth in production and reserves over the last several decades'.[40] Attesting to this fact, Al-Kasim et al also observe that the Angolan '… regime is generally perceived as corrupt, but while the population suffers from welfare negligence, the oil sector is perceived to be professionally managed with better control systems than oil sectors in neighbouring countries'.[41]

Angola's local content regime can be found in a series of petroleum related laws, and in commitments contained in PSCs.[42] For example, Article 27 of Angola's Petroleum Activities Law 10/2004 requires companies to procure goods and services from Angolan providers where they are of the same or approximately the same quality as what is available on international markets, and where their prices do not exceed what is offered by their foreign competitors by a 10 per cent margin. Commenting on this Article, Heller notes that 'in reality, the operating committees and other technical units of Sonangol actually push operating

36 Nwaokoro, 2012, at p 63.

37 Proven reserves are estimated at around nine billion barrels, see OPEC, 'Angola: Facts and Figures' http://www.opec.org/opec_web/en/about_us/147.htm, accessed 17 May 2017.

38 See Soares de Oliveira, 2007.

39 For more readings, see Clarke, 2010, at pp 115–135; see also Oliveira, 2015. See also Stratfor Global Intelligence, 2014.

40 Thurber et al, 2011.

41 Al-Kasim, Søreide T and Williams, 2010, at p 21.

42 They include the General Petroleum Activities Law, with No. 10/2004, A Customs and Taxation Law with Law No. 11/04, Decree No. 48/2006, which contains Rules and Procedures of Public Procurement Competitions in the Petroleum Sector. There is the Training Law with No. 116/2008 which relates to capacity building for local content development, another Training Decree Law with No. 17/2009, and there is an Executive Decree with No. 14/2010, which relates to the Functioning and Management of the Petroleum Training Fund.

companies to contract locally at far higher thresholds'.[43] Sonangol is also vested with extensive PSC powers which it utilises to further the Angolan content. For example, because it must approve the majority of the procurements related to these PSCs, the firm shortlists companies before they bid for supply or service contracts. According to Ovadia:

> Sonangol's strength and dominance over the Angolan oil sector has in practice allowed D.PRO and DEC[44] to put pressure on operating companies to not only accept a 10% difference, but to take differences of 20–30% in some cases. Sonangol also has strong powers to enforce local content because it can give preferential treatment to any company it chooses-not just those with 51% Angolan ownership. Sonangol can examine where materials will be made, where goods will be assembled, and who the subcontractors will be. Even a 100% foreign company can get preferential treatment, and can even get the 10% difference allowed to national companies, if it is making products in Angola or incorporating a large amount of local content. Taken together, the legal framework provided by legislation and the PSA regime not only enable the government to promote local content in the Angolan oil industry, but also enable the presidency, through Sonangol, to exercise enormous influence over billions of dollars spent annually by the IOCs on service contracts.[45]

Corroborating Ovadia, Heller observes that while 'local content and local staffing are important goals of most NOCs that work with international partners … most international officials who work in Angola indicate that Sonangol is tougher about local content and places more emphasis on it than counterpart companies in other countries'.[46]

Like Sonangol, Malaysia relies extensively on Petronas for the monitoring of its PSC partners in order to ensure compliance with local content regulations. It is usual for the firm, as Malaysia's NOC, to insist that priority be given to Malaysian firms in contracts for procurements, supplies, and services. In fact, in Malaysia, contracts may only be awarded to foreign firms where there are no Malaysian firms available to execute such jobs. Furthermore, all firms which desire to execute oil servicing contracts in Malaysia must be licensed by Petronas, after fulfilling specified requirements.[47] From its vantage position, Petronas is able to insist that its PSC partners 'comply with the national objective of maximizing Malaysian participation in the use of local equipment, facilities, goods, materials, supplies and services in petroleum operations'.[48]

43 Heller, 2012.
44 These are its Directorate of Production and Directorate of Economy and Concessions.
45 Ovadia, 2012.
46 Heller, 2012, at p 865.
47 Heller, 2012, at p 64.
48 Bank Pembangunan, 'Report On Malaysia Oil and Gas Exploration and Production' (2011) http://www.bpmb.com.my/GUI/pdf/annual_report/2011/20.pdf, at p 63.

The Sonangol and Petronas examples demonstrate that committed and efficient NOCs can actually ramp up the promotion of local content by harnessing their strategic positions. For this to happen, the managers of such firms should be made to fully appreciate the value of local content, and to ensure that their goals align with those of their home states.

Besides monitoring their JV/PSC partners, NOCs may also drive local content by patronising locally made goods and services in their sole operations. NOCs which play dominant operator roles in their home states, such as Petrobras, Statoil, Aramco, NIOC, Petronas, and Sonatrach, are in a stronger position to patronise local industries than NOCs which have minor operator roles. The fact that they are state owned should also make it easier for their home states to require them to give preference to local suppliers. Sadly, this is not always the case. In fact, some NOCs may not enthusiastically pursue the local content policies of their home states if their managers consider LCRs as being unrealistic, in the light of capacity challenges. Where such is the case, these firms may either use their influence to request that the requirements be relaxed or waived, or in extreme cases, they may violate them. What this means is that even in those countries where PPCs have adequate in-country capacity, their NOCs may elect to patronise foreign suppliers and service companies, either for selfish corrupt reasons, or where they consider such foreign goods and services as being far superior to locally produced goods. In essence, weakly regulated NOCs may not necessarily advance local content. NOCs may also advance local content through direct employment. Because these firms are unusually large, and comprise of several subsidiaries, they are thus positioned to employ an appreciable number of persons at home. For instance, Petrochina has about 548,355 employees, while Gazprom, Pemex, Lukoil, Rosneft, and Sonatrach have about 404,400, 150,884, 150,000, 106,000, and 41,204, employees, respectively.[49]

NOCs may also foster local content by initiating a host of other programmes which have a bearing on the development of local content such as the provision of loans for local suppliers and service firms or the provision of a database of local suppliers. In this regard, Chapter 4 shows that NNPC established the Joint Qualification System through which it created a database of local suppliers and services in the industry, and made same available to petroleum firms for the facilitation of the contracting and the streamlining of the prequalification process.[50]

8.3 NOCs and the acquisition and development of petroleum related technology

NOCs may indirectly drive local content by promoting research and developing petroleum related technology. In this regard, an efficiently run NOC is a strategic

49 'Top 20 Largest Oil & Gas Employers' *The Oil and Gas Post* http://www.oilgaspost.com/2013/04/25/top-20-largest-oil-gas-employers/, accessed 15 September 2016.

50 NNPC, 'Nigerian Content Implementation Framework' http://www.nigcontent.com/index.php?option¼com_content&task¼view&id¼30&Itemid¼57#4, accessed 9 March 2016.

asset for the development and acquisition of petroleum related technology. It is a fact that the technology-intensive nature of the petroleum industry makes the acquisition of up-to-date technologies not only necessary, but also imperative. And as petroleum firms increasingly operate in difficult terrains such as swamps, and deep and ultra-deep offshore frontiers, there is the need for sustained investment to ensure that relevant technologies are acquired to tackle the challenges of the industry. This means that PPCs which seek to exercise functional dominion over their petroleum industries in areas such as drilling, fabrication, supply, and services, etc., may have to sustain their investment in training and retraining in order to produce skilled human capacity to meet the needs of the industry. For that purpose, some have established well-funded research centres which collaborate with the industry and academia, in addition to funding research, and awarding scholarships, etc. And because NOCs are often repertoires of vast amount of funds, they are often used by their home states in financing these initiatives. Besides, these funds are routinely invested in research and development (R&D), and are used to promote human capacity development through the training and retraining of local personnel.[51] These technologies may ultimately benefit local content.

Furthermore, NOCs are in a position to harness their collaborations with E&P firms in order to ensure some degree of technology transfer for the benefit of their home countries. Thus an NOC may build capacity and acquire relevant technology by understudying its partners in the course of JV/PSC collaborations, which it can use to further local content over time. Statoil and Petronas, for example, were able to build their capabilities by making the most of their collaborations with IOCs.[52] In addition to promoting local content, the acquisition of petroleum related technological knowledge and expertise by NOCs also results in the training of local personnel. These personnel thus empowered can be employed in regulatory and policy making institutions, while the technological expertise acquired can also be relayed back to other economic sectors such as shipping, steel, manufacturing, and fabrication, etc.[53] This accounts for why NOCs which have acquired petroleum related technology sometimes veer off into petrochemicals, fertilizers, ethanol, construction, and aviation, etc. The chapter now considers

51 S.5(1)f of the NNPC Act 1977 authorises NNPC to carry out research relevant to petroleum activities. Similarly Brazil's Law 12.276 of 2010, which regulates the capitalisation of Petrobras, authorises the federal government to cede at a cost to Petrobras the exercise of research and production of oil, natural gas, and other fluid hydrocarbons in the areas of pre-salt.

52 For example, although Statoil began to collaborate with IOCs in the early 1970s, it was only in 1981 that it operated its first Gullfaks field. See Olsen, 2013, at p 619.

53 Countries such as Norway, Malaysia, and Brazil relied extensively on their NOCs in furthering their technological advances. For instance, Petronas has established a university of technology, the Universiti Teknologi Petronas (UTP), see UTP, 'About Us' https://www.utp.edu.my/The%20University/About-Us/SitePages/Home.aspx, accessed 22 November 2016. While in 2011, Brazil budgeted $4.5 billion for R&D alone. See also B Ellsworth, 'Brazil's Petrobras to invest $4.5 billion in research' *Reuters* (11 February 2011) https://www.reuters.com/article/petrobras-rd/brazils-petrobras-to-invest-4-5-billion-in-research-idUSN0413807520110204, accessed 21 July 2018.

some of the strategies employed by some selected NOCs in fostering petroleum related technology and building human capacity.

First, there is Petrobras of Brazil, which following its establishment in 1953, set about realizing its objective of becoming the sole driver of the Brazilian Petroleum Industry. To that end, it invested heavily in R&D and concentrated on cultivating indigenous technology. As far back as 1955, the firm established a centre for the promotion of innovative technologies and for manpower development.[54] The centre, which today is reputed as being the largest research centre in the southern hemisphere, has remained closely integrated within the firm's operations and strategic objectives, and has recorded some notable breakthroughs in the field of petroleum technology.[55] Currently, it engages more than 600 professionals who hold master's and doctorate degrees in the conduct of R&D as well as in other engineering activities. Petrobras has also developed E&P solutions such as basin mapping and old field revitalization processes. The firm also continues to invest heavily in the centre in its bid to produce capable manpower for the furthering of the Brazilian content.[56]

Petrobras also collaborates with universities and research institutions all over Brazil in funding local and overseas scholarships.[57] Some of these collaborations have resulted in a better understanding of how ocean waves and currents affect the operations of floating platforms, while anchored hundreds of kilometres from the coast.[58] In 2016 alone, the firm invested over $1.8 billion in R&D.[59] That these massive investments in R&D have paid off is evidenced from the fact that Petrobras is globally recognised as having appreciable expertise in deep-water and ultra-deep-water E&P.[60]

Like Petrobras, Saudi Aramco invests heavily in R&D. It currently has 11 operational research centres and technology offices worldwide. In 2015 alone, the firm obtained 123 patents from the US Patent and Trademark Office.[61] Recognising the need for training in order to bridge experience and knowledge gaps in

54 Petrobras, 'Technology and Innovation' http://www.petrobras.com/en/energy-and-technology/technology-and-research/, accessed 9 August 2016.

55 They include: first offshore oil discovery in the Guaricema field in 1968, geological mapping of the national coast in 1978, setting the new world record of deep-water oil in 1999, designing of a new concept of building floating platforms on a single column in 2005, and pre-salt discoveries in 2007. See Tordo and Anouti, 2013, at p 52.

56 Wertheim and Abrantes, 2015.

57 See Oliveira, 2012, at p 515.

58 Petrobras, 'Technology and Innovation' (n 19).

59 Petrobras, 'Sustainability Report' (2016) http://www.petrobras.com.br/en/society-and-environment/sustainability-report/, accessed 11 March 2017.

60 Petrobras won the Offshore Technology Conference (OTC) merit award in 1992, 2001 and 2015 for its exploits in deep water technology, see http://www.otcnet.org/Content/OTC-Distinguished-Achievement-Awards-for-Companies-Organizations-and-Institutions, accessed 6 November 2016.

61 Aramco, 'A Focus on Technology', http://www.saudiaramco.com/en/home/innovation/research-centres.html, accessed 20 October 2016.

the industry, Saudi Aramco established an Upstream Professional Development Centre, which provides integrated training programmes for its workforce.[62]

Petronas of Malaysia is another NOC which invests heavily in R&D and in human capacity development as part of its overall strategy. It established a research fund into which all its PSC partners are required to contribute 0.5 percent of their cost oil and profit oil.[63] The firm has also invested heavily in building a skilled workforce and relevant technology. In 1997, Petronas established the Universiti Teknologi Petronas (UTP) as a fully owned subsidiary for the furtherance of research in areas such as enhanced oil recovery, and carbon dioxide management. Other areas of research conducted by the university include deep-water technology, nanotechnology, green technology, biomedical technology, hybrid energy systems, intelligent cities, and sustainable resources, etc.[64]

Adopting a similar approach, Norway, from the inception of its petroleum industry, used Statoil as a conduit for technology transfer and economic growth,[65] and Statoil continues to invest heavily in R&D.[66] Its R&D endeavours are organised around three research centres and a five-pronged research programme which includes exploration, enhanced recovery, development of new solutions, oil and gas processing, and new energy and new ideas.[67]

8.4 Discussions and analysis

The roles NOCs play in furthering local content have been the focus of this chapter. It was seen that these firms can take advantage of their collaborations with E&P firms to insist on the patronage of indigenous supply and service firms. In addition, they may also support local content policies by ensuring that they utilise domestic suppliers, employ their citizens, and by instituting initiatives such as investment in R&D, and funding scholarships, etc. Because of their viability, size, and strategic relations with private petroleum firms, they are often suited for the furtherance of local content in their home country.

In spite of arguments against them, NOCs remain relevant for many developing countries which are yet to reap the full benefits of the industrial

62 Aramco, 'Preparing Employees for Challenges Ahead' http://www.saudiaramco.com/en/home/innovation/stories-of-progress/preparing-employees-for-challenges-ahead.html, accessed 7 November 2016.

63 Under Art.9.1 of its Model PSC. See 'Local Content: Malaysia' (2014) Columbia Centre on Sustainable Investment http://ccsi.columbia.edu/files/2014/03/Local-Content-Malaysia-Petroleum-CCSI-Sept-2016.pdf, accessed 22 November 2016.

64 UTP, 'About Us' https://www.utp.edu.my/The%20University/About-Us/SitePages/Home.aspx, accessed 7 November 2016.

65 Gordon and Stenvoll, 2007, at p 23.

66 It is estimated that Statoil invests about 2 billion Kroner annually on R&D, an amount in excess of $200 million See Statoil, 'R&D Program' http://www.statoil.com/en/technologyinnovation/technologymanagement/FoUprogram/Pages/FoUprogram.aspx, accessed 21 November 2016.

67 Ibid.

revolution.[68] This is particularly so in Africa. The absence of strong government regulators and developed service sectors means that, for some time to come, NOCs will continue to play important roles in furthering of local content in their home states. The success of these firms in driving local content is, nevertheless, dependent on whether certain crucial elements are in place. To start with, these firms should be competent, capable, and competitive. They should also be focused and committed, while issues such as corruption and nepotism should be reduced to a minimum. Lastly, African PPCs should devise ways of checking their NOCs in order to ensure that they remain committed to advancing local content.

The point being put forward here is that NOCs do not always further local content in their home states. It is, in fact, interesting that NOCs may be less enthusiastic than IOCs on the need to develop local capabilities. For while an IOC may consider it beneficial to its long-term interests if it partners with local firms as well as supporting budding local suppliers, ironically, corrupt NOC managers may consider 'importing' goods and services as better suited to meet their selfish interests. It is therefore crucial that the owners of NOCs are aware of these issues, and take steps to ensure that factors are put in place that would ensure that their NOCs play active roles in local content development. First, these NOCs should consciously create the necessary linkages between the industry and the rest of the economy. This would require making the local content objectives clear and discernible for the managers and employees of the NOC, while the extent to which such firms further local content should be used as performance criteria. Then there is the need to ensure that these NOCs are actually capable, competitive, and efficient.

The most successful NOCs bring global managerial and operational standards to bear in their workings.[69] Firms such as Statoil, Aramco, and Petrobras not only rake in billions of dollars annually for their home states, but they also deploy their capabilities, experience, and resources for the development of domestic capabilities. Taking advantage of their depth of experience, and immense capabilities, these firms are positioned to insist on the patronage of local suppliers by their E&P partners, and to advance local content directly. In contrast, some NOCs are inefficient, corrupt, and opaque. Sadly, African NOCs, such as NNPC, GePetrol of Equatorial Guinea, and Nilepet of South Sudan, fit this profile. To a large extent, these firms have not been able to develop their local capabilities over time, but continue to depend extensively on IOCs for the provision of technology, and in most cases, funds. Their extensive dependence on their partners naturally weakens their monitoring capabilities.

It is therefore important that African PPCs make building vibrant operator NOCs a primary focus of their local content agenda. This is because viable NOCs, which operate efficiently, transparently, and competitively, will be better suited to

68 These firms are routinely accused of being corrupt, inefficient, wasteful, and bogus. See Eller et al, 2007. See also Thurber et al, 2012, at p 701.

69 Olsen, 2013, at p 619.

advance local content than those which are opaque and inefficient. If African NOCs are required to concentrate and develop their upstream capacities, they would be in a better position to strengthen local content especially in their sole operations. What this means is that firms such as NNPC and Sonangol should take on increasingly challenging roles in their upstream industries, and shirk from relaxing asset managers and non-operator roles. These firms would, in turn, be able to invest in R&D in the mould of Petronas, Petrobras, and Aramco, which will invariably impact local content in the long run, besides directly patronising local suppliers, and generating employment for thousands of their citizens at home.

In order to achieve NOC viability, it is suggested that African PPCs should consider restructuring their NOCs in order to enable them focus on their core operations. This may require the excision of non-core operations from such firms which have the tendency of distracting them from their core roles, besides draining their profits and limited resources. In addition, these countries should also require their NOCs to function in fully or partially liberalised petroleum industries as a means of removing their automatic entitlement to state patronage and shoring up their competitiveness. Liberalisation will put NOCs at the forefront of devising local solutions to local problems, rather than relying entirely on state patronage to be kept afloat.

In this respect, African PPCs should also consider partially privatising their NOCs. All over the world, it is a fact that some of the most capable NOCs, such as Rosneft, Gazprom, Petrobras, and Statoil, are partially privatised.[70] Partial privatisation, if done properly, will enable NOCs in Africa to raise funds more quickly and easily, access technology from their private partners, and confer them with some level of autonomy. It will also enable the managers of these firms to be more professional in their outlook, while conferring transparency and governance benefits as well.

In addition to all these, there is the need to address NOC corruption head on. Across Africa, several NOCs are routinely used as tools for corrupt patronage and rent seeking by politicians and government officials. This means that contracting in their petroleum industries is often used as a means to defraud the state rather than to protect the interest of the public. In effect, the managers of an NOC may not welcome the long-term benefits of prioritising domestic firms. In fact, corrupt managers of NOCs may prefer to establish 'shell companies' abroad through which they may supply to the NOC and its affiliates, items which can be sourced at home, at exorbitant costs.

The propensity of the managers of NOCs to be corrupt makes it imperative that PPCs which desire to shore up their local content take steps to ensure that these firms operate under policies and frameworks which would give room for transparent and effective monitoring. This may require subjecting African NOCs to efficient regulatory oversight. These firms should thus be made to comply with the

70 Some fully owned NOCs such as NIOC of Iran and Aramco of Saudi Arabia are, however, quite efficient at what they do.

laws of the land and with the policy directives of their home states, especially as far as local content is concerned. And where breaches occur, they should be visited with stiff fines and sanctions.[71] There is thus need for African PPCs to maintain some reasonable level of control over their NOCs as a means of ensuring goal congruence.

The case for strengthening regulation is very apt in Africa, a continent in which formal regulators are, more often than not, marginalised in favour of NOCs. This is because the latter, as revenue earners, are often regarded as being more important. This has meant that while several PPCs actually take steps to establish regulatory institutions to which they confer regulatory oversight over their petroleum industries, in practice these regulators remain ineffective and underfunded. For instance, from 1985 to 2010, NNPC operated side by side with DPR, the primary regulator of the NPI. But because DPR was, and is still, largely viewed as a subsidiary of NNPC rather than its overseer, it struggled to regulate NNPC. This contributed in no small measure to NNPC's inability to further the Nigerian content pre-NOGICDA. Like Nigeria, Angola, which has a Ministry of Petroleum with formal oversight over its petroleum industry, practically places actual control over its petroleum industry on Sonangol, with the Ministry performing only marginal duties in the industry.[72] Thankfully, the firm has been largely successful in carrying out its mandate. However, this is not necessarily because of its subjection to an independent regulator, but perhaps by virtue of a combination of its professional outlook as well as certain historical factors which inclined it towards efficiency in the discharge of its mandate.[73]

This, again, is where some level of privatisation or sector liberalisation becomes relevant in aiding African PPCs to exert stronger oversight over their NOCs. In essence, the less entitled these firms are to state patronage, the lesser their powers and influence would be. Where that is the case, it would make for easier regulation and oversight than would be the case where all the hopes of the country are placed in a single firm. It is hoped that if the above suggestions are

71 In 2011, for instance, Petrobras was fined the sum of $18 million for breaching local content rules in development of 44 concessions 'ANP Slaps Petrobras with $18 million Fine' *Upstream* (1 September 2011) http://www.upstreamonline.com/live/article276020.ece, accessed 22 November 2016.

72 See the Petroleum Activities Law 2004 and the Law on Taxation of Petroleum Activities 2004. See also Advogados and FCB Sociedade de Advogados, n.d.

73 Sonangol's relative successes as manager of Angola's petroleum resources can be largely attributed to its history and to its strategy. Historically, the firm has long benefited from the services of highly rated professionals whose expertise has shored up its performance. Sonangol was established in 1976, following Angola's nationalization of Angol, then a subsidiary of Portugal's Petrogal. A memorandum of understanding between the Angolan government and Petrogal, however, allowed Angol's employees who continued with the newly created Sonangol to count their years of service to Sonangol as service to the Portuguese government. The firm was thus given a head start by being staffed from inception, by persons with relative technical expertise and know-how in petroleum operations. See Heller, 2012, at p 865, see also Oliveira, 2007.

put in place, they would better position African NOCs to play their roles in driving local content at home. An NOC which advances the interests of its home state would stand as an inspiration to other local firms in the development of their capabilities.

8.5 Conclusion

This chapter analysed how NOCs further local content at home. It noted that NOCs advance local content by directly patronising locally made goods and services, investing in R&D, harnessing technology transfer commitments from their POC partners, and insisting that their JV/PSC partners utilise locally made goods and services. In order to demonstrate the criticality of efficient NOCs to fostering local content, the chapter examined the roles of Sonangol and Petronas, while also noting that NNPC was not efficient in advancing the Nigerian content despite the enormous powers at its disposal to do so. It therefore explored the prospects of petroleum sector liberalisation, partial privatisation, and NOC restructuring in improving NOC performance in general, which would also have consequences for local content development.

Bibliography

Advogados EV and FCB Sociedade de Advogados, 'Key Legislation and Regulatory Structure in the Angolan Oil and Gas Sector' (n.d.) https://www.hg.org/article.asp?id=30556, accessed 21 November 2016.

Al-Kasim F, Søreide T and Williams A, 'Shrinking Oil: Does Weak Governance and Corruption Reduce Volumes of Oil Produced?' (2010) (3) *U4 Issue*, 1 https://www.u4.no/publications/shrinking-oil-does-weak-governance-and-corruption-reduce-volumes-of-oil-produced.pdf, accessed 5 February 2016.

Brumberg D and Ahram AI, 'The National Iranian Oil Company in Iranian Politics' (2007) James A. Baker III Institute for Public Policy of Rice University and Japan Petroleum Energy Center, http://www.bakerinstitute.org/files/3903/, accessed 21 November 2016.

Clarke D, *Africa: Crude Continent: The Struggle for Africa's Oil Prize* (Profile, London, 2010).

Eller SL et al, 'Empirical Evidence on the Operational Efficiency of National Oil Companies' (2007) James A. Baker III Institute for Public Policy of Rice University and Japan Petroleum Energy Center.

Fry JD and Ibrahim E, 'Reassessing Venezuela's Organic Hydrocarbon Law: a Balance between Sovereignty and Efficiency?' (2013) 6(3) *Journal of World Energy Law & Business*, 234.

Gordon R and Stenvoll T, 'Statoil: A Study in Political Entrepreneurship' (2007) James A. Baker III Institute for Public Policy of Rice University and Japan Petroleum Energy Center, https://www.bakerinstitute.org/media/files/page/9ffcb110/noc_statoil_gordon_stenvoll.pdf, accessed 7 July 2017.

Grayson LE, *National Oil Companies* (John Wiley, London, 1981).

Heller PRP, 'Angola's Sonangol: Dexterous Right Hand of the State' in DG Victor et al (eds) *Oil and Governance State-owned Enterprises and the World Energy Supply* (Cambridge University Press, Cambridge, 2012).

Hernández I, 'Why is Venezuela's Oil Sector so shattered?' *Natural Resource Governance* (8 February 2018) https://resourcegovernance.org/blog/why-venezuela-oil-sector-so-shattered, accessed 15 May 2018.

Hults D, 'Petróleos de Venezuela, S.A. (PDVSA): From Independence to Subservience in Gridlock' in DG Victor et al (eds) *Oil and Governance State-owned Enterprises and the World Energy Supply* (Cambridge University Press, Cambridge, 2012).

Leis J et al, 'National Oil Companies Reshape the Playing Field' *Bain and Company* (10 October 2012) http://www.bain.com/publications/articles/national-oil-companies-reshape-the-playing-field.aspx, accessed 12 July 2017.

Noreng O, *Oil and Islam: Social and Economic Issues* (John Wiley and Sons, Chichester, 1997).

Nwaokoro JE, 'Signed, Sealed but will it Deliver? Nigeria's local content Bill and Cross-Sectoral Growth' (2012) 4(1) *Journal of World Energy Law & Business*, 56.

Oliveira A, 'Brazil's Petrobras: Strategy and Performance' in DG Victor et al (eds) *Oil and Governance State-owned Enterprises and the World Energy Supply* (Cambridge University Press, Cambridge, 2012).

Oliveira RS, 'Business Success, Angola-style: Postcolonial Politics and the Rise and Rise of Sonangol' (2007) 45(4) *The Journal of Modern African Studies*, 595.

Oliveira RS, *Magnificent and Beggar Land: Angola since the Civil War* (Oxford University Press, Oxford, 2015).

Olsen M, 'The Future of National Oil Companies in Russia and How they May Improve their Global Competitiveness' (2013) 35 *Hous. J. Int'l L.*, 617.

Ovadia JS, 'The Dual Nature of Local Content in Angola's Oil and Gas Industry: Development vs. Elite Accumulation (2012) 30 *Journal of Contemporary African Studies*, 403.

Samples TR and Vittor JL, 'Energy Reform and the Future of Mexico's Oil Industry: The Pemex Bidding Rounds and Integrated Service Contracts' (2011) 7(2) *Texas Journal of Oil Gas & Energy*, 215.

Stevens P, 'National Oil Companies and International Oil Companies in the Middle East: Under the Shadow of Government and the Resource Nationalism Cycle' (2008) 1(1) *Journal of World Energy Law & Business*, 5.

Stevens S, 'Sonangol: Angola's Charm Offensive' (2016) *Natural Resource Charter Case Study* http://www.resourcegovernance.org/sites/default/files/documents/sonangol-angolas-charm-offensive.pdf, accessed 22 November 2016.

Stratfor Global Intelligence, 'Angola's National Oil Company Continues to Be the Government's Backbone' (2014) https://www.stratfor.com/analysis/angolas-national, accessed 5 February 2016.

Thurber MC, et al 'NNPC and Nigeria's Oil Patronage Ecosystem', in DG Victor et al (eds) *Oil and Governance State-owned Enterprises and the World Energy Supply* (Cambridge University Press, Cambridge, 2012).

Thurber MC, et al, 'Exporting the Norwegian Model: the Effect Administrative Design on Oil Sector Performance' (2011) 8 *Energy Policy*, 8.

Tordo S and Anouti Y, *Local Content in the Oil and Gas Sector: Case Studies* (World Bank Publications, 2013), http://extrayendotransparencia.grupofaro.org/wp-content/uploads/2014/12/LC-in-the-oil-and-gas-sector-Case-Studies.pdf, accessed 8 March 2017.

Tordo S, Tracy BS and Arfaa N, 'NOCs and Value Creation' (2011) *World Bank Working Paper No. 218* http://siteresources.worldbank.org/INTOGMC/Resources/9780821388310.pdf, accessed 2 January 2016.

Wang W, 'Impact of Western Sanctions on Russia in the Ukraine Crisis Null' (2015) 8(2) *Journal of Politics and Law*, 1.

Wertheim PH and Abrantes D, 'Cenpes Petrobras R&D Centre Became the Biggest in Latin America' *Scandinavian Oil and Gas Magazine* (29 April 2015) http://www.scandoil.com/moxie-bm2/news/spot_news/cenpes-petrobras-rd-centre-became-the-biggest-in-l.shtml, accessed 9 December 2016.

9 Local content and resource rich regions: a case study of Nigeria's Niger Delta Region

9.1 Introduction

The improper response of resource rich countries (RRCs) to the aspirations of resource rich regions (RRRs) for the right to control or share in their natural resources is widely recognized as a potential source of unrest and conflict in many parts of the world.[1] History has shown that perceptions of marginalization of one group by another with regards to the use and control of natural resources can give rise to secession, internal conflicts, civil war, and the disruption of RRCs. From Sudan's long, bitter, and bloody civil wars,[2] Indonesia's invasion of Timor, Kurdistan's yearnings for the control of its petroleum resources, to Scotland's aspirations for independence, the desire by RRRs to either own or control natural resources remains a very sensitive matter which requires tact, fairness, and honesty to address.

The Natural Resource Charter notes that failure to '... provide reasonable compensation as well as equitable participation in the national benefits can give rise to citizens' frustration and may lead to disruption of extractive projects or to conflict'.[3] In a similar vein, Article 26 of the United Nations Declaration on the Rights of Indigenous Peoples which was adopted by the UN General Assembly in 2007, recognises the right of indigenous people to the lands, territories, and resources which they have traditionally owned, occupied, or otherwise used or acquired.[4] The Declaration also recognises the rights of indigenous peoples to own, use, develop, and control the lands, territories, and resources they possess by reason of traditional ownership or other traditional occupation or use, as well as those which they have otherwise acquired. As such, it mandates countries to give

1 The term "resource rich regions" is used to mean geographical or geopolitical regions in which natural resources are found in abundant measure when compared to other regions of a country. For example, Bahia is an RRR in Brazil, while Scotland, although a country in its own right, may equally be regarded as an RRR in the UK. The Niger Delta Region (NDR) of Nigeria and Kurdistan in Iraq are all RRRs.

2 In 1955–1972 and 1983–2005, the southern and northern regions of Sudan were embroiled in a bloody civil war that claimed the lives of untold thousands.

3 Natural Resource Charter, 'Overarching Domestic Governance' http://naturalresourcecharter.org/sites/default/files/Natural%20Resource%20Charter%20second%20edition%20-%20DRAFT.pdf, accessed 27 February 2016.

4 A/RES/61/295.

legal recognition and protection to these lands, territories, and resources, and to accord due respect to the customs, traditions, and land tenure systems of the indigenous peoples concerned.[5] Similarly, the Natural Resources Charter recommends that RRCs 'should pursue opportunities for local benefits, and account for, mitigate and offset the environmental and social costs of resource projects'.[6]

Conscious of the need to specially provide for, or accommodate some of the yearnings of RRRs, some federal constitutions either grant them some level of fiscal autonomy, or remit a certain percentage of resource-based revenues to them.[7] Whether these measures adequately address genuine concerns of marginalisation is another thing entirely, as unrest, suspicion, and turmoil can still be found in some countries whose constitutions attempt to cater for some of the concerns of their RRRs.[8] For example, although Nigeria has increased the derivation of the Niger Delta Region (NDR), as well as introduced a series of extra-legal initiatives in its bid to give the region some benefits from its petroleum resources, the impact of these measures have been minimal. Consequently, the NDR remains one of the poorest of Nigeria's geo-political regions. Using the NDR as its case study, this chapter examines some of the challenges of RRRs (poverty, inflation, environmental degradation, and civil unrest, etc.), the measures put in place to address them (derivation, and special interventionist agencies, etc.), and their marginal impact so far. In the light of which, the chapter argues that rather than focus on increasing derivation and revenue sharing, RRCs should focus on developing a localised local content as a more sustainable way of ensuring that benefits derived from resource extraction impact the people more positively.

9.1.1 The NDR's struggle within the context of Nigeria's federalism

Nigeria is ethnically and religiously diverse. Its majority tribes are the Hausa/Fulanis who occupy most of the Northern region of the country, the Igbos of South-Eastern Nigeria and the Yorubas of the South-West. Then there are also minorities such as the Nupes, Birom, Tivs, and Idomas of the North Central regions. Other minorities are found in the NDR or South-South region, such as the Ijaws, Ikwerres, Itsekiri's, Ibibios, Urhobos, and Effiks, etc.[9] Perhaps by a twist of providence, over 90 percent of Nigeria's petroleum resources are located in the NDR.[10] Like Qatar, Kuwait, or Saudi Arabia, most of the region sits on top

5 See also Arts 27, 28, 29, 31 and 32.

6 Precept 5.

7 Countries which have these arrangements include Indonesia, Iraq, Nigeria, and Brazil. On the Indonesian arrangement, see Augustina and Ahmad, 2012. On the Iraqi arrangement, see Gunter, 2011, and for Brazil, see Postali, 2016, and Gobetti, 2010.

8 The yearnings of Iraq's Kurdish minorities for independence has not been assuaged by access to greater control of their petroleum revenues; see Gunter, 2011.

9 The region originally referred mainly to Delta, Rivers, and Bayelsa States. It has recently been politically interpreted to include Cross River, Akwa Ibom, Edo, Imo, Abia, and Ondo States.

10 Akpabio and Akpan, 2010.

of vast and immense crude oil and natural gas resources. And perhaps with the exception of Cross River State, all the states in the NDR are petroleum producing. Despite its vast petroleum resources, though, the NDR remains one of the poorest regions in Nigeria, besides struggling from environmental degradation from petroleum operations.[11] This paradox of poverty in the midst of plenty has engaged the minds of scholars for some time now. An understanding of the historical factors behind the region's underdevelopment will aid in placing the NDR struggle in proper perspective.[12]

Nigeria's Independence and Republican constitutions of 1960 and 1963, respectively, provided adequately for the NDR to benefit from petroleum-based revenues derived from it. For example, section 140 of the Republican Constitution had provided that each of Nigeria's Eastern, Northern, and Western Regions at the time were to be entitled to 50 percent of royalties and rents from natural resources situated in their regions.[13] The Constitution also entitled RRRs to share from a distributable account into which 30 percent of resource-based revenues was paid. The remaining 20 percent was the entitlement of the central government. And, for purposes of derivation, the Constitution made no distinction between RRRs and their coastal regions. This allowed the littoral states of the NDR (Akwa Ibom, Rivers, Bayelsa, Cross River, Delta, and Ondo) to benefit from their offshore and onshore petroleum resources.

In essence, while management and control of the petroleum resources of the NDR was vested in the Federal Government of Nigeria (FGN), the region's right to participate in sharing the benefits of its petroleum resources was duly recognised and catered for under the 1960 and 1963 Constitutions. This otherwise relatively agreeable arrangement was stymied when the military overthrew the democratically elected government of Nigeria in 1966. The military, which ruled by decrees, immediately suspended portions of the 1963 Constitution, including section 140. Following that, it passed decrees which all but expropriated the NDR's petroleum resources in favour of the FGN. For instance, section 1 of the Petroleum Act 1969 expressly vested ownership and control of all petroleum resources in Nigeria in the federation.[14] While the Offshore Oil Revenues Act of 1971 created a dichotomy between onshore and offshore petroleum resources, thus disentitling the NDR from any offshore benefits which had been available to it under the Republican Constitution of 1963.[15] In a similar vein, section 1 of the Land Use Act of 1978 expropriated all lands in Nigeria's federating states and vested them in military governors who were beholden to the military head of state

11 Banks and Sokolowski, 2010, at p 275.
12 For a historical perspective on the underdevelopment of the NDR, see Okorobia, 1999.
13 The NDR was during this time a part of the Eastern Region.
14 The provision is replicated in s.44 of the 1999 Constitution which gives the FGN's authority over petroleum in Nigeria, its territorial waters of Nigeria, its continental shelf and exclusive economic zone.
15 See *Attorney General of the Federation v Attorney General of Abia State and 35 others* (2002) 6 NWLR (Pt.764).

Table 9.1 Demonstration of the downward slope of the NDR's derivation from its petroleum resources

Year	*Derivation*
1960–1965	50% of royalties and rents of onshore and offshore petroleum The NDR also shared in 30% of petroleum rents paid in the distributable account
1965–1974	45% derivation No offshore entitlements
1975–1979	20%
1979–1981	0%
1982–1992	1.5%
1992–1999	3%
1999–present	13%

at the time. The effect of these decrees was to diminish the relevance of the NDR economically by depriving it of the right to benefit from its petroleum resources. See Table 9.1. The incursion of the military into Nigeria's politics thus paved the way for the systematic and gradual economic deprivation, marginalisation, and environmental despoliation of the NDR, under the dubious guise of legality.[16] Denied the right to participate in petroleum revenues, the NDR suffered from environmental degradation from oil spills and gas flaring. The traditional livelihood of the people was destroyed as its farms and rivers were either forcefully taken by the FGN, or destroyed by oil spills. The region also suffered economically from the fact that it lost its rights to special revenues which had existed on the basis of the time honoured principle of derivation. Furthermore, the absence of accountability and transparency in the management of petroleum revenues meant that revenues which were paid to the FGN by petroleum firms were not ploughed back into the region, but were largely misappropriated by military rulers and their cohorts. Limited dissenting voices from the NDR were brutally crushed by the government, sometimes with the support of its international oil company (IOC) partners.[17] One commentator noted that the '... use of overwhelming military force at the slightest suggestion of non-state "provocation" in the Niger Delta had been standard federal practice since the late 1980s'.[18]

The perception of injustice in the NDR was heightened by the fact that political and military leadership in Nigeria is dominated by the Hausa/Fulanis, Ibos, and

16 Several works have been written on the deprivation of the NDR, see for instance Worika, 2002.

17 The unjust and brutal 1995 hanging of Ken Saro Wiwa and eight other environmentalists from Ogoniland still haunts Shell in Nigeria, which was seen as being complicit in the whole affair. See generally Amnesty International, 'Nigeria: Petroleum, Pollution and Poverty in The Niger Delta' (2009) http://www.amnesty.org/en/library/asset/AFR44/017/2009/en/e2415061-da5c-44f8-a73c-a7a4766ee21d/afr440172009en.pdf, accessed 9 July 2016.

18 Nwajiaku-Dahou, 2012.

Yorubas, which constitute the majority. This created a feeling of oppression and colonisation, on the part of the NDR. According to one author:

> By 1967 and certainly by 1969, petroleum, particularly the mineral oil, was becoming the major resource in terms of total income and foreign exchange earnings in the country. It was therefore, not difficult for the majority groups who are in control of the Federal Government to reverse the basis of revenue allocation with regard to petroleum resources from derivations to the Federal Government's exclusive ownership.[19]

When Nigeria returned to democracy in 1999, its Constitution guaranteed the NDR the right to at least 13 percent of all revenues derived from petroleum extracted from it.[20] This development was an appreciable improvement from the near absence of any form of derivation which had been the norm since 1966. And because democracy reintroduced free speech, and some rule of law into the Nigerian political space, it emboldened leaders of thought and civil society organisations in the NDR to clamour for a return to the 1963 revenue sharing formula, which had been far better, as well as for reparation for the decades of deprivation and despoliation the region had been subjected to.[21] Furthermore, democracy and the return to civil rule, led to the release of pent-up emotions by certain elements in the NDR against the FGN, and petroleum firms operating in the region. The clamour for increased participation of the NDR in the revenues that are derived from it now assumed multifaceted dimensions, some legal and some extra-legal. The legal manifestations of the agitations of the NDR people include human rights and environmental advocacy, litigation, lobbying, regional politicking, and calls for economic restructuring. The extra-legal measures adopted by some youths in the NDR include militancy, sabotage of petroleum installations, oil theft, illegal bunkering and refining of petroleum products, and the abduction of oil workers.[22] These agitations, needless to say, have caused untold economic, environmental, and security hardships, not only to the NDR people, but also to the Nigerian state in general.

For example, the 'theft' of Nigeria's crude at an industrial level at its zenith cost the Nigerian state about $1 billion monthly.[23] And because the Nigerian economy is heavily reliant on petroleum revenues, the monumental losses caused by oil theft, coupled with record low oil prices between 2014 and 2016, were largely responsible for the first economic recession Nigeria had seen in about two decades.[24] The extra-legal aspects of the agitation also had negative consequences for

19 Kalu, 2011.
20 S.162 of the Constitution of the Federal Republic of Nigeria ('the Constitution').
21 See Adangor, 2015.
22 Some NDR activists are, however, quick to distance themselves from the criminal manifestations of the problem.
23 Assi, Amah and Edeke, 2016, at p 73.
24 The bombings and destruction of petroleum infrastructure by various militant groups were curtailed following an amnesty programme of the FGN in 2009. Following this,

the NDR environment. Presently, the region has to contend not only with oil spills and gas flaring which are a consequence of the operations of petroleum firms, but also with spills which occur as a result of acts of sabotage, breaking of pipelines, illegal bunkering, and illegal refining of petroleum.[25]

There is also the security dimension. Beginning from the late 1990s and early 2000s, expatriate petroleum workers were subjected to targeted abductions with a view to pressing the demands of various agitators in the NDR. These abductions later transmogrified into whole-scale kidnappings at an industrial scale – not only oil workers, but also of citizens perceived to be persons of means. Today, the length and breadth of the NDR reels with insecurity at a scale never seen hitherto. Petroleum firms are compelled to expend billions of naira in order to secure their staff and assets, while the FGN also spends billions to police the region in order to allow for the smooth operations of the NPI. The security challenge is exacerbated by the fact that funds generated from oil theft and illegal refining are sometimes used to fund militant and criminal activities in the region, in an endless cycle of violence and criminality.

The FGN has adopted a multilateral approach to the agitations of the NDR. They include the securitisation and militarisation of the region, the establishment of specialised developmental agencies, and the increased derivation of NDR states from petroleum resources generated from the region. These are in addition to corporate social responsibility projects of petroleum firms operating in the region, such as scholarships, and the building of cottage hospitals and link roads, etc. The adoption of these measures notwithstanding, the problems of the NDR continue.

Although the agitations of the NDR people with respect to their petroleum resources have environmental, political, and management dimensions, the greater consensus points to the fact that the most consistent demand of the region is for the right to benefit from petroleum revenues. This, in effect, puts most of the agitations in an economic perspective. Unlike Scotland or Kurdistan, which clamour for independence in order to control their natural resources, the NDR struggle is less about control than it is with the right to benefit directly from petroleum revenues. This means that were Nigeria to return to its 1963 constitutional revenue sharing arrangement, in all probability, the agitations of the NDR people vis à vis the FGN would reduce significantly.[26] The question at this stage is

the NPI enjoyed some relative peace, and production continued until 2015, although other acts of criminality have continued unabated such as oil theft and oil bunkering. See Hinshaw and Kent, 2016.

25 Oil theft occurs when oil thieves tap into Nigeria's oil pipelines which carry crude oil from the swampy oil-rich NDR to Nigeria's various exports. Much of the stolen crude is loaded into large barges and sold on the 'black market' internationally, although about 25 percent is reportedly refined locally. The activities of pipeline vandals also result in the spill of large amounts of crude oil – sometimes deliberately and other times accidently. These spills severely damage the NDR environment and pollute rivers, economic crops, nets, and fauna. See SDN, 2013.

26 Other suggestions include the need to eradicate endemic poverty and under-development in the region, improve transparency in the management of petroleum revenues, greater regulation of petroleum companies in order to better protect the environment,

whether or not the NDR states are justified in advocating for increased derivation for the region. Put in another way: is increased petroleum revenue the way out of under-development for the NDR? In effect, would an increase in the region's finances impact the lives of the common people appreciably? In order to answer these questions, it may be necessary to analyse the impact of the 13 percent derivation which the region has received since 1999, as that would serve as a template to determine how far perhaps a 25 percent or a 50 percent derivation would go in developing the NDR.

9.2 Derivation and the NDR economy since 1999

The call for increased derivation may be justified mainly on the ground that most of Nigeria's petroleum resources belong to the NDR people. This call is further justified in the light of Article 26 of the United Nations Declaration on the Rights of Indigenous Peoples 2007, which as already shown, recognises the right of indigenous people to the lands, territories, and resources which they have traditionally owned, occupied, or otherwise used or acquired.[27] In principle, increased derivation would make more funds available for the NDR states to develop infrastructure, advance education, healthcare, and reduce poverty. As such, increased derivation and proper management have the potential to transform the NDR into an industrial and tourist hub similar in many ways to Qatar and Dubai. But this requires capable leadership who are brought into power through transparent electoral processes. The challenge with the NDR is that it is largely governed by persons who 'force' their way into power fraudulently. These leaders have little or no incentive to be accountable to the people, nor are there structures or frameworks to bring them to account.

For while the NDR and most of Nigeria practice western democracy, at least in form, the country is still relatively young in its practice of rule of law. Years of military rule have ushered in totalitarian governors who rule like monarchs, and acquire political offices not necessarily through credible electioneering processes. The institutions in the NDR, and in most of Nigeria, are not strong or credible enough to restrain the excesses of the political class. The legislatures and judiciaries in the NDR are, more often than not, appendages of the executive class. Weak leadership and poor visionary capacity on the part of the ruling class of the NDR have all but meant that the region has, for the most part, lacked any lasting policy for the effective utilisation of its petroleum wealth for the common good of the people. As such, the current political and governance structures in the NDR are not suited for the prudent management of vast petroleum revenues.

What is being said is that increased funds may not automatically translate into prosperity in the absence of visionary and disciplined leadership by those who have capacity to plan and prudently apply such funds. In the absence of these, more

and increased derivation for the NDR. See Abiboa and Maiangwa, 2012; see also Ifedi and Ndume, 2011.

27 A/RES/61/295.

funds may as well translate into more poverty and instability. This has been the experience of countries such as Equatorial Guinea, South Sudan, and the Democratic Republic of the Congo, etc. The key issue, then, is whether or not the NDR states as they stand currently have the governance capacity to adequately manage increased derivation. To resolve this question, it is important to enquire into the stewardship of the NDR states since 1999.

As noted above, since 1999, the NDR states have been receiving 13 percent of all petroleum revenues extracted from their states, which is a somewhat considerable amount. For example, it has been estimated that NDR receipts from petroleum sales actually exceed the budgets of some neighbouring African countries with relatively higher populations and development needs. For instance, in 2013 when the price of petroleum was quite high on the international market, Akwa Ibom, Rivers, and Bayelsa States received $1.7 billion, $1.5 billion, and $1.1 billion respectively, considerably higher than the budgets of: Liberia at $433 million, and Gambia at $210 million in the same year.[28] The curious thing is that there has been little to show for these receipts by way of infrastructural and human development in most of the NDR states.[29] Put into context, the region which earns considerably more from Nigeria's federation account than most of Nigeria's other federating states does not appear to fare better than the rest in terms of standard of living, or other metrics for measuring development.[30]

Rather than promote development, the petroleum revenues accruing to the NDR have largely served the purposes of corrupt government officials and politicians.[31] In essence, while the call for increased justification may have some merit, the judicious utilisation of petroleum revenues already received so far by the NDR states would have meaningfully transformed the region.[32] However, that has not been the case because although the 1999 Constitution increased the derivation of

28 See Okafor, 2014.

29 In 2016, Nigeria's Junior Petroleum Minister, Dr Ibe Kachikwu, noted that the NDR had received over $40 billion from oil companies, interventionist agencies and from the 13 percent derivation, with little to show for it. Idowu, 2016.

30 Wallis, 2012.

31 Some governors in the NDR have been either implicated in one act of corruption or another, or convicted in a court of law. For instance, Chief Diepreye Alamieseigha, who ruled Bayelsa State for nearly seven years (1999–2006), was arrested in London in 2005 for money laundering, and was later convicted in Nigeria in 2007 on six charges related to corruption. In 2012, Chief James Ibori, former governor of Delta state, was convicted in London for money laundering and for fraud. Chief Lucky Igbenidion of Edo State (1999–2007) was convicted in London in 2012 for the theft of over $250 million. Similarly, other governors of other states have had pending matters in court for fraud related offences.

32 For instance, Rivers state (an NDR state), received N1,053 billion between 1999 and 2008 in federal allocations, in contrast to the north-eastern states of Yobe and Borno which received N175 billion and N213 billion, respectively. On a per capita basis, by 2008 the 18.97 million people who lived in the six states in the north-east received on average N1,156 per person, while in contrast, Rivers state was allocated N3,965 per capita, and on average the oil producing South-South region received on average N3,332 per capita. See Abiboa and Maiangwa, 2012.

the NDR to 13 percent, it did not create sustainable frameworks to ensure that those funds are prudently utilised for the benefit of the masses. For example, there were no savings or investment mechanisms introduced by law, which would mandate these governors to save these revenues in interest/profit-yielding facilities.[33] Nor were the governors of the region required, or mandated, to utilise these revenues for the benefit of the communities which actually produce these resources. The result has been that the NDR governors have, for the most part, been unprepared to manage such huge revenues. And consequently most of these funds have been either mismanaged, or stolen.

In fact, in the light of the inability of most of the NDR governors to adequately manage their petroleum revenues for the good of their people, the agitation for increased derivation has lost its edge, and justification, since the response of the other regions of Nigeria to the NDR has been, 'account for what you have received so far, before crying out for more'. Increased derivation without putting in place structures to guide the utilisation and management of petroleum revenues, may rather than develop a region, further under-develop it. In relation to the NDR, it made the region largely resource-dependent. The recent drop in crude oil prices between 2015 and 2016 exposed the volatile nature of the region's over-dependence on crude oil revenues and its neglect of other sectors of its economy. Incidentally, while most of the NDR states struggled during this period, Lagos, Ogun, and Anambra states, which are not rich in petroleum, fared better in terms of infrastructure, payment of salaries, and other metrics of measuring development.[34] Viewed holistically, it may be argued that dependence on 13 percent derivation may have actually under-developed the NDR further. For example, because increased derivation made funds available to unaccountable politicians, it may have been responsible for the exacerbation of insecurity in the region. This is because these funds are often used to purchase arms and ammunitions for various criminal groups scattered across the region for the purpose of enabling politicians cling to power at all costs.[35] These criminals, when discarded by their political bosses post-elections, in turn, use their weapons for robberies, kidnapping, assassinations, and arsons, etc. Watts also notes that the many militant groups that sprawled all over the NDR were bankrolled by governors in the region who benefitted from the 13 percent oil revenues.[36] The fallout of which has been to scare away investors and companies from the region to less troubled states.

The NDR may well benefit from lessons that can be extracted from the experiences of countries such as Norway, Saudi Arabia, and Kuwait, etc. Norway, for instance, has admirably managed its petroleum revenues because it formulated

33 For example, from inception, the Ghana Petroleum Revenue Management Act of 2011 (PRMA) which establishes a framework for the collection, allocation and management of petroleum revenues derived from upstream and midstream operations in a responsible, transparent, accountable, and sustainable manner for the benefits of the citizens of Ghana.

34 Onyekakeyah, 2016.

35 See Nwajiaku-Dahou, 2012.

36 See Watts, 2007.

policies which were aimed at promoting prudence and accountability, while ensuring that Norwegians were significantly involved in its petroleum industry. It was aided in so doing by its vibrant democracy, a culture for respect of rule of law, and a Scandinavian aversion to corruption.[37] These virtues and values are required for adequate management of petroleum revenues in a democratic setting. And although Kuwait, UAE, and Qatar do not practice western democracy, they benefited immensely from their vast petroleum deposits, and the oversight of visionary leaders who sought to boost their international profiles through infrastructural development and the establishment of sovereign wealth funds.

Deliberate and sustained efforts are therefore required to address the challenges of the NDR. Half-hearted measures have only addressed the symptoms, not the root causes, which like cancers manifest themselves in one form or another, within a short period. For example, the FGN, in a bid to address the issue of militancy in the NDR, resorted to an expensive amnesty programme in 2009, without necessarily addressing the root causes. It was therefore not surprising that, not long after, it was faced with the issue of oil theft, which in no time became a multibillion dollar predicament. The FGN has also established special development agencies from time to time for the development of the NDR, but these have also yielded little results due to funding and corruption issues.[38]

It is therefore suggested that there is need for the formulation of policies aimed at guaranteeing the proper application of petroleum revenues for the benefit of the NDR people.[39] Furthermore, it is imperative that good governance and accountable leadership be entrenched at the centre as well as at the NDR level. But perhaps what is more important is for the Nigerian state to devise a strategy which bypasses the NDR political class and reaches the grass roots directly, through wealth-creation initiatives. These strategies should

37 Norway, Finland, Sweden, and Denmark are consistently rated as being among the least corrupt countries on earth. See Transparency International, 'Corruption Perceptions Index 2016' https://www.transparency.org/news/feature/corruption_perceptions_index_2016, accessed 4 July 2017.

38 In response to a 1958 report by the Willinks commission that there were genuine developmental challenges in the NDR, and that the region had genuine fears of marginalisation from the major tribes, the Niger Delta Development Board (NDDB) was established. It was, however, not very effective in fulfilling its mandate to develop the NDR due to a lack of political will to develop the region. In 1992, the military government of Ibrahim Babangida (1985–1993) established the Oil Minerals Producing Areas Development Commission (OMPADEC) to perform functions similar to those of the NDDB. The OMPADEC was again unsuccessful due to a marginal allocation, and internal corruption. It was replaced by the Niger Delta Development Commission (NDDC) in 2000. NDDC, however, suffers typically from the same challenges of OMPADEC. See Idemudia, 2012; see also Ebeku, 2003. They include the Oil Mineral Producing Areas Development Commission, which was taken over by the NDDC, and the Niger Delta Ministry, etc.

39 For instance, although Alaska and Alberta are states within the USA and Canada, respectively, they were able to establish sovereign wealth funds for the management of their petroleum revenues. See Heck, 2014.

advance entrepreneurial schemes which engage the NDR youths in the NPI with the aim of addressing their restiveness. The aim of these initiatives should be to integrate the NDR indigenes directly into the NPI. The FGN, the NDR, as well as petroleum firms should collaborate in devising structures aimed at the effective participation of the NDR in the value chain of the NPI via an NDR content. The benefits of an NDR content will include improved entrepreneurship, job creation, development of skills and capacity development, and linkages with other subsectors of the region, etc.[40] Attention is now turned on strategies that can be employed in the development of an NDR content in the NPI.

9.3 The case for an NDR content

It is proposed that Nigeria should, through a legislatively guaranteed NDR content, integrate the NDR directly into the NPI in a bid to address some of the challenges currently faced by the region. This strategy, in contrast to increased derivation, will give the NDR a better sense of belonging and ownership in the NPI. It will also ensure that the benefits of the region's petroleum resources are not left in the hands of the ruling class, but flow directly to the people. Direct participation of the region in terms of ownership of equipment and upstream firms, contracting, or employment, will also quell significantly the perceptions of marginalisation and alienation, which have increased the anxiety and tension in the region.

What is being said here is that there is the need for the people of the NDR to be actively involved in every phase of the NPI. Firms from the region should thus be awarded oil blocks, while service firms from the NDR should be considered in the award of contracts. For example, a specified percentage of indigenes of the region should be considered for employment by all the firms operating in the NPI, while the FGN should also ensure that firms from the NDR are awarded term contracts for the lifting of crude oil and other equally important contracts. It is also important that steps be taken to revamp the NDR ports in order for vessels and cargo ships to easily berth in the region.[41]

As already shown in the course of this book, the policy of awarding discretional oil blocks to indigenous exploration and production (E&P) firms has seen these firms increasingly taking on important roles in the NPI. The issue is that the degree to which these firms are fully or partly owned by Niger Deltans is dismally low. Currently, about 59 indigenous petroleum E&P firms operate in the NPI, and they produce about 7 percent of Nigeria's daily crude oil production. A review of their shareholders and directors, however, reveals that perhaps only the Bayelsa Oil Company,[42] Universal Energy,[43] Prime Petroleum Limited, Suffold

40 See Isidiho and Sabran, 2015.
41 The NDR is home to the Calabar, Onne, Port Harcourt, and Delta Ports. However, these ports are not viable due, in part, to neglect by the FGN. As such, most ships now berth at Lagos State, to the loss of the region. See Akinola, 2016.
42 The firm operates the Atala marginal oil field in oil mining lease (OML) 46.
43 OML 13/14.

Petroleum,[44] the Niger Delta Company,[45] Ashbert Petroleum,[46] Moni Pulo, and Sahara Energy appear to have some connection to the NDR in terms of share ownership/directorships.[47] There is thus need for indigenous E&Ps from the NDR to be awarded not only in onshore operations, but also in swamps and offshore. In this vein, Nwapi observes that 'community dissatisfaction resulting from seeing lucrative jobs going to "outsiders" can stir up conflicts'.[48]

Currently, unlicensed refineries run throughout the length and breadth of the NDR. While they have had deleterious effects on the environment of the region and on the Nigerian economy in general, they also demonstrate the yearnings of the NDR people to participate in the NPI either at the downstream or upstream levels. It is thus important that the FGN integrate these refiners into the NPI by refining their skills through training, and licensing them to operate modular refineries. Besides the benefits which the FGN stands to gain in terms of taxes and application of better environmental protection practices, there is also the effect that youth restiveness in the region may also be curtailed.[49]

This requires the formulation of a policy aimed at awarding a certain percentage of upstream and downstream petroleum licences to firms owned by NDR indigenes, and ensuring that firms operating in the region create an NDR content in their employment and contracting as well. This policy should be followed through by the passage of a law, which stipulates that at least 30 percent of the roughly 70 percent of Nigerian content targeted by the Nigerian Oil and Gas Industry Content Development Act 2010 (NOGICDA), be reserved for the NDR states. This law may also provide that certain jobs should be executed by firms from outside the region provided they partner with firms owned by Niger Deltans as a means of boosting technology transfer, addressing funding issues, and developing local capacity over time.

As it stands, NOGICDA does not specifically benefit the NDR. The framers of the law ignored the peculiar challenges of the region, and its rights to special privileges in the NPI. The Act has no direct mention of the NDR, and its only provisions that may have a bearing on the region are stipulations which require operators to establish project offices in the catchment areas where their projects are situated,[50] and to locate personnel with decision making authority in the same

44 OML 11.
45 OML 54.
46 Oil prospecting licence (OPL) 325.
47 OPL 114, 239, 234 and 231.
48 Nwapi, 2015. For example, the decision of the Nigerian Liquefied Natural Gas Company Ltd (NLNG) to site a $1.5 billion project at Badagry in Lagos State, rather than in the NDR, where most of Nigeria's gas resources are located, stirred up controversy as youths of the NDR threatened the management of the firm for what they perceived as a deliberate ploy to deprive the region of the benefits that would accrue from the project. The management of the NLNG has, however, denied being the 'owners' of the said dry dock. See Iheanachor, 2015.
49 For a slightly similar proposal with respect to a local 'local' content, see Nwapi, 2015.
50 S.25.

office.[51] Then there is the requirement that the Nigerian Content Development and Monitoring Board is to require operators to maintain offices in communities where they have their operations,[52] and to maintain a reasonable number of personnel from those areas,[53] while its head office is to be situated in an oil producing state.[54] With the exception of the above provisions which have a marginal bearing on the NDR, NOGICDA does not appear to distinguish the NDR from the rest of Nigeria. Nwapi notes that this approach of providing a 'generalised' local content without distinguishing RRRs and communities, 'impedes the potential of LCRs to engender real economic development. If policymakers do not pay closer attention to the definition of "local," the potential benefits of LCRs may not be maximized'.[55] This is justified on the basis that although the Nigerian federation is an indivisible sovereign entity, when peculiar challenges are faced by specific regions, they may require peculiar strategies to address them.

In effect, the NDR content should aim at attaining what NOGICDA aspires for Nigeria as a whole, and as such it should reflect NOGICDA's underlying philosophies. The premise upon which NOGICDA seeks to protect the NPI from being dominated by foreign firms should also be the basis upon which the NDR should be protected from competition from non-NDR states. The direct integration of the NDR into the NPI will not only address poverty issues, but will also reduce the perceptions of marginalisation and oppression that have developed through the years, thereby pitting the NDR against the FGN and petroleum firms operating in the region. And because an NDR content will ensure that a sizeable chunk of the industry is in the 'hands' of the indigenes, it has the potential to empower a vast number of people in the region. In addition, other sectors of the NDR will benefit immensely from the linkages that will result from an NDR content.

The passage of the proposed legal framework will ensure that the NDR benefits from lucrative term contracts for the lifting of oil, refining of crude, E&P contracts, and major oil servicing jobs such as fabrication, and construction etc. The benefit of this approach is that it will result in the formation of a workable partnership for the development of the region between progressive elements, on the one hand, and with the FGN and petroleum firms, on the other hand. The effective implementation of such a framework will positively impact other subsectors of the NDR economy, such as manufacturing, shipping, transportation, insurance, banking, and construction.[56]

An NDR content will also have other benefits for the NPI. First, if more Niger Deltans are involved in the NPI, they may be in a better position to negotiate and dialogue with other Niger Deltans who are involved in the sabotage of petroleum

51 S.26.
52 S.27.
53 S.28(2).
54 S.71.
55 Nwapi, 2015, at p 188.
56 See Ovadia, 2012, at p 19.

resources. Thus a RG feeling of 'ownership' may, while assuaging the grievances of the NDR, result in a reduction in sabotage and pipelines vandalism. If an NDR content leads to job creation, it would invariably result in crime reduction in the region, which would allow for smooth operations of the NPI. In effect, it is in the long-term interests of the FGN to integrate the NDR into the NPI, not through derivation alone, but more importantly through a localised local content.

It may, however, be argued that the NDR already benefits immensely from the NPI and that in addition to the 13 percent being paid to it, many petroleum producing communities in the region benefit from the petroleum firms which operate in their areas through contracts awarded in pursuance of the Global Memorandum of Understandings (GMOUs) entered into between them and these firms. It may also be contended that they also benefit from some corporate social initiatives of these firms, which provide scholarships, fund cottage hospitals, build roads, and provide access to electricity in some cases. In addition to all these, it may be pointed that the FGN has also awarded upstream petroleum licences to some NDR states. For example, the FGN awarded the Atala marginal field in OML 46 to the Bayelsa state government in 2003, while the administration of President Goodluck Jonathan also awarded surveillance contracts to 'repentant' militants from the NDR to secure NNPC's pipelines.[57]

Conceded that these initiatives were the right step in the right direction, the issue is that they did not go far enough. For example, there is no independent monitoring of the implementation of the GMOUs, coupled with the fact that they cannot be enforced in court. These have given rise to claims that the commitments made by IOCs are not adequately implemented.[58] Furthermore, as laudable as the objectives behind the GMOUs are, they are limited in scope to E&P firms which operate in the NDR, but do not cover supply and service firms which execute jobs outside the NDR which are used in the region. In the same vein, although some NDR communities may have benefited from communally arranged contracts awarded to their indigenes by E&P firms, the bulk of these contracts are menial, and relate to non-essential services such as pipeline surveillance, grass clearing, and minor supplies, etc. They are thus not extensive or meaningful enough to integrate the NDR into the core of the NPI. The award of marginal fields and surveillance contracts to some states and individuals in the NDR are laudable efforts which have some potential for the integration of the region to the NPI, but there is the need for a more sustained effort in that direction on a wider scale.

The question is whether it is justified for the NDR to have a special content in the NPI since Nigeria is a federation. The answer is that the region requires a special content, first, on the basis of the fact that it 'owns' most of Nigeria's petroleum resources, has lost most of its livelihood, and has suffered environmental

57 See Adibe, Nwagwu and Albert, 2018; see also Nwokolo, 2018.

58 This relationship, which is often captured in numerous GMOUs executed between host communities and oil companies, often includes the construction of hospitals, and roads, and the award of minor contracts to host communities.

degradation through the years. Secondly, a special NDR content is required in the NPI in order to 'protect' the region, in view of its peculiar economic and developmental weaknesses, from other stronger regions of Nigeria. These views are developed below.

The first justification for a special NDR content is premised on the fact that years of economic and infrastructural neglect, discrimination, and marginalisation have weakened the NDR's ability to compete favourably with other regions of Nigeria for jobs and contracts in the NPI. As one of the most backward regions in Nigeria, the NDR lags behind the rest, perhaps with the exception of the North East, in manpower, capacity, funds, and experience in the petroleum industry. Therefore, if the region is to participate in the NPI, it would require strategic legislatively conferred privileges which entitle it to jobs and contracts in the NPI. At present, a number of the indigenous firms operating in the NPI are domiciled in the Western part of Nigeria (notably Lagos State).[59] In addition, most of the IOCs operating in the NDR are headquartered in Lagos State, despite having most of their operations in the NDR. The consequence for this is that these firms employ their staff in Lagos State and not in Bayelsa, Akwa Ibom, or Rivers State. This arrangement places the NDR at a disadvantage, since its professionals and skilled personnel are only given 'left-overs' by petroleum firms, despite the fact that their operations directly impact the NDR environment and its social fabric. Furthermore, the domiciliation of the operations of these firms outside the NDR deprives the region of much needed financial resources, since personal income taxes of these professionals are paid to, for instance, Lagos State, rather than to the NDR states.[60]

Secondly, a special NDR content is justified on the basis that most of Nigeria's petroleum resources are 'owned' by the NDR people. This pre-eminently qualifies the region to special benefits beyond derivation. Prior to 1956, the NDR was largely dependent on farming and on fishing. The advent of the petroleum industry has, however, resulted in the loss of arable lands and waters, with deleterious effects on the livelihood of the people in the region. Petroleum exploration has invariably meant the expropriation of vast lands and waters which were owned by the NDR people from time immemorial. These expropriations have altered the livelihood and culture of the NDR people in many ways. Fishes and economic crops have been destroyed by environmental pollution, to the bane of the people. Years of neglect and injustice should, and can only, be addressed when steps are taken to redress these wrongs. Clearly, the NDR people require a viable and sustainable source of livelihood, especially as derivation appears not to have met this need, but may have further impoverished the region by making it depend almost

59 Most of these firms are in Lagos State, although some of them can be found in Ogun and Oyo states.

60 The Bayelsa State government has for a long time charged IOCs with short-changing the state of taxes due to it. IOCs staff employed in Lagos and domiciled there are often flown into Bayelsa to work, but they do not pay taxes to the state. See 'Bayelsa to Seal Oil Firms for Tax Evasion' *Vanguard* (31 July 2016) http://www.vanguardngr.com/2016/07/bayelsa-seal-oil-firms-tax-evasion/, accessed 2 February 2017.

entirely on monthly 'handouts' from Nigeria's Federation Account. An NDR content in the NPI will, therefore, not only compensate for the loss of livelihood and occupation, but will also create occupational opportunities for the people of the region who can translate the knowledge gained in the sciences, technology, welding, fabrication, banking, and insurance, etc., to other segments of the NDR economy.

The issue, however, is that the NDR states may struggle with capacity in terms of funding, expertise, and human resources, which may make it impracticable to reserve a sizeable chunk of jobs executed in the NPI for them. While that may be true, it is also true that implementing a local content policy may not always depend on the availability of capacity at the present, which may be acquired over time. To wait for a country to develop capacity before formulating a local content policy is to ignore the fact that individuals and firms may only develop as they face challenges. And the fact that Nigerian firms struggled, and still struggle, with capacity did not deter the FGN from legislating on local content and taking steps to implement certain aspects of NOGICDA. The same line of reasoning should apply to the NDR. What the FGN should do is to encourage local NDR firms to partner and collaborate with partners from outside the NDR. After all, the same strategy was adopted with respect to the Ladol/Samsung in the development of a floating, production, storage, and offloading platform in the multibillion dollar Egina deep water oil field project.[61] An NDR content may also be shored up immensely if NDR firms collaborate with other partners which have capacity. Again, the FGN may formulate a policy of awarding upstream or downstream licences to two or more NDR firms jointly, where it is clear that acting alone, they may lack the capacity to execute such jobs.

Attaining a meaningful NDR content will not only depend on the FGN though. It will require the participation of NDR states, which should take the lead by encouraging capacity development, promoting the development of local firms, and establishing state owned E&P firms, and service firms, etc.[62] It will also require the participation of IOCs and other E&P firms operating in the NPI, which should sustain their patronage of the region and move away from handouts towards ensuring that they recognise the aspirations of the region to participate directly in the NPI. Already, E&P firms operating in the NPI, as shown earlier, are playing crucial roles in driving the Nigerian content.[63] But they will need to be more focused, deliberate, and determined to integrate petroleum producing communities in their operations, through contracting, employment, and mutual respect. The culture of treating as a nuisance NDR communities' yearning for

61 The LADOL/SHI partnership in the construction of Total's Upstream Floating Production Storage Offloading vessel at its Egina Deepwater field is discussed in Chapter 1, 1.1, as well as in Chapter 6, 6.2.

62 In this regard, the Bayelsa State Oil Company was incorporated by the Bayelsa State government and it was awarded the Atala Marginal Oil Field licence by the FGN in 2002.

63 See Chapter 5, 5.1 for more in the local content milestones recorded in Nigeria. See also Ayoola, 2017, at p 53.

participation, and of treating NDR people with distain, should give way to meaningful engagement, based on trust and dependability. Rather than rely on the military or on politicians to secure their participatory rights, petroleum firms should engage consistently and transparently with the grassroots, particularly in those communities where they operate. This will not only confer on them a social licence to operate, it will also engender peace, and trust, while also stabilising their operations in the NDR.[64]

9.4 Conclusion

This chapter argued for an NDR content in the NPI. It sought to demonstrate that derivation has not helped the region significantly, and as such, more derivation may not address the problems confronting the region. Rather, it argued that there should be a deliberate strategy aimed at giving the NDR people a direct stake in the industry. What the NDR requires is not necessarily more interventionist agencies, a host communities fund, etc., or more funds, but rather, engagement, employment, and contracts, etc. During the course of the writing of this book, the Pan Niger Delta Forum, a Pan Niger Delta group, published its 16-point agenda for peace in the region. Remarkably, it demanded that the NDR be included in the participation in the oil industry and ownership of oil blocks, and for the enunciation of policies and actions that would address the lack of participation, as well as the imbalance in the ownership of oil and gas assets.[65] The demand of the Forum in this respect is not out of reality. All over the world, communities and RRRs are being recognised as important stakeholders in the extraction of their natural resources. In addition to providing special derivation for RRRs, some states also give them the right to be involved in the contracting process, and environmental impact assessment, as well as the right to information of the activities of petroleum or mining firms.[66] This right naturally endears the people to the central government, while also conferring a social licence on the firms that operate in their terrains.[67] The chapter also showed that poverty within the NDR has resulted in militancy and oil theft, with the outcome being the loss of billions of dollars, social upheavals, and environmental damage. It noted that the NDR problem requires a holistic, effective, and sustainable solution, which should come primarily from an NDR content, combined with other initiatives already on ground.

It is also pertinent to reiterate that the success of an NDR content, will depend on other equally important factors. For instance, there has to be willingness on the part of the people of the region to work and to take on challenges as they arise. There have been reports of cases where jobs granted to

64 See Pardo, 2017, see also Moffat and Zhang, 2014.

65 Soniyi, 2016.

66 For a more insightful analysis of the rights of communities to participate in their natural resources, see Giurco et al, 2014; Smith, 2016, at p 123.

67 Pardo, 2017.

some NDR youths by oil companies are 'sold' by those youths to non-NDR indigenes. There is the need for governors of the region to encourage entrepreneurship within the region by investing in infrastructure and research, and in carefully utilising the 13 percent derivation that is granted to them.

There is also need for the FGN to double its efforts in developing strict monitoring regimes to prevent fraud and money laundering, since mismanagement of funds by NDR governors has also increased the tension between the common people and the NPI. Should an NDR content be provided for by law, it is proposed that there should also be some effort to link contracts to community co-operation. Thus the level of co-operation of a particular local government or community should be proportional to the amount of NDR content it receives in terms of jobs and contracts. This will further motivate the beneficiaries of such contracts to act as ambassadors by encouraging their kinsmen not to break into oil pipelines, and reporting those who do so to the relevant authorities. Lastly, there is need for the people of the NDR to rise above the sentiments of the past and to move into the future. This will require commitment, dedication, and resolution. For although oil theft may generate revenues for some NDR indigenes, its impact in a post-petroleum NDR may be disastrous, and may erode what limited gains the region has gained from the NPI.

Bibliography

Aaron K and Patrick JM, 'Corporate Social Responsibility Patterns and Conflicts in Nigeria's Oil-rich Region' http://citeseerx.ist.psu.edu/viewdoc/download?doi=10.1.1.910.3864&rep=rep1&type=pdf, accessed 17 May 2018.

Abiboa DE and Maiangwa B, 'Corruption and the Underdevelopment of the Niger Delta in Nigeria' (2012) 5(8) *Journal of Pan African Studies*, 108.

Adangor Z, 'The Principle of Derivation and the Search for Distributive Justice in the Niger Delta Region of Nigeria: The Journey So Far' (2015) 41 *Journal of Law, Policy and Globalization*, 115.

Adibe R, Nwagwu E and Albert O, 'Rentierism and security privatisation in the Nigerian petroleum industry: Assessment of oil pipeline surveillance and protection contracts' (2018) 45(156) *Review of African Political Economy*, 345.

Akinola B, 'Deep Sea Ports Everywhere, But which will be Viable?' *Thisday* (29 August 2016).

Akpabio E and Akpan N, 'Governance and Oil Politics: in Nigeria's Niger Delta: the Question of Distributive Equity' (2010) 30(2) *Journal of Human Ecology*, 111.

Assi VE, Amah OI and Edeke SO, 'Oil Theft and Corruption: Pathways to Underdevelopment in the Niger Delta' (2016) 6(3) *Research on Humanities and Social Sciences*, 70.

Augustina CD and Ahmad E, 'Political Economy of Revenue Sharing in Indonesia' (2012) *Asia Research Working Paper No. 55.*

Ayoola OT, 'Nigerian Oil and Gas Industry Content Development Act's Perceived Performance Impact' (PhD Thesis, Walden University 2017).

Banks CM and Sokolowski JA, 'Modeling the Niger Delta Insurgency' (2010) 47 *The Social Science Journal*, 271.

Ebeku KSA, 'Critical Appraisal of Nigeria's Niger Delta Development Commission Act 2000' (2003) 6 *International Energy Law and Taxation Review*, 203.
Elamade O, 'The Inter-face of Ethnicity and Revenue Allocation in Nigeria's First Republic' (2012) 10 *African Identities*, 95.
Giurco D et al, 'Responsible Mineral and Energy Futures: Views at the Nexus' (2014) 84 *Journal of Cleaner Production*, 327.
Gobetti SW, 'Federalism and Royalties in Brazil: what does change in the Pre-salt Context' Conference on Oil and Gas in Federal Systems (3–4 March 2010) World Bank, Washington, DC http://siteresources.worldbank.org/EXTOGMC/Resources/336929-1266445624608/6790249-1268936241851/O&G_Conference_session3_BrazilGobetti.pdf, accessed 23 August 2018.
Gunter MM, 'Arab-Kurdish Relations and the Future of Iraq' (2011) 32 *Third World Quarterly*, 1623.
Heck C, '"We Are All Millionaires Now": Norway's Astounding Fiscal Reserve' *Huffington Post* (3 June 2014) http://www.huffingtonpost.com/charles-heck/we-are-all-millionaires-n_b_4906237.html, accessed 2 February 2017.
Hinshaw D and Kent S, 'Niger Delta Avengers Sabotage Oil Output' *Wall Street Journal* (16 June 2016) https://www.wsj.com/articles/niger-delta-avengers-sabotage-oil-output-1465165361, accessed 2 February 2016.
Idemudia U, 'The Resource Curse and the Decentralization of Oil Revenue: the Case of Nigeria' (2012) 35 *Journal of Cleaner Production*, 183.
Idowu S, 'Kachikwu: $40bn Spent on Niger Delta in 12 Years without Result' *Thisday* (27 August 2016) https://www.thisdaylive.com/index.php/2016/08/27/kachikwu-40bn-spent-on-niger-delta-in-12-years-without-result/, accessed 4 July 2017.
Ifedi AJP and Ndume AJ, 'Blood Oil, Ethnicity, and Conflict in the Niger Delta Region of Nigeria' (2011) 22(1) *Mediterranean Quarterly*, 74.
Iheanachor D, 'N-Delta Youths Kick against Building of NLNG Dry Dock in Badagry' *Vanguard* (7 August 2015) https://www.vanguardngr.com/2015/08/n-delta-youths-kick-against-building-of-nlng-dry-dock-in-badagry/, accessed 21 May 2018.
Isidiho AO and Sabran MSB, 'Challenges Facing Niger Delta Development Commission (NDDC) Projects in Imo State and Niger Delta Region in Nigeria' (2015) 5(6) *International Journal of Humanities and Social Science*, 38.
Kalu I, 'Fiscal Federalism in Nigeria Practices and Issues' (2011) http://www.rmafc.gov.ng/…/PAPER.Fiscal%20Federalism%20in%20Nigeria%2., accessed 27 February 2016.
Moffat K and Zhang A, 'The Paths to Social Licence to Operate: An Integrative Model Explaining Community Acceptance of Mining' (2014) 39 *Resources Policy*, 61.
Murdock H, 'Oil Theft Dilemma Stymies Nigeria's Niger Delta' *VOA* (27 March 2014) http://www.voanews.com/content/oil-theft-dilemma-stymies-nigerias-niger-delta/1880431.html, accessed 2 June 2014.
Nwajiaku-Dahou K, 'The political economy of oil and "rebellion" in Nigeria's Niger Delta' (2012) 39(132) *Review of African Political Economy*, 303.
Nwapi C, 'Defining the "Local" in Local Content Requirements in the Oil and Gas and Mining Sectors in Developing Countries' (2015) 8(1) *Law and Development Review*, 187.
Nwokolo N, 'Consolidating or Corrupting the Peace? The Power Elite and Amnesty Policy in the Niger Delta Region of Nigeria' (2018) *Chinese Political Science Review*, 1.
Okafor C, 'Akwa Ibom, Rivers, Delta, Others Accounted for Top 10 Federation Account Allocations in 2013' *Thisday* (2 June 2014) http://www.thisdaylive.com/articles/akwa-ibom-rivers-delta-others-accounted-for-top-10-federation-account-allocations-in-2013/180004/, accessed 2 June 2016.

Okorobia A, 'A History of the Underdevelopment of the Eastern Niger Delta, AD 1500–1993' (PhD Dissertation, University of Port Harcourt, Nigeria, 1999).

Onyekakeyah L, 'How Obiano is Setting Anambra State Apart' *Guardian* (26 July 2016) https://guardian.ng/opinion/how-obiano-is-setting-anambra-state-apart-part-1/, accessed 2 February 2017.

Ovadia JS, 'The Making of Oil-backed Indigenous Capitalism in Nigeria' (2012) 18 *New Political Economy*, 19.

Pardo MFM, 'The New Reality of Participation of Local Authorities in Mining Projects In Colombia: Interpretation of Constitutional Principles, New Opportunities and Participation Mechanisms' (2017) 35(4) *JERNL*, 392.

Postali FAS, 'Tax Effort and Royalties in the Brazilian Municipalities' (2016) 16 *Economia*, 395.

SDN, 'Communities not Criminals – Illegal Oil Refining in the Niger Delta' (2013) *SDN Report*.

Smith D, 'Social License to Operate in Unconventional Oil and Gas Development Sector: The Colorado Experience' in L Barrera-Hernández et al (eds), *Sharing the Costs and Benefits of Energy and Resource Activity: Legal Change and Impact on Communities* (Oxford University Press, Oxford, 2016).

Soniyi T, 'Niger Delta Gives Buhari 16 Conditions for Peace' *Thisday* (2 November 2016) https://www.thisdaylive.com/index.php/2016/11/02/niger-delta-gives-buhari-16-conditions-for-peace/, accessed 6 March 2017.

Wallis W, 'Nigeria's Central Banker Calls for an End to Imbalances' *Financial Times* (26 January 2012) http://www.ft.com/cms/s/0/02ce9e7e-4837-11e1-b1b4-00144feabdc0.html#axzz2VGfBd8T8, accessed 9 July 2013.

Watts M, 'Petro-insurgency or Criminal Syndicate? Conflict and Violence in the Niger Delta' (2007) 34 *Review of African Political Economy*, 652.

Worika IL, 'Deprivation, Despoliation and Destitution: Whither Environment and Human Rights in Nigeria's Niger Delta? (2002) 8 *ILSA J. Int'l & Comp. L.*, 1.

Conclusion

This book has analysed and examined local content oil and gas law in Africa, with Nigeria as its primary case study. To that end, it attempted to address several important and relevant aspects of local content. From the role of national oil companies (NOCs) in advancing local content, its potential role in meeting the yearnings of resource rich regions (RRRs), its implication in international trade law, as well as the underlying factors behind their rise. It examined the Nigerian legal framework, while also drawing lessons from other jurisdictions, notably Norway, Brazil, and Angola.

Chapter 1 noted that protectionist and liberalised models exist for the advancement of local content among petroleum producing countries (PPCs), and examined the merits and demerits of each model. The chapter also sought to explain the reasons behind the adoption of local content requirements (LCRs) among several PPCs, their perceived benefits, as well as criticisms against them. Moving on, Chapter 2 examined the legal and institutional frameworks for local content development. It compared the legislative approach to local content with the contractual approach. It also noted that PPCs may either rely on NOCs or on formal regulators to drive their local content policies. The chapter concluded by examining the Norwegian and Brazilian experiences with regard to local content development.

Chapter 3 examined the historical factors that shaped the development of the Nigerian content in the Nigerian petroleum industry (NPI), as well as certain reasons why the Nigerian content was weak pre-Nigerian Oil and Gas Industry Content Development Act 2010 (NOGICDA). While Chapter 4 was an overview of NOGICDA. It examined the Nigerian Content Division (NCD) of the Nigerian National Petroleum Corporation (NNPC), the factors leading up to it, its gains, as well as its drawbacks. Going forward, it noted that NOGICDA was an improvement of the NCD regime in that it applied not only to the partners of NNPC, but also to the whole NPI. The salient provisions of the Act were thereafter analysed.

Chapter 5 assessed the impact of the Act since its enactment, the suitability of NOGICIDA as a more viable alternative to the contractual approach which had been largely relied upon by Nigeria pre-NOGICDA. The chapter concluded by noting that the successful implementation of NOGICDA may be hindered by in-country capacity challenges in Nigeria. To buttress the point, lessons were extracted from Nigeria's experience with gas flaring, as well as with its maritime sector.

Chapter 6 examined the enforcement mechanisms employed by the Nigerian Content Development and Monitoring Board (NCDMB), its procedures, as well as the sanctions regime in NOGICDA. It enquired into whether the regulator's powers are adequate and sufficient for the discharge of its mandate, and also enquired into its independence in the light of NNPC's collaborations with IOCs. Lastly, the chapter explored the enforcement potential of private citizens' local content litigation, and enquired into whether they have the legal jurisdiction to enforce the provisions of the Act.

Chapter 7 was essentially an analysis of the legality of protectionist LCRs in the light of international trade law. It analysed the World Trade Organization (WTO) system as well as bilateral investment treaties (BITs), and compared same with the provisions of NOGICDA. It concluded by noting that while the Act may prima facie risk violating Nigeria's WTO and BIT obligations, a closer scrutiny may reveal some policy spaces which may allow it to further local content measures. It concluded by arguing that even if some of these laws violate Nigeria's WTO or BIT obligations, certain justifications may be cited in favour of LCRs as far as developing PPCs are concerned.

Chapter 8 concentrated on NOCs and local content. It enquired into why PPCs participate directly in their petroleum industries through NOCs in the first place, and narrowed its analysis to the roles NOCs play in the advancement of local content, drawing lessons from NNPC, Statoil, Sonangol, and Petrobras, etc. The chapter noted that not all NOCs would willingly pursue the local content policies of their home states, and for that reason, it advocated stronger NOC monitoring. It also advocated NOC restructuring as far as Africa is concerned, and in addition, suggested that African PPCs should explore the possibility of petroleum sector liberalisation as well as partial privatisation.

Chapter 9 examined the role of local content in addressing the grievances of RRRs, using Nigeria as a primary case study. It was shown that the Niger Delta Region (NDR) has suffered years of neglect and deprivation mainly from the Federal Government of Nigeria (FGN). And that Nigeria's return to democratic rule and the provision of 13 per cent derivation in Nigeria's constitution has not bettered the lot of the NDR people. It therefore examined whether calls for increased derivation from Nigeria's federation account are justified in the light of the fact that the governance structures in the NDR do not engender accountability and transparency. The chapter therefore argued that, as an alternative to increased derivation, the FGN should consider providing for a Niger Delta content in the NDR. This initiative should be cemented by legislation, as with NOGICDA. This call was justified on the basis that an NDR content will integrate the masses of the region directly into the core aspects of the NPI, and will thus give them a sense of belonging in the industry. It argued that minor corporate social responsibility initiatives of IOCs and their counterparts, while laudable, do not go far enough to integrate the region. That gap would, however, be addressed by a Niger Delta content.

The African continent is rising. The realisation that ownership of petroleum resources does not automatically translate into improved standards of living has engendered a sense of caution among new entrants to the industry such as Ghana, Tanzania, Uganda, and Kenya. The more established provinces such as Nigeria and Angola, in a race of time, are attempting to overturn years of failure to improve the lot of their people through efficient management of their natural resources. And as the citizens of these countries acquire relevant knowledge of petroleum technology, law, geology, and engineering, their confidence in their ability to play more integral roles in their petroleum industries has grown significantly.

This has given rise to LCRs. The birth of indigenous exploration and production firms in Nigeria, for instance, as well as several service firms, signals an end to the era of total reliance on IOCs and their service counterparts. In the past, grievances with their interactions with IOCs gave rise to the expropriation and nationalisation of the assets of foreign firms operating in countries such as Libya, Saudi Arabia, and Venezuela. But expropriation is often resisted and visited with huge sanctions. Rather than resort to these extreme forms of resource nationalism, several PPCs have opted for LCRs, which as protectionist as they are, still leave room for foreign players to operate, particularly in increasingly challenging projects.

The sustainability of LCRs in the developing countries of Africa and in the emerging economies of South America and the Middle East will, however, require several factors. From the perspective of these PPCs, there would be the need for commitment on the part of regulatory and government institutions to follow through. For without commitment, laudable as these objectives are, they would not automatically translate into success. There is the need for strong regulation and monitoring. However, governments should not only commit to efficient regulation, but also to efficient collaboration. As the Nigerian example demonstrates, local content development does not only depend on regulation – some form of collaboration is required. Governments should engage and continue to engage not only with IOCs and their service counterparts, but with local firms as well.

There is the need for constant interaction between academia, research institutions, and the petroleum industry. Hands-on practical experience and technical know-how should be integrated with academic knowledge in order to ensure that graduates and trainees of African tertiary institutions are poised to tackle the challenges associated with the petroleum industry. This will breach the gaps often associated with the industry, where graduates of African universities are unsuited to confront the challenges of the petroleum industry.

Nigeria's refusal to rely exclusively on top-down LCRs as against the stiff approach adopted by the National Agency for Petroleum, Natural Gas, and Biofuels in Brazil is laudable. Engagement, enlightenment, and constant interactions between regulators and the industry should be the first option in local content development. But at the same time, regulators should be ready to use the stick and impose sanctions, where necessary. This again requires that the institutional arrangements for local content development, whether through NOCs, formal regulators, or a hybrid of both, should have the capacity to execute their mandate, and should also operate with the support of governments. Regulators should therefore not be marginalised in the favour of the industry, but should be held out as championing the cause of the people.

It is also important that PPCs be ready to 'back down' where it is necessary that they do so. LCRs should also not be overly ambitious to the extent that hinders the progress of the petroleum industries of developing countries. The Brazilian example was shown to have hindered the growth of the Brazilian petroleum industry, besides weakening the performance of Petrobras. The country's adaptability to change as shown in reforms introduced from 2016, however, has enabled it to attract investors again. As African PPCs strive to develop capacity, they should also be ready to whittle down their LCRs where necessary, but again care is needed here. The example of the Associated Gas Reinjection Act 1979 was shown to have hindered Nigeria's resolve to end gas flaring, mainly because of the availability of waivers and exceptions which, in the end, frustrated the country's desire to protect its environment from harmful greenhouse gases.

LCR advancement requires some form of co-operation and sacrifice not only from governments, but also from foreign players. Some of these firms such as Shell, Mobil, Chevron, and Agip, etc., have operated in Africa for decades, and have made billions of dollars for their shareholders over the years. These firms should have invested in the development of local capabilities in their areas of operations, but did little in the past. There is the need for a paradigm shift in their thinking. Protectionist LCRs have come to stay. As noted in this book, rather than going away, they seem to be rising, with Middle Eastern countries currently embracing the local content movement, which started mainly in South America, and was given more impetus in Africa. What these firms should do is to collaborate with their host countries in recognition of the fact that LCRs are the new normal. Just as several of them rationalised and adapted in order to remain relevant in the 1950s and 1960s, following the birth of NOCs, so they must do again. Rather than antagonise LCRs, they should constantly engage with their host countries, while at the same time take efforts not only to comply, but also to encourage domestic contracting. The Nigerian example can serve as a template for other countries, where IOCs have, to some extent, encouraged the growth and development of Nigerian content in the NPI. The interesting thing is that, in the long run, IOCs which invest in the development of local content will not only obtain a social licence to operate, but they will also benefit from the experiences and capabilities of vibrant local firms.

Lastly, it is important to remind developing PPCs that local content is not an end in itself. Nor is it the solution to all the problems associated with petroleum extraction and development. It is only one of several policies which, if implemented effectively, will play its part in ensuring effective resource management. Thus rather than rely entirely on local content, developing PPCs should develop elaborate frameworks for efficient resource management. This would include addressing corruption, diversifying from petroleum at the earliest time, promoting transparency and accountability in the management of petroleum revenues, strengthening regulation, and providing adequate savings and investment mechanisms. These policies, if adequately implemented and added to viable local content policies, will augur well not only for new entrants into the petroleum industry, but for the older players as well. Ignored, they would not only entrench the resource curse phenomenon, but may also frustrate the objectives which LCRs were meant to achieve in the first place.

Index

For Product Safety Concerns and Information please contact our EU representative GPSR@taylorandfrancis.com
Taylor & Francis Verlag GmbH, Kaufingerstraße 24, 80331 München, Germany

www.ingramcontent.com/pod-product-compliance
Ingram Content Group UK Ltd.
Pitfield, Milton Keynes, MK11 3LW, UK
UKHW011010180926
475701UK00004B/665

* 9 7 8 1 0 3 2 2 4 1 5 7 9 *